The KBMT Project:

A Case Study in Knowledge-Based
Machine Translation

The KBMT Project:

A Case Study in Knowledge-Based

Edited by

Kenneth Goodman
Sergei Nirenburg

Morgan Kaufmann Publishers
San Mateo, California

Sponsoring Editor   Michael B. Morgan
Production Editor   Yonie Overton
Cover Designer   Patty King
Copyeditor/Proofreader   Barbara Beidler Kendrick

Morgan Kaufmann Publishers, Inc.
Editorial Office:
2929 Campus Drive, Suite 260
San Mateo, CA 94403

Library of Congress Cataloging-in-Publication Data

The KBMT project : a case study in knowledge-based machine translation
  / edited by Kenneth Goodman, Sergei Nirenburg.
        p.   cm.
   Includes bibliographical references (p.   ) and index.
   ISBN 1-55860-129-5 : $34.95
   1. Machine translating--Case studies. 2. Japanese language-
  -Machine translating. 3. English language--Machine translating.
   I. Goodman, Kenneth W., 1954- . II. Nirenburg, Sergei.
  P308.K37   1991
  418'.02'0285--dc20   91-16547
                                                         CIP

Contents

Contents

ix

Contents

List of Figures

List of Tables

Preface

Machine translation of natural languages is one of the most complex and comprehensive applications of computational linguistics and artificial intelligence. This is especially true of knowledge-based machine translation systems, which require a large number of knowledge resources and processing modules. These modules carry out all levels of linguistic analysis, representation and generation of form and meaning.

The number of concrete problems, tasks and solutions involved in developing any realistic-size knowledge-based machine translation system is enormous. It is usually beyond the scope of a journal or conference proceedings article, or even a sequence of such articles, to describe a knowledge-based machine translation project in sufficient detail. It is therefore quite difficult for workers in the field to learn what a system "really does." This book fills the need for a comprehensive and detailed case study of a particular project.

IBM decided in 1987 to fund a two-year research project in knowledge-based machine translation at the Center for Machine Translation of Carnegie Mellon University. The idea for this project came from researchers at IBM's Tokyo Research Laboratory, specifically Dr. Norihisa Suzuki and Dr. Taijiro Tsutsumi. The objective was to develop a large prototype machine translation system in the knowledge-based paradigm. The original specifications for the project were developed by Jaime Carbonell and Masaru Tomita, and an original system was demonstrated in February 1988. In the second year of the project, under the direction of Sergei Nirenburg, the structure and content of the interlingua and the lexicons were expanded, and the semantic interpretation processes in analysis and in generation were developed. Architecturally, the augmentor, an interactive editor, was added.

The final system, named KBMT-89, was demonstrated in February 1989. The development team consisted of CMT staff and students and a researcher from IBM Japan, Koichi Takeda. Not all the group members worked on the project for its entire duration, but all contributed to its successful completion. Ralf Brown developed the augmentor module; Donna Gates wrote the English grammar and mapping rules for English, both for analysis and generation; Dawn Haberlach contributed to the ontology and lexicon acquisition; Todd Kaufmann provided systems support and was the main implementor of the Ontos knowledge acquisition system; Marion Kee contributed to lexicon writing and parser development for English; Lori Levin served as associate director of the project and contributed to the development of the grammar and mapping rule formalism and the acquisition of grammars; Rita McCardell contributed to the development of the generator, notably the generation lexicon; Teruko Mitamura developed the analysis lexicon and grammar for Japanese; Ira Monarch contributed to the development of Ontos; Stephen Morrisson maintained and extended the parser and the mapping rule interpreters; Eric Nyberg developed the generator module; Koichi Takeda developed the Japanese generation grammar and lexicon; and Margalit Zabludowski contributed to the development of the English lexicon and mapping rules.

We would like to extend special thanks to Jaime Carbonell, director of the Center for Machine Translation, for advice on design and for participation in many key discussions; Masaru Tomita for maintaining and improving the parser technology; and Radha Rao for able administrative support.

Earlier versions of the basic material in this book appeared in a special double issue of the journal *Machine Translation* (4, nos. 1, 2 [1989]). Although most examples and some descriptions are practically unchanged, most of the material has been extensively reworked and expanded to produce the most comprehensive account of KBMT-89. We gratefully acknowledge the cooperation of Kluwer Academic Publishers, the publishers of *Machine Translation.*

We are also grateful to W. Scott Bennett, Victor Raskin and Allen B. Tucker for very useful comments on an early version of the manuscript.

Mark Boggs, Inna Nirenburg, Barbara Moore and Tom Jennings helped in several ways to prepare the volume for publication.

Kenneth Goodman and Sergei Nirenburg
Pittsburgh, 1991

Chapter 1

Introduction

■ SERGEI NIRENBURG

Machine translation (MT) systems have been of three major types: direct, transfer and interlingua. (Detailed descriptions of the three approaches, with all their modifications and varieties, can be found in Hutchins 1986 and Zarechnak 1979.)

Briefly, direct translation systems typically rely on a large set of language-pair-dependent idiosyncratic rules to carry out the translation of a text. These rules take separate grammatical and lexical phenomena of the source language (SL) and their realizations in the target language (TL) and put the two in correspondence. Examples of such systems are SYSTRAN (Wheeler 1984) and older versions of SPANAM (Vasconcellos and Leon 1985).

Transfer systems involve a good measure of source-language analysis that is independent of the target language. This analysis is usually syntactic. It allows substitution of source language lexical units with target language lexical units *in context*. That is, it permits taking into account the types of syntactic sentence constituents in which lexical units appear. Among the transfer translation systems are EUROTRA (Arnold and des Tombe 1987) and METAL (Bennett 1982).

In interlingua systems the source language and the target language are never in direct contact. The processing in such systems has traditionally been understood to involve two major stages: representing the meaning of a source language text in a language-independent formal language, an *interlingua*, and then expressing this meaning using the lexical units and syntactic constructions of the target language. Few interlingua systems have been fully implemented because of the very significant complexity (both theoretical and empirical) of extracting a "deep" meaning from a natural language text. Among the systems conforming to the interlingua design are TRANSLATOR (Nirenburg et al. 1987a) and Ultra (Farwell and Wilks 1991).

Direct translation systems are known to be inadequate in a number of ways, and no recent system is based on this paradigm. A major distinction between the interlingua- and transfer-based systems is, in fact, not so much the presence or absence of a bilingual lexicon but rather the attitude toward comprehensive analysis of meaning. Inherently, a transfer system can involve many levels of meaning analysis. These analyses are constrained so that the language in which the meanings of source language lexical units are expressed will not be an artificial knowledge representation language but instead the target language itself, through a bilingual lexicon that features disambiguation information. In interlingua systems the meanings are represented in an artificial language—precisely because such a language better facilitates the formulation of disambiguation rules necessary for producing an adequate representation of meaning for a source text.

As a rule, however, machine translation researchers who believe in translating without "deep" understanding (or perhaps who believe in the unattainability of "deep" understanding) of the source text tend to prefer the transfer paradigm. The price paid for avoiding meaning analysis is the need for an extra step in the translation process, namely, postediting.[1]

Builders of interlingua systems, on the other hand, must devise new knowledge-based natural language understanding techniques to account for some of the more difficult problems in natural language processing. The complexity of this task induces knowledge-based machine translation researchers to constrain the range of phenomena processed by their systems. This is usually done by restricting the sublanguage of translation to a relatively small fragment of a natural language.

The first 40 years of MT experience teach us that significant long-term progress depends on advances in our basic knowledge of how to model natural language understanding using computers. It may be argued that, while systems with limited understanding might be immediately more useful and practical, systems that extend and strengthen our grasp of translation problems must strive for understanding.

---

[1]The relative functions and purposes of pre-editing, postediting and interactive editing are for the most part intuitively clear. For a more detailed discussion, see the papers in Nirenburg 1987a. For a review of some semantic issues in machine translation, see Nirenburg and Goodman 1990.

This will be true even if, at the beginning, the lack of knowledge about specific types of disambiguation and meaning representation require the introduction of a measure of human involvement in the form of interactive editing. A detailed theoretical and methodological discussion of knowledge-based machine translation is given in the companion to this volume (Nirenburg et al. 1991).

1.1 Specifications and Architecture

The KBMT-89 system has the following specifications:

- *Source languages*: English and Japanese;

- *Target languages*: English and Japanese;

- *Translation paradigm*: interlingua;

- *Computational architecture*: a distributed, coarsely parallel system; and

- *Subworld (domain) of translation*: personal computer installation and maintenance manuals.

The knowledge acquired for the system includes:

- An *ontology* (domain model) of about 1,500 concepts;

- *Analysis lexicons*: about 800 lexical units of Japanese and about 900 units of English;

- *Generation lexicons*: about 800 lexical units of Japanese and about 900 units of English;

- *Analysis grammars* for English and Japanese;

- *Generation grammars* for English and Japanese; and

- Specialized syntax ↔ semantics *structural mapping rules*.

The underlying formalisms that were developed for the use in this system are:

- The knowledge representation system FRAMEKIT;

- A language for representing domain models (a semantic extension of FRAMEKIT);

- Specialized grammar formalisms, based on Lexical Functional Grammar (LFG);

- A specially constructed language for representing text meanings (the *interlingua*); and

- The languages of analysis and generation lexicon entries and of the structural mapping rules.

The procedural components of the system include:

- A *syntactic parser* with a semantic constraint interpreter;

- A *semantic mapper* for treating additional types of semantic constraints;

- An *interactive augmentor* for treating residual ambiguities;

- A *semantic generator* producing syntactic structures of the target language, complete with lexical insertion; and

- A *syntactic generator*, producing output strings based on the output of the semantic generator.

The support and environment facilities include:

- Ontos, a knowledge acquisition tool for acquiring ontologies and lexicons;

- A knowledge acquisition tool for acquiring grammars; and

- Testing environments for analysis, augmentation and generation.

The discrete computational modules that compose the system are an English parser, English generator, Japanese parser, Japanese generator, Ontos and an augmentor. Each module runs in a separate LISP process on a separate IBM-RT/PC, each with 12M RAM. The system uses Carnegie Mellon University's COMMONLISP under its Mach UNIX operating system. The LISP processes communicated over a 10Mbits/second Ethernet network using TCP/IP sockets. A seventh workstation running the X window system (V10) was used to display the output from the processes. Appendix C to this volume gives a brief account of the processes involved in loading and running the system.

1.2   The KBMT-89 Approach to Machine Translation

The KBMT-89 approach to *knowledge representation* is an immediate descendant of that in Nirenburg et al. 1987a. The other direct influence is Carbonell et al. 1981. Some ideas about representation (in particular, the nature of a frame slot filler, dictated by the need to prepare the data for preference processing) are related to work by Wilks (e.g., 1975). In some other respects (for instance, in treating properties as full-fledged concepts), Wilensky 1984 must be cited as an influence. Ultimately, the knowledge representation substrate of KBMT-89 belongs to the family of frame-based, non-truth-value-oriented empirical semantic and pragmatic knowledge representation systems.

The project corpora were based on two instruction manuals for personal computers (International Business Machines 1983, 1986). The system was tested on 300 sentences, although a subset was initially selected at random to provide a foundation for developing and tuning the system. None of the sentences was pre-edited, and not all corpus sentences could be translated fully automatically. Instruction manuals for personal computers are notorious for their opaque style, even when written by native speakers for other native speakers. The domain and sublanguage of personal computers thus represented a significant challenge.

A further challenge consisted of the need to devise an internal representation for *textual* features; the ability to handle such features is crucial if there is to be any hope of designing systems for actual application in commerce, industry and scholarship. For instance, enumerated lists are quite common in much documentation and must be handled if automatic translation is to be successful. Consider the following list (from the introduction to the English version of the computer manual):

1. Remove the Diagnostics diskette from the back of this manual.

2. Set the Power switch on the system unit (and expansion unit, if attached) to Off.

3. Set all external Power switches Off (printer, TV, etc.).

What is the best way to represent the numerals that begin each line? Do they have semantic content? A syntactic role? How should it be represented? The decision to encode the numerals and their accompanying periods as a `number-bullet` slot in the concept `*proposition` is one way of solving this problem (see chapters 6 and 7). Additional, similar problems include how to represent self-referential text like *back of this manual* and how to handle use-mention phenomena (such as the terms *Off* and *On* in items 2 and 3 just above).

In the chapters that follow, we attempt to convey as much as possible about the decision making that went into building the KBMT-89 system, in addition to a description of the system itself. This will involve the highlighting of areas that were particularly problematic and in which either no solutions were found or the solutions adopted were less than optimal. As in any scientific venture, results are largely dependent on method; and an evaluation of the approach taken, its advantages and shortcomings, can be valuable for other researchers. Thus the purpose of this volume is to reveal and address problems as much as to report results.

The KBMT-89 system and its components are undergoing continuous revision. At no point in the research did the system achieve stasis. This posed interesting problems in the task of describing the system. When, for instance, should the system be "frozen" for the sake of description? Or should an attempt be made to detail all the latest developments? The solution was to try to strike a balance, basing most of the text on the system as it was first demonstrated in February 1989 but updating material to improve reader understanding. Mistakes made in the initial implementations are noted only if they are instructive. Some of the latest developments in the knowledge-based machine translation work at Carnegie Mellon University are described in Nirenburg et al. 1991.

KBMT-89 is a research prototype, not a commercial system, as is evident from the sizes of the lexicons and domain models. The project mandate has been to provide a "proof of concept" for knowledge-based machine translation in a non-toy domain, using full-blown knowledge support facilities and processing modules designed to operate with large grammars and lexicons.

1.3   An Overview of the System and the Book

KBMT-89 takes as input single sentences of English or Japanese and produces representations of their meanings in a specially devised notation, called the *interlingua*. The representation resulting from analyzing a unit of input is called an *interlingua text* or ILT. Taking an ILT as input, the generator produces sentences in Japanese or English that are translations of the original input sentences. Figure 1.1 illustrates the global architecture of the system.

Chapter 2 describes the knowledge base in which the system's domain is modeled and the interlingual text knowledge-representation language. The domain knowledge base, also known as an "ontology" or "concept lexicon," contains representations of items—objects, events and their interactions—from the domain of

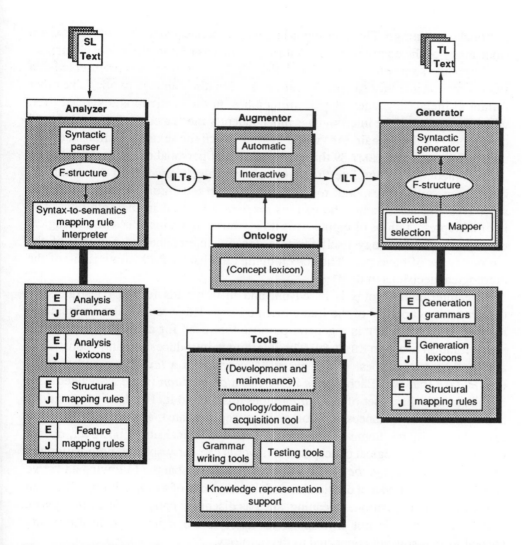

Figure 1.1: **Architecture of the KBMT-89 system. 'E' and 'J' designate English and Japanese, the languages used in KBMT-89. Analysis of source language text and generation of target language text are based on ensembles of knowl-edge bases, including grammars, lexicons and mapping rules. Analysis may produce ambiguous interlingua representations, which are resolved by the automatic or interactive augmentor. This produces a single ILT, from which the generator produces the target text. The knowledge bases and augmen-tor draw from the domain model or ontology. The system is developed and maintained by various tools, shown as parts of a distinct module.**

personal computing.[2] The interlingua language is connected to the concept lexicon since many of the components of an ILT are instances of domain model elements.

To go into somewhat greater detail, the KBMT-89 interlingua is represented in a frame notation and thus can be viewed as a kind of a semantic network. Like other formal artificial languages, the interlingua has its own lexicon and syntax. Yet, while the syntax of the interlingua is independently motivated, its lexicon is based on a model of the domain (or "world") from which the texts to be translated are taken. In the case of KBMT-89 this is the domain of personal computer installation and maintenance. Thus interlingua nouns are *object* concepts in the ontology; interlingua verbs correspond, roughly, to *events* in the ontology; and interlingua adjectives and adverbs are the various *properties* defined in the ontology. The internal representations of inputs—the ILTs—thus contain instances of ontological concepts. The ontology itself forms a densely interconnected network of the various types of concepts. The screen dumps in chapter 2 illustrate some of the ontological decisions in KBMT-89.

The interlingua syntax is based on, and in turn adds further constraints to, the syntactic properties of the frame-oriented knowledge representation language FRAMEKIT. FRAMEKIT is a general-purpose tool used for almost all knowledge representation needs in KBMT-89. The interlingua introduces semantic constraints and marked frame types. Thus, every ILT consists of a *text* frame and a set of (ILT-)*clause* frames.[3] Each *clause* frame has a *proposition* frame associated with it; this, in turn, has a set of *case role* frames attached to it. Heads of propositions and case roles are instances of ontological concepts, as are many of the proposition and role modifiers. Some of the source language lexical units, however, do not correspond to ontological concepts. Such words can carry special, propositionally relevant meanings (e.g., *be* can be a marker signifying that the following adjective should be understood as a predicative and thus the head of a proposition). They can also carry nonpropositional meaning, such as discourse cohesion (e.g., *therefore*). Lexical units that do not correspond to concepts are represented in ILTs using special formalisms not connected to the ontology.

Chapter 3 gives an account of KBMT-89's syntactic substrate. The chapter provides an introduction to salient issues in linguistic theory and describes the use of Lexical Functional Grammar in KBMT-89. This formalism is central to understanding the workings and interactions of KBMT-89 components. Issues and

---

[2]We use the terms "ontology" and "concept lexicon" interchangeably.

[3]KBMT-89 inputs were restricted to single sentences, and so the need for the text-level index did not arise. However, cf. the discussion of anaphora in chapter 8.

problems in grammar writing are highlighted in this and especially the following chapter.

The grammars for source language analysis and target language generation are introduced in chapter 4. The goal here is to give a sense of how English and Japanese syntactic phenomena are treated in KBMT-89. No attempt is made to present an exhaustive account. Instead, particularly interesting and difficult problems in natural language processing are discussed. Similarly, as it would not be feasible to review all major issues in both English and Japanese syntax, descriptions of English phenomena are given greater exposure.

The analysis and generation lexicons are featured in chapters 5 and 6. The former describes the English and Japanese dictionaries used during parsing. The latter provides an account of the lexicons and mapping rules employed during target language generation by the lexical selection submodule.

The remaining chapters describe the program modules for analysis, augmentation and generation.

Chapter 7 contains an overview of the analysis process in KBMT-89. The analyzer consists of two intimately interconnected components, a syntactic parser and a semantic interpreter called a "mapping rule interpreter." The syntactic parser obtains the source language input and produces a syntactic structure for it. The parser uses an LFG-type grammar, so that the resultant syntactic structure is, in fact, an LFG *f-structure*.

Briefly, as soon as the f-structure for the source language sentence is created, the semantic interpreter starts applying mapping rules for substituting source language lexical units and syntactic constructions with their interlingua translations.[4] Roughly, lexical units map into instances of domain concepts (e.g., the English *data* will map into an instance of the ontological concept `information`), while syntactic dependency structures map into conceptual relations (e.g., *subjects* of English sentences often map into the *agent* relations). Ambiguities are eliminated by applying semantic constraints, largely selectional restrictions, on co-occurrences of various concept instances.

Figure 1.2 illustrates processing in KBMT-89 as seen from the point of view of data connections among the analysis, generation and concept lexicons and the ILT. There are three concept lexicon hierarchies, for "sound," "legal events" and "perceptual events." The second is included to illustrate polysemy in analysis (a legal hearing versus the hearing of sound). The analysis lexicon entries crucially

---

[4]This description is simplified for clarity. In reality, mapping rule application starts as soon as an f-structure is produced for any structure component, not after the entire sentence is processed.

contain either links to concept lexicon elements or direct links to particular ILT components. Thus, the solid lines starting at analysis lexicon entries point to the meanings of the corresponding lexical units. For instance, the meaning of *should* is given as the value (> 0.8) of the "epistemic modality" property of an ILT clause. While some source language lexical units are directly connected to their interlingua representations, others, the so-called open-class items, have instances of their (possibly multiple) corresponding ontological concepts included in the ILT during semantic analysis. This is illustrated in the figure by broken lines labeled "instantiation." The figure also suggests the lack of symmetry in the treatment of lexical semantics in analysis and generation. The main problem in analysis is polysemy, while in generation it is synonymy, as is illustrated by the differences in the analysis and generation lexicon entries.

Parser output is sometimes ambiguous and must in any case be reformatted from its native LFG-like formalism into the ILT formalism. Residual disambiguation and reformatting are performed by a special KBMT-89 component, the augmentor, which is described in chapter 8.

In practice, the augmentor first reformats the output of the analyzer in the canonical formalism. Second, it helps eliminate any residual ambiguities (that is, multiple candidate ILTs for a given input sentence) by applying additional semantic and pragmatic constraints. This is called *automatic augmentation*. Should that fail, typically due to the unavailability of a knowledge element, the augmentor enters into a dialogue mode with system users and facilitates their decisions about disambiguation. This is known as *interactive augmentation*.

KBMT-89's generation component takes an ILT as its input and produces a target language text as its output. The generator consists of two major modules, one semantic and one syntactic. The former, sometimes referred to as an "f-structure builder," performs the tasks of target language lexical selection and of choosing among target language syntactic constructions. It is aided in these tasks by the generation lexicon and the generation structural mapping rules, respectively. The output of this module is an f-structure of the target language sentence that will be output by the system. As its syntactic module, the generator uses the f-structure-to-string converter GENKIT (Tomita and Nyberg 1988). The KBMT-89 generator is a subset of the DIOGENES generator (Nirenburg et al. 1988a).

A system of KBMT-89's size and complexity cannot be built successfully in the absence of a set of tools that aids in (i) the acquisition of world and linguistic (lexical and grammatical) knowledge and (ii) the process of testing and debugging the system's processing modules.

The major knowledge acquisition aid in KBMT-89 is Ontos, a system for inter-

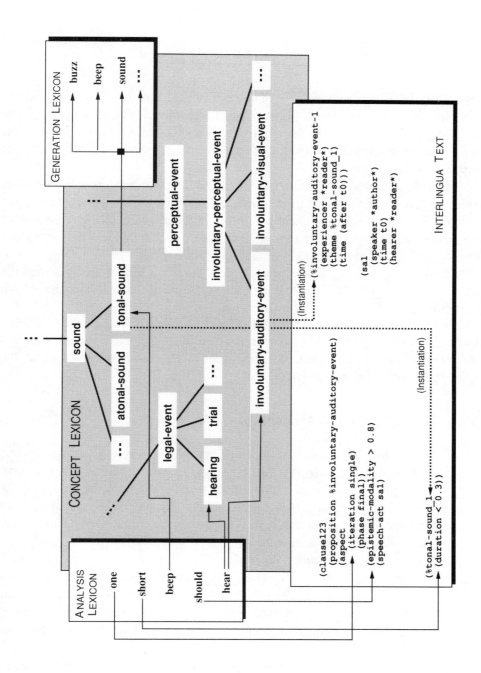

Figure 1.2: **The interaction among lexicons and ILT, illustrating the process of constructing an ILT for the sentence "One short beep should be heard."** Note that some source language lexical units are connected to their interlingua meanings directly, bypassing the concept lexicon. Others, the open-class items, are instantiated in the ILT.

active acquisition and maintenance of domain models; it is also used for acquiring the analysis and generation lexicons. Ontos was specifically developed for use in KBMT-89; however, it can be applied in a number of situations wherein the acquisition of large quantities of knowledge is required. Some Ontos features are described in chapter 2.

The volume contains three appendices. The first two are runtime traces that illustrate KBMT-89 processing from source language input through target language output. The traces have technical preambles and are annotated. The preambles expand on issues in parsing first raised in chapter 7, and in this way they introduce details needed for a complete understanding of the traces.

The final appendix is a very brief "user's guide" to loading and running the KBMT-89 system. It is included to give a feel for some of the tasks associated with using the system.

KBMT-89 programs use a variety of standard and invented symbols and operators. Most are either commonly known or introduced in appropriate chapters, although some few are not. To ease understanding of the text's examples and traces, all the symbols are collected in Table 1.1.

1.4   Extensions and Prospects

As any builder of a large-scale software system knows, there is seemingly no end to potential improvements in system design and implementation. The *practical* impetus to improvements of the current system will come from the growth in the size and complexity of the sublanguages that the system will be called upon to process. New syntactic structures, lexical units and types of meanings will have to be included in the system's inventory.

KBMT-89 specifications called for sentence-level processing. One of the most important extensions of KBMT-89 would thus be the treatment of multisentential text. The system's representational substrate is sufficiently broad to allow an experiment in treating multisentential text (as is taking place in the DIONYSUS project at the Center for Machine Translation; see, e.g., Nirenburg and Defrise, forthcoming).

The ILT contains a provision for representing intersentential discourse cohesion markers and flexible-scope focus values. The DIOGENES generator is already able to process intersentential anaphora and, as noted previously, KBMT-89's generator constitutes a subset of this system. The automatic augmentor module is also geared to processing intersentential anaphora (see the discussion of multiple anaphor resolution strategies in chapter 8). In many cases during the development of KBMT-

SYMBOL	USAGE	EXAMPLE(S)
*...	Designates concept name	*computer, *on-state, *physical-object
*...	Designates FRAMEKIT frame names	*proposition, *clause
...	Designates grammar operator to distinguish sets of equations	*or*
...	Designates syntactic filler for entity controlled by a higher clause	*subj-controlled*
...	Designates type of feature structure in parser output	*sem*, *multiple*, *or*
...*	Kleene star designates 0 or more in BNFs	(features (<feat-val>)*)
...+	Kleene plus sign designates 1 or more in BNFs	(opt <thematic-role>+)
...+	Used in Japanese analysis to introduce coordination	NP+, S+
%...	Designates slot name	%location, %referent-of
&...	Designates atomic or literal value	&red
$...	Designates slot-name created by parser to distinguish from user-defined names	$is-token-of, $map-data
$...	Tool for future handling of kanji characters	$ko, $si
$...$	Designates concept not in concept lexicon	$pronoun$
?...	Designates optionality in BNFs	?(class), ?(local)
<...>	Designates syntactic category	<N>, <NP>, <V>
<$...$>	Designates special phrase structure category; inserted into grammar by parser	<$WORD$>
!...(!)	FRAMEKIT variable	feature!, !slotfs
@...	FRAMEKIT variable	@frame.completion
@...	Tool for future handling of hiragana characters	@si
@^	Tool for future handling of single-character hiragana consonant clusters	@^ --> K
'...	LISP quote mark	'convey, 'purpose
:...	LISP keyword argument	:exclusive
#...	Temporary LISP variable	#1=, #2= and #1# ... where the contents to the right of #1= is returned at the 1 in #1#

Table 1.1: **Symbols appearing in examples and traces. Note that some symbols (e.g., ∗ . . . ∗) can be used for different purposes if they appear in distinct programs.**

89, the absence of intersentential context was a serious hindrance. Without such context, special solutions were needed for many phenomena, among these the translation of deictic elements and discourse cohesion markers such as *also, then* and *however.*

Other major extensions will involve the addition of source and target languages and the provision of translation support in new domains.

The expressive power of the interlingua will have to be extended to cover more lexical and pragmatic meanings. The existing grammars and lexicons will have to be enhanced both in their coverage and organization. Better treatment of multisense lexemes is required, for instance, as well as a re-evaluation of the size of the set of lexical categories used by the grammar. From a practical point of view, special preprocessors are needed to deal with such issues as the treatment of translatable and untranslatable material in figures and tables, translating abbreviations and special symbols and reproducing the layout characteristics of the input text in the output. Other subsystems must be designed and written. These include a general-purpose morphological processor for the analyzers and the generators and an accompanying acquisition tool for morphological knowledge.

A separate set of improvements concerns performance optimization. KBMT-89 was built as a working prototype of an interlingua system in a nontrivial domain model. A number of steps can be taken to improve the performance of the system. Unambiguous grammars can be written, and the lexicons can be tuned to the needs of a particular, however large, corpus so that no extra lexical mappings occur and there are no unused concepts in the domain model. At the same time, a number of techniques can be used to speed up the component programs. Thus, for instance, the LISP code that is automatically generated for the generation grammars may be improved by adding optimizing steps in the compiler. We found it necessary to begin adding optimizing steps during the final stages of the project, when the English generation grammar became very large. Currently, lexical insertion is achieved by rules in the grammar. In the future, this will be supplanted by a separate dictionary and morphology rules so that each inflected form of a root noun or verb need not be coded directly in the grammar. This will have two positive effects: it will decrease the size of the compiled grammar, and it will increase the productivity of the grammar writer.

In addition to its utility as an MT shell, KBMT-89 can be profitably used as a research tool and testbed in computational linguistics and artificial intelligence.

In its current state, the system provides a tool for devising and testing new and more powerful specialized semantic interpretation algorithms, such as noun-noun compound understanding or prepositional phrase attachment. With more types of semantic and pragmatic knowledge appearing in the ILT, more specialized "microtheories" (as described in chapter 2) will need to be devised and incorporated into the process.[5] The modularity of the KBMT-89 architecture will facilitate this. In fact, the system already allows a greater measure of modularity, which has been tested partially in the DIOGENES project and will probably have a blackboard-based architecture underlying it in its next incarnation (see Leavitt 1991; Leavitt and Nyberg 1990).

KBMT-89's generation component is also a good substrate on which to build more sophisticated generators. In particular, it facilitates the interaction of syntactic, lexical and prosodic processing and offers a level of reliance on world knowledge that is unusual in most natural language generators.

An additional advantage of using KBMT-89 as a research vehicle is that it is a *comprehensive* system allowing immediate testing of a new component in a context in which a genuine output can be obtained.

KBMT-89's interface can serve as a medium for building other interfaces, notably for computer-aided instruction and, in particular, for teaching foreign languages. A comprehensive understanding-and-generation system such as KBMT-89 can also be used as a component in a cognitive agent model, integrated with components for planning and problem solving, perception and action simulation. It can be useful in machine learning systems, especially those studying learning from text or learning by being told, or in systems that investigate hybrid learning processes.

The ontological knowledge facet of the system can be quite useful for research in the area of acquisition and maintenance of very large, multifunctional knowledge bases. Ontos is already used in more than half a dozen different projects at Carnegie Mellon University and elsewhere.

The computing technology embodied by KBMT-89 has a number of potential practical applications outside the field of machine translation. One of the areas in which it will yield practical results is in design and development of translator's workstations. The interaction environment can be extended to include other types of human-computer communication. Additional knowledge sources, such as human-readable dictionaries and encyclopedias, could be connected to the system.

---

[5]Provided that a comprehensive, computationally relevant theory of semantic and pragmatic interpretation is *not* about to be formulated, the best policy for computational linguists in building comprehensive (although sublanguage-dependent) natural language processing systems seems to be to combine the results offered by partial theories—microtheories—of particular semantic and pragmatic phenomena (e.g., quantification, reference, thematic structure, discourse cohesion, aspect, time and tense, metaphor, metonymy, etc.). Under this approach, we can use different theories once we represent the findings uniformly and introduce the computational control structure that will assign a high degree of autonomy to the component microtheory-based modules.

And the presence of the analyzer and the generator would allow the system to suggest solutions to the human translator. This feature is lacking in all current translator's workstations.

The technology developed in KBMT-89 is readily useful in applications that require different types of inputs to and/or outputs from a natural language processor. Thus, instead of forwarding an ILT to the generator, one could pass it to a special reasoning program to produce an abstract of the input text, to answer questions based on it or to place the input text into one of a number of taxonomic classes. KBMT-89 can also be reconfigured for supporting natural language interfaces to database systems. Indeed, if a data manipulation (query) language is substituted for the interlingua, the task of query formulation could become quite similar to that of analyzing a natural language input for translation.

Chapter 2

World Knowledge and Text Meaning

■ SERGEI NIRENBURG, IRA MONARCH AND TODD KAUFMANN

Few tasks are of as much importance and interdisciplinary interest as the representation of world knowledge and text meaning. In KBMT-89, domain knowledge is represented in a "concept lexicon" or domain model or "ontology," a collection of representations of objects and interactions from the world of personal computers. The meaning of English and Japanese texts is represented in a specially designed knowledge representation language, an interlingua. In KBMT-89, the interlingua is in turn given in a frame notation—an interlingua text—and thus can be viewed as a kind of semantic network. Like other artificial or formal languages, the interlingua has its own lexicon and syntax. Yet while the syntax of the interlingua is independently motivated, its lexicon—the concept lexicon—is based on the domain of personal computer installation and maintenance. This chapter gives an introduction and overview of the concept lexicon and interlingua used in KBMT-89.

In brief, interlingua nouns are *object* concepts in the ontology; verbs correspond, roughly, to *events*; and adjectives and adverbs are the various *properties* defined in the ontology. The representations of source language inputs, the ILTs, thus contain (numbered) instances of concepts from the concept lexicon. The ontology itself forms a densely interconnected network of the various types of concepts.

The interlingua syntax adds further constraints to the syntactic properties of the general-purpose, frame-oriented knowledge representation language FRAMEKIT, which is used for almost all of KBMT-89's knowledge representation needs. The interlingua introduces semantic constraints and marked frame types. Thus, every ILT consists of a *text* frame[1] and a set of (ILT-)*clause* frames. Each clause frame has a *proposition* frame associated with it; each proposition frame, in turn, has a set of *case role* frames attached to it. The heads of the propositions and case roles are instances of ontological concepts, as are many of the proposition and role modifiers. However, some of the source language lexical units do not correspond to ontological concepts. Such words can carry special, propositionally relevant meanings. For instance, *be* can be a marker signifying that the following adjective should be understood as predicative and, as such, the head of a proposition. These forms can also transmit various nonpropositional meanings, such as discourse cohesion (e.g., *therefore*). Nonpropositional meanings are represented in the ILT using special formalisms not connected with the ontology.

2.1   The Concept Lexicon

The KBMT-89 concept lexicon is, as noted, a language-independent conceptual representation of the interactions between personal computers and their users. It provides the semantic information needed in the sublanguage domain for parsing source texts into ILTs and generating target texts from ILTs. Although node-names and slot-names of the encoding use English strings, they represent language-independent concepts in the sense that both English speakers and Japanese speakers can use them to make meaning assignments to lexical items in their respective languages. For instance, the concept *remove is used to make meaning assignments to the English *remove* and the Japanese *torinozoku*.

To be sure, one ought not be too sanguine about this crucial and difficult issue. Work to extend and modify the KBMT-89 ontological model is an ongoing and difficult task; successive approximations seek the level of detail required for specifying the semantic restrictions needed to constrain the output of the parser and generator. To give sufficient semantic restrictions, the ontological model must provide uniform definitions of fundamental categories that are employed in crafting descriptions of particular domains. The theoretical and methodological aspects of this research are reviewed in Nirenburg et al. 1991.

---

[1]In KBMT-89 the inputs were restricted to single sentences, and the need for the text-level index did not arise.

2.1.1 Knowledge Acquisition and Maintenance

Ontological and domain models are acquired with the knowledge acquisition and maintenance system ONTOS. The system provides an interactive environment that includes facilities for interacting in multiple windows through menus and graphics. Ontos contains ontological postulates that are the basis for:

- Memory and decision aids to help users find the appropriate way to describe a newly entered concept; and

- A filtering capability that helps identify potential inconsistencies and problems in the knowledge base.

These ontological postulates are computationally inscribed in a frame network representation of objects, events and situations, characterized by attributes and relations and organized in subcategorical and partonomical hierarchies. Integrated acquisition of domain concepts proceeds through elaboration and specification of concepts framing ontological postulates. The result is an *ontology*. Such an environment should eventually—it does not now—support both of the following:

- Knowledge update by humans through intelligent interactive aids; and

- Semiautomatic and automatic knowledge update, in which a knowledge acquisition maintenance system learns from texts by suggesting new, partially characterized concepts to be elaborated on, refined and sometimes deleted by humans or by the system itself as new information is encountered.

Most important, the second of these two requirements is essentially dependent on the first in the sense that automating knowledge and lexicon building depends on handcrafting a substantial base of real-world knowledge (Lenat et al. 1985) for limited subworlds (Nirenburg and Raskin 1987b) and sublanguages (Kittredge and Grishman 1986).

2.1.2 Ontological Postulates

World knowledge is organized as a multiply interconnected, hierarchical network of frames constructed with Ontos. Ontological postulates resident in Ontos are encoded in the higher, more abstract nodes of this network and serve as a map to help knowledge enterers determine where domain concepts fit into the knowledge hierarchy. They are also a source of properties and constraints that can be further specified into domain concepts.

The knowledge representation language FRAMEKIT (Nyberg 1988) represents Ontos concepts and serves as a grammar of the *lingua mentalis* or language-independent description of the subworld of human-computer interaction. Attention must be focused on the task of defining and creating the concept lexicon for this *lingua mentalis*, that is, for the set of interrelated concepts.

In this section we present five postulates that regulate the relations between and among Ontos concepts and their properties. We first discuss some of the extensions to any general-purpose knowledge representation system that enable it to facilitate ontological modeling. Next, we discuss the types of knowledge in a domain model and how that domain model is used in representations of text meaning.

To construct ontological domain models, we need to extend the semantic definitions and constraints already available in FRAMEKIT. These extensions provide an ontological interpretation or semantics for the FRAMEKIT representation language.

Thus, the first four postulates are:

1. *Each frame represents an Ontos concept.*

2. *Concepts are subdivided into the types of things that can be referred to, such as objects, events and their properties.*

3. *Properties of concepts are divided into relations and attributes, with each slot corresponding to a property.*

4. *Relations map concepts into concepts, while attributes map concepts into value sets. The elements of value sets are literals, not concepts.*

So, for instance, `part-of` is a relation. (Consider `((part-of) disk_drive computer)`.) On the other hand, `age` is an attribute whose value set is defined in Ontos as a semiopen integer range (> 0) whose dimensionality is seconds.[2] `color` is an attribute that maps physical objects into a set of symbols (a value set) without a strict ordering.[3]

---

[2]In general, the goal was to define all scalar attributes using standard units of measurement, e.g., seconds in the case of temporal ranges. However, qualitative restrictions on ranges were sufficient for KBMT-89. We use such literal value-set elements as "small," "medium" and "large" instead of numerical ranges.

[3]We considered using a quantitative standard for color, such as the Munsell color notation, which specifies colors on numerical scales of hue, value and chroma and can be expressed as accurately as desired. The boundaries of each color name can be fixed and defined in terms of this or some like numerical notation. As with scalar attributes in KBMT-89, we have adopted the qualitative or "literal" representation of color.

The distinction between relations and attributes captures an intuitive distinction between them, namely, that relations involve two or more things in the world, whereas attributes only involve one. Making reference to an element in a value set is not referring to one thing in terms of another but referring to a given thing in a certain way. This method of encoding an ontological distinction has computational benefits as well. It establishes a syntactic criterion that facilitates consistency and type checking in creating and extending a knowledge base. Moreover, the distinction provides the device for restricting the conceptual granularity of an ontology. For example, while there should be a concept of *number* or *numeral*, it is not necessary for there to be a concept for *every* integer (1, 2, 3, . . .). Similarly, while there needs to be a concept of color, there does not need to be a concept for every color (red, blue, black . . .). However, with regard to representing particular numerals, we discovered in the process of integrating the ontology into the analysis lexicon that virtual frames, or frames created by the parser at run time rather than retrieved from the ontology, made it easier to build parts of ILTs to represent those numbers. Further, special lexical entries were needed to facilitate building ILTs involving value-set elements.

A number of legal facet fillers are allowed in the knowledge representation language.[4] There are five kinds of directly listed values: single concept names, multiple concept names, single value-set elements, multiple symbolic value-set elements and multiple numerical value-set elements.

Recall that concepts include representations of objects, events and properties. Any hope that relatively straightforward intuitions would suffice to assemble representations of objects, say, would have been dashed early on. For instance, among the difficulties in acquiring concepts in the domain of personal computers was how to represent computer screens as *media*. That is, the physical objects that are computer screens might well be understood as appropriately shaped pieces of glass, or particular components or parts of video display tubes. But the KBMT-89 corpus—manuals for operating a personal computer—repeatedly includes instructions that direct a user's attention to messages that are displayed on the screen or to other transient or contingent properties. We will return to this issue later. For now, note that figure 2.1 shows several subnetworks of the ontology produced by Ontos from its resident ontology and with the help of its browsing facility. This output displays some of the ontological commitments that were made during the acquisition of the KBMT-89 domain. These concepts in aggregate constitute the

---

[4]Note that the underlying knowledge representation language guarantees the uniqueness of all (frame slot) pairs.

"semantic memory."

A general-purpose world model also must cover the union of needs for multiple application domains and for any type of rational process. The knowledge required to solve problems in various domains and types of activity includes not only an ontological world model, as described above, but also records of past experiences (including learned or reported ones). To resume the earlier analogy, we find that in addition to grammar and lexicon, our *lingua mentalis* makes itself manifest in "texts" encoded in it. In KBMT-89, ILTs are literally such texts. Hence the final postulate is:

> 5. *The* lingua mentalis *equivalent of a text is an* episode—*a unit of knowledge that encapsulates a particular experience of an intelligent agent and that is typically represented as a temporally and causally ordered subnetwork of frames.*

The ontology and the episodes are sometimes discussed in terms of the contents of two different types of memory: semantic and episodic (Tulving 1985). This distinction seems useful in computational modeling as well. In KBMT-89, ontological concepts and episodes have been represented with varying degree of specificity. The same knowledge representation apparatus is used for storing the contents of both the ontology and the episode cluster.

It becomes important from the theoretical, descriptive and implementational points of view to define an adequate interface between the two memories. We suggest the following approach. The episodes (remembered experiences) are temporally and hierarchically organized sets of tokens of event-types. They are indexed through the type they correspond to and can be interrelated on temporal, causal and other such links. The participant roles in the episodes can be either instantiations of object- and event-types in the semantic memory or references to existing named instances, stored outside semantic memory but having links to their corresponding types (again see figure 2.1).

The presence of a systematic representation and indexing method for episodic knowledge is a prerequisite for case-based reasoning (Kolodner 1984; Schank 1982) and analogical inference (Carbonell 1983a, 1986).

2.1.3   The Domain Ontology

The concept lexicon comprises the domain ontology and the lexical mapping rules entered as the fillers of lexical slots in frames encoding concepts. The addition of the lexical mapping rules is not an addition to the content of the ontology. Rather,

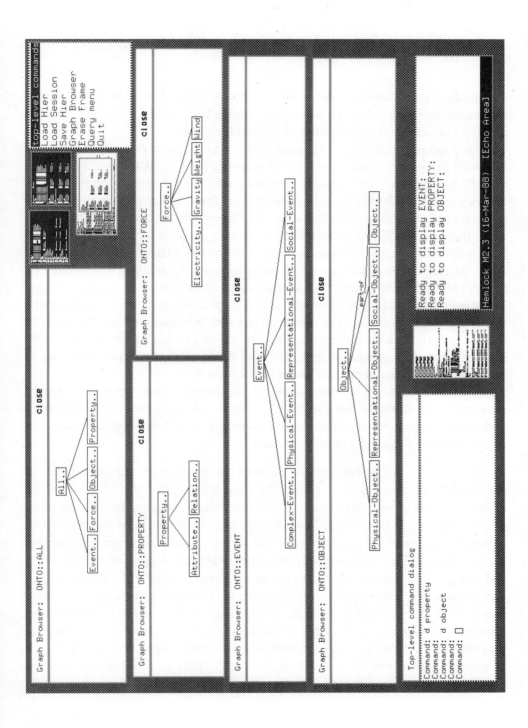

Figure 2.1: **Top-level concept lexicon objects.**

the ontology provides the basis for assigning meanings to lexical items by way of the lexical mapping rules. However, associating lexical items with items in the ontology has required modification of the ontology itself.

The concept lexicon plays an important role throughout the KBMT-89 system. It is used to assign semantics via lexical mapping rules to all the lexical items of the 150 English and 150 Japanese sentences selected for experimentation. The analysis lexicons are built by adding information from the lexical mapping rules to syntactic and morphological information associated with the corresponding lexical items (see chapter 5). At parse time, f-structures are built from source language text by the syntactic parser. A mapping rule interpreter analyzes these f-structures using lexical mapping rules, structural mapping rules, the analysis lexicon and the concept lexicon (here to determine semantic restrictions) to produce parser output. The augmentor builds an ILT from the parser output. When there is an ambiguous parse, the augmentor uses the parser output and information from the concept lexicon to formulate alternative meaning options and builds an ILT in accord with user response. The generation lexicon is also based on the concept lexicon and is used by the generator to produce target language text.

In what follows, we describe some of the decisions that were made during creation of the KBMT-89 concept lexicon. As noted in chapter 1, the system is undergoing continuous revision and improvement. The following represents the system at a key stage in its implementation.

Types and tokens: We distinguish between the meaning of *concepts* on the one hand and the meaning of *propositions* (ILT structures) on the other. The meanings of concepts are types. The meanings of propositions are composed of instances of these types.[5] The concept lexicon specifies, for example, the concept of a computer, the concept of having parts and the concepts of a computer's components. (Figure 2.2 illustrates both the concept lexicon frame for `*computer` and the graph browser's representation of the concept tree.) The ILT represents actual states of affairs in the world, for example, that a particular computer has as components a central processing unit, a keyboard, a disk drive and a monitor. One important implication of this is that the concept lexicon cannot reference particular propositions. It is only permitted to reference *heads* of propositions, such as events or properties that may be understood to classify *types* of propositions—that is, propositions describing changes, relationships and attributes.

---

[5]Actually, other information is also included, but it is not immediately relevant; see the description of ILTs following.

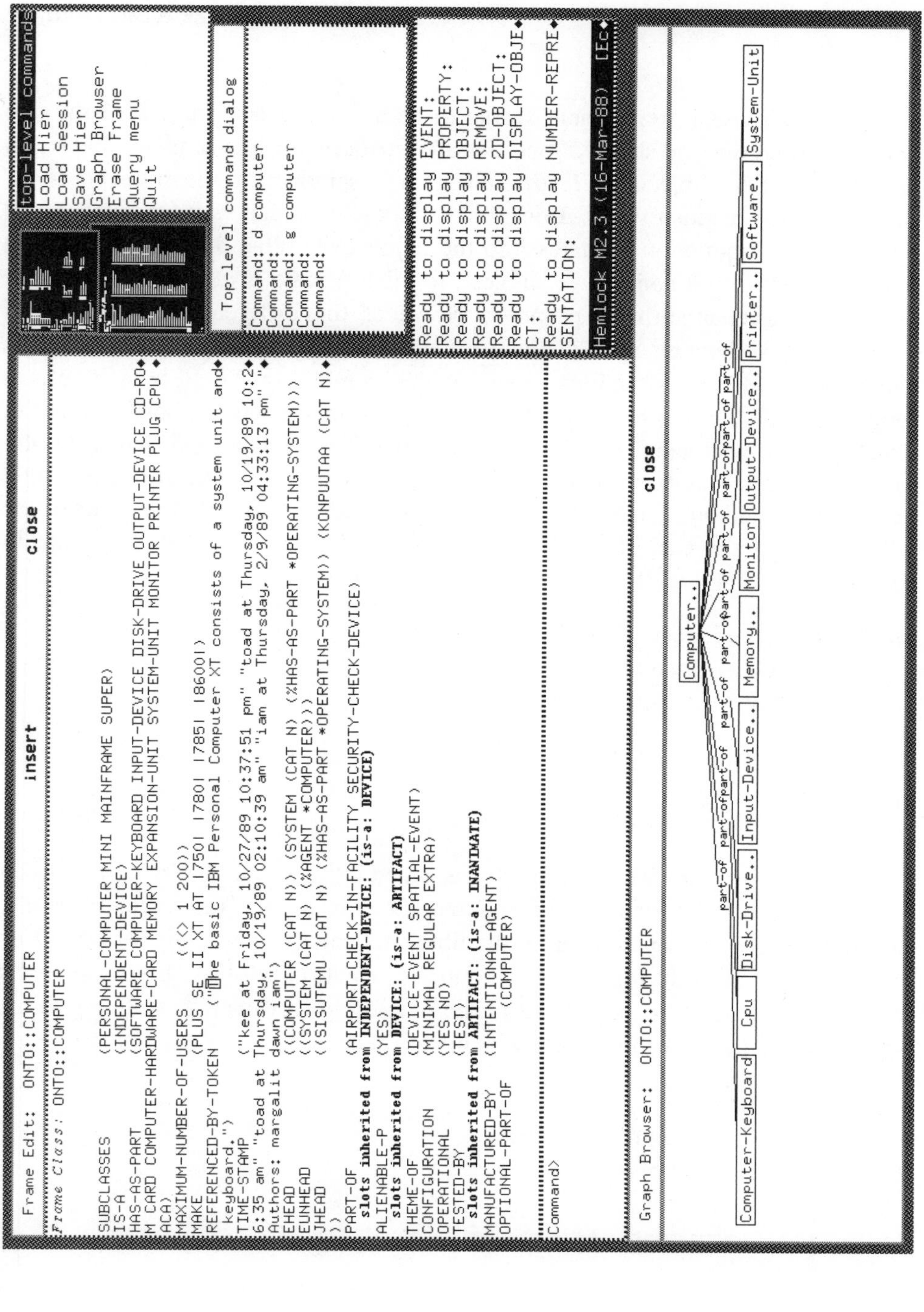

Frame Edit: ONTO::COMPUTER   insert   close

Frame Class: ONTO::COMPUTER

```
SUBCLASSES            (PERSONAL-COMPUTER MINI MAINFRAME SUPER)
IS-A                  (INDEPENDENT-DEVICE)
HAS-AS-PART           (SOFTWARE COMPUTER-KEYBOARD INPUT-DEVICE DISK-DRIVE OUTPUT-DEVICE CD-RO◆
M CARD COMPUTER-HARDWARE-CARD MEMORY EXPANSION-UNIT SYSTEM-UNIT MONITOR PRINTER PLUG CPU ◆
ACA)
MAXIMUM-NUMBER-OF-USERS   ((<> 1 200))
MAKE                  (PLUS SE II XT AT (7501 (7801 (7851 (86001))
REFERENCED-BY-TOKEN   ("The basic IBM Personal Computer XT consists of a system unit and◆
keyboard.")          ("kee at Friday, 10/27/89 10:37:51 pm" "toad at Thursday, 10/19/89 10:2◆
TIME-STAMP
6:35 am" "toad at Thursday, 10/19/89 02:10:39 am" "iam at Thursday, 2/9/89 04:33:13 pm" ""◆
Authors: margalit dawn iam")
EHEAD                 ((COMPUTER (CAT N)) (SYSTEM (CAT N)) (%HAS-AS-PART *OPERATING-SYSTEM)))
EUNHEAD               ((SYSTEM (CAT N) (%AGENT *COMPUTER))
JHEAD                 ((SISUTEMU (CAT N) (%HAS-AS-PART *OPERATING-SYSTEM)) (KONPUUTAA (CAT N))◆
)))
PART-OF               (AIRPORT-CHECK-IN-FACILITY SECURITY-CHECK-DEVICE)
   slots inherited from INDEPENDENT-DEVICE: (is-a: DEVICE)
ALIENABLE-P           (YES)
   slots inherited from DEVICE: (is-a: ARTIFACT)
THEME-OF              (DEVICE-EVENT SPATIAL-EVENT)
CONFIGURATION         (MINIMAL REGULAR EXTRA)
OPERATIONAL           (YES NO)
TESTED-BY             (TEST)
   slots inherited from ARTIFACT: (is-a: INANIMATE)
MANUFACTURED-BY       (INTENTIONAL-AGENT)
OPTIONAL-PART-OF      (COMPUTER)

Command>
```

top-level commands
```
Load Hier
Load Session
Save Hier
Graph Browser
Erase Frame
Query menu
Quit
```

Top-level command dialog
```
Command: d computer
Command:
Command: g computer
Command:
```

```
Ready to display EVENT:
Ready to display PROPERTY:
Ready to display OBJECT:
Ready to display REMOVE:
Ready to display 2D-OBJECT:
Ready to display DISPLAY-OBJE◆
CT:
Ready to display NUMBER-REPRE◆
SENTATION:
Hemlock M2.3 (16-Mar-88)   [Ec◆
```

Graph Browser: ONTO::COMPUTER   close

```
                         Computer..
 part-of  part-of  part-of  part-of  part-of  part-of  part-of  part-of
Disk-Drive.. Input-Device.. Memory.. Monitor Output-Device.. Printer.. Software.. System-Unit
Computer-Keyboard  Cpu
```

Figure 2.2: **Concept lexicon frame for** *computer **and graph browser representation of the concept tree.**

Properties and states: There seems to be a fairly clear intuitive distinction between properties and states. Properties are *attributes* objects can *have* and states are *conditions* that objects are *in*. However, on closer scrutiny, the initial clarity of this distinction begins to fade. Does the distinction between states and properties warrant the introduction of states into the ontology? What does the distinction really amount to? It comes, we suggest, to this: A state is more temporary and more likely to change than a property. However, this difference only represents a difference of degree. Such distinctions allow different users to make different decisions in different situations about whether something should be a state or a property. But this is precisely what ontological analysis is supposed to avoid. Consequently, what are deemed "states" are treated from a commonsensical point of view as properties in our ontology. Thus states such as `*on-state` in example (2.1a) were ruled out. Rather, the meaning of *on* and *off* is handled in terms of the value-set elements `%on` or `%off` of the attribute `*electric-current`, as in (b).

(2.1)   a. `(*on-state`
           `(is-a *state)`
           `(theme *light-switch))`

        b. `(*light-switch`
           `(is-a *switch)`
           `(electrical-current %on %off))`

States and events: We also initially assumed a traditional distinction between states and events. For example, in analyzing the meaning of the sentence *John is hitting the ball*, one can say that in the time between the beginning of the *hitting* event and the end of the *hitting* event, John is in a state of hitting. This again seems to require that states be postulated in the ontology. However, postulating states would require the creation of nearly identical frames:

(2.2)   a. `(*hit`
           `(is-a *physical-event)`
           `(agent *intentional-agent)`
           `(theme *physical-object)`
           `(instrument *stick))`

        b. `(*hitting`
           `(is-a *physical-state)`
           `(agent *intentional-agent)`

```
(theme *physical-object)
(instrument *stick))
```

Rather than create more frames than needed, we handle the meaning of present progressives by instantiating an appropriate event frame and recording aspectual information. Specifically, an `aspect` frame containing a `(phase)` slot filled with `[(and begin (not end))]` is instantiated and embedded in the event frame. Only the event frame is part of the concept lexicon.

The concept `*event` as specified in the lexicon is used in the analysis of tense and aspect. The meaning of most nominalizations can be mapped to events, so that a sentence such as *The destruction of the city was a mistake* can be paraphrased as "It was a mistake to destroy the city." By taking *the destruction* as an event, we gain the generalization that the frame should contain an agent and a theme.

The complete concept lexicon frame for *event* follows. While much of the frame should be transparent or intuitively obvious, some aspects will not be. They are motivated in the next section, and in chapters 5, 6 and 7.

```
(make-frame
   event
   (is-a
      (value
         (common all)))
   (subclasses
      (value
         (common superordinate-event physical-event effect-event cause-event
            complex-event social-event representational-event temporal-event)))
   (part-of
      (value
         (common complex-event)))
   (path
      (sem
         (common physical-object)))
   (theme-of
      (sem
         (common superordinate-event)))
   (agent
      (sem
         (common intentional-agent computer)))
   (goal
      (sem
         (common object)))
   (spatial-relation
      (sem
         (common physical-object event)))
   (beneficiary
      (sem
         (common intentional-agent)))
   (literal-iteration
```

```
        (sem
            (common again always rare frequent)))
    (phase
        (sem
            (common end begin not-end not-begin begin-end during)))
    (frequency
        (sem
            (common literal-iteration)))
    (location
        (sem
            (common event physical-object)))
    (source
        (sem
            (common object)))
    (theme
        (sem
            (common event object force property)))
    (theme-property
        (sem
            (common property)))
    (relative-sequence
        (sem
            (common last this next latest)))
    (definition
        (sem
            (common "any event")))
    (effect
        (sem
            (common event property object)))
    (effect-of
        (sem
            (common event property)))
    (precondition
        (sem
            (common property object event)))
    (condition
        (sem
            (common (not event :dot effect = event :dot precondition))))
    (instrument
        (sem
            (common force event property object)))
    (duration
        (sem
            (common short medium long)))
    (caused-by
        (sem
            (common force object event property
             (*except* intentional-agent computer))))
    (cause-of
        (sem
            (common event property)))
    (before
        (sem
            (common event property)))
```

```
(after
   (sem
      (common event property)))
(temporal-part-of
   (sem
      (common temporal-object)))
(until
   (sem
      (common property)))
(complete
   (sem
      (common yes no)))
(correct
   (sem
      (common yes no)))
(ease-of-task
   (sem
      (common low high medium medium-low medium-high)))
(start
   (sem
      (common event)))
(finish
   (sem
      (common event)))
(degree-of-care
   (sem
      (common low low-mid mid high-mid high)))
(degree-of-force
   (sem
      (common low low-mid mid high-mid high)))
(manner
   (sem
      (common badly ok well)))
(default-manner-p
   (sem
      (common yes no)))
(probability
   (sem
      (common low high medium medium-low medium-high)))
(displayed-on
   (sem
      (common physical-object)))
(referenced-by-token
   (sem
      (common
       "a discussion of the proper and improper use of diskettes
        gave you a better understanding of how to handle diskettes"
       "it is recommended that all files be backed up onto diskettes
        before continuing with this procedure")))
(time-stamp
   (sem
      (common )))
(ehead
   (sem
```

```
    (common (accomplish (cat V)) (use (cat V))
     (procedure (cat N) (%referent-of *procedure))
     (step (cat N) (%referent-of *procedure)
      (%ref-of-display-object *display-object))
     (do (cat V)) (perform (cat V)) (use (cat N)) (step (cat N)))))
 (jhead
    (sem
     (common (tasseisuru (cat V)) (oku (cat V)) (hataraku (cat V))
      (motiiru (cat V)) (siyousuru (cat V)) (tasukeru (cat V))
      (kinou (cat N)) (suru (cat N)) (henkasuru (cat V)) (kaeru (cat V))
      (tezyun (cat N) (%referent-of *procedure))
      (suteppu (cat N) (%referent-of *procedure)
       (%ref-of-display-object *display-object))
      (suteppu (cat N)) (okonau (cat V)) (zikkousuru (cat V))
      (zikkousuru (cat N)) (siyousuru (cat N)))))))
```

Complex events: From the point of view of the concept lexicon, an event is complex just in case it *has-as-part other events in the concept lexicon. Thus, even though an event might seem outwardly complex (e.g., a computer test), we do not make it a complex event unless there is a need to refer to an overriding event and talk about its component events.[6]

A primary example of this is the complex event *to-press-button, which can be divided into three subevents: *press-button, *hold-down-button and *release-button. These subevents are temporally related; this relation is captured in the concept lexicon through slots internal to representations of the subevents. For instance, the *press-button concept contains a *before relational slot filled with *hold-down-button, and *hold-down-button in turn contains an *after slot filled with *press-button and a *before slot filled with *release-button.

So, to capture the meaning of the English sentences

(2.3)   a. Hold down the key for 10 seconds.

         b. Release the key.

it is necessary to posit subevents for the complex event *to-press-button. In Japanese, however, the concept of holding down a key might be expressed as "pressing," with an aspectual marker suggesting "long duration," thus requiring only one event. (In Japanese, one expresses a subevent for "release-button" but not "hold-down-button.")

---

[6]In order to distinguish syntactically *complex-events from other events, we simply prefix *complex-events with to. For example, *to-press-button is a complex event, and *press-button is a simple event. This convention has reduced confusion for users.

In the English analysis lexicon, sentences that mean "type a button" are mapped onto the `*to-press-button` frame, while those meaning either "hold down" or "release" are mapped onto the subevents. The `*duration` attribute tells the system that if a duration is expressed in the subevent `*hold-down-button`, that duration is also the duration of the complex event.

In the Japanese analysis lexicon, we would map the sentence meaning "hold down the key for 10 seconds" onto the `*to-press-button` frame and insert '10 seconds' into the `*duration` slot of the complex event. The `*duration` slot tells the system that if a duration is expressed in the complex event, then it is also the duration of the subevent, in this case `*hold-down-button`. In this way, the (English) generator will produce *hold down the key for 10 seconds* as opposed to *type the key for 10 seconds*. This is what is wanted, as the latter sentence has the preferred meaning "type the key over and over again for 10 seconds."

While the notation described previously is adequate for this project, it is perhaps flawed in that two complex events might share some subevents but order them differently. Similarly, a single subevent of two different complex events might have a different cause or effect depending on the complex event. An ideal notation for complex events must therefore relate the subevents within the complex event.

Determining lexical unit boundaries ontologically: Semantically, the determination of lexical unit boundaries is dictated by conceptual unit boundaries specified ontologically. We offer two examples, reflecting problems that arose as we began to associate lexical mapping rules with the ontology. The first example exhibits a problem arising from the guiding principle that ontology and meaning are language-independent. In the context of KBMT-89, however, such problems were easily handled and in any event were not very numerous. This may be said to vindicate, to some degree, the assumption. Even if the assumption were philosophically flawed, however—and we believe it is not—ensuing problems can be overcome, at least in a restricted domain.

The first example is based on sentences in the corpora giving instructions for unpacking the box that contains a personal computer. It became necessary to decide whether the English *shipping cardboard* should be one lexical unit or two. Its lexical mapping is to the concept `*protection-material`. Now, in Japanese the corresponding lexical unit is *hogosiito*, which has a more specific meaning than `*protection-material` and as such is lexically mapped to a more specific concept— `*protection-sheet`. Hence, in this case, the Japanese lexical unit has a more specific corresponding concept than the English. The solution was to make *shipping cardboard* one lexical unit associated with

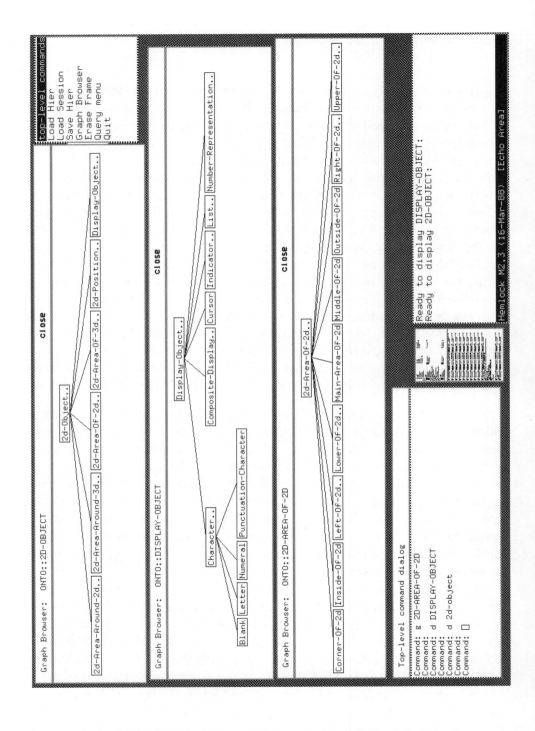

Figure 2.3: **The** *2d-object **hierarchy and some descendants.**

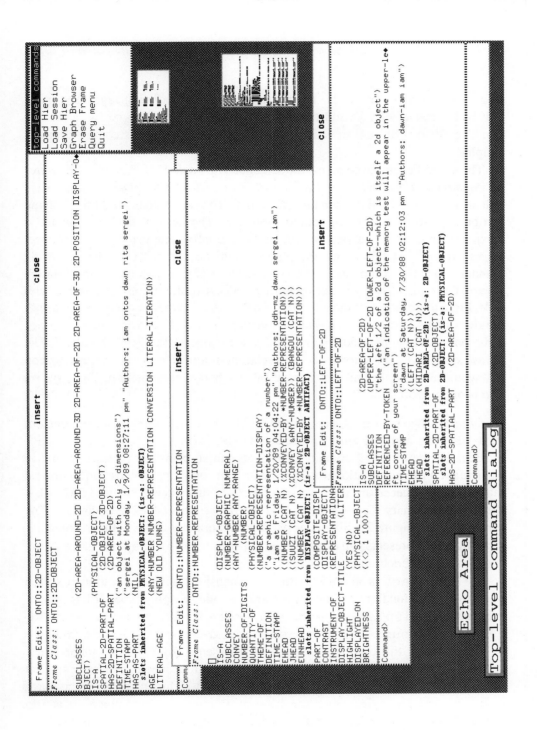

Figure 2.4: **Part of the** `*2d-object` **and related frames.**

*protection-material. Further, since the corresponding Japanese lexical unit is associated with a child concept of *protection-material, namely *protection-sheet, locating it for translation purposes is computationally simple.

The second example concerns the sentence *The basic IBM Personal Computer XT consists of a system unit and keyboard.* For KBMT-89, *system unit* is one lexical unit while *IBM Personal Computer XT* is not. The rationale behind this decision can be explained in terms of compositionality. The head of the latter phrase is *computer* and, after analysis, would be (structurally) mapped into the concept *computer. At this point, the phrase could be composed in the following manner: In order to go from *computer to *ibm-computer, the relation *manufactured-by (which is another concept in the ontology) is filled with *IBM*. From there, the attribute *number-of-users (also a concept) is filled with the slot value single (which is indicative of personal) and goes to *ibm-pc. This concept's relational slot *make (likewise a concept) then is filled with *XT*. The phrase *system unit* does not access any relation or attribute in the concept lexicon that would allow for a comparable traversal and, hence, composition. Thus, *system unit* is one lexical unit.

Objects: Two sorts of objects caused problems in building the concept lexicon: *2d-object and *representational-object.

Because the KBMT-89 domain focuses on human-computer interaction and in particular on the information that is presented on computer screens and in printed manuals, it was necessary to create two classes of the concept *physical-object: the ordinary *3d-object and the rather unusual *2d-object. The screen dump in figure 2.3 illustrates part of the hierarchy for two-dimensional objects; figure 2.4 presents part of the *2d-object, number-representation and left-of-2d frames.

A *2d-object is an object with two dimensions, such as a computer screen understood as a medium and not as a part of a video-display tube. It has several subclasses: *display-object, *2d-area-of-2d, *2d-area-of-3d, *2d-area-around-2d, *2d-area-around-3d and *2d-position.

It is not clear that objects such as those represented by *display-object are physical in nature, in part because of the strong tendency to think of physical objects as three-dimensional. But it is clear that two-dimensional objects have many physical properties—they can be seen by more than one person, stand in spatial relations, be pointed to and so forth. Once the decision was made to consider display objects as two-dimensional physical objects, it was easier to introduce other two-dimensional objects to handle a related but somewhat different problem. Consider the sentences:

(2.4)   a. An indication of the memory test will appear in the upper-left corner of your screen.

         b. Before arranging your system read the note below.

What sort of meaning should be ascribed to *upper-left corner* and *below*? There is a strong tendency to think of *below* as expressing a relation, for example, "A is below B." But in sentence (2.4b), what is *note* related to? Again, there is a strong tendency to think of *left-of* as being relational as well—"A is to the left of B." However, in both the case of *below* and *upper-left-corner*, the lexical items seem to be referring to objects; now, these objects might be insubstantial, but they are nevertheless in some sense physical. It was decided to make these `*2d-objects` as well. In this way, a `*2d-object` like `*display-object` and a `*corner` can be `*spatially-part-of` another `*2d-object`, such as `*2d-area`.

What are called "representational objects" in KBMT-89 also required difficult decisions. A `*representational-object` has three subdivisions: `*information`, `*temporal-object` and `*language`. We maintain that postulating objects such as `*information` in the ontology is necessary to capture a unique relation such as "convey/conveyed-by," which is a relation not between physical objects but between a physical object and a nonphysical object or representational object. For example, we maintain that a picture of a house does not `*convey` a house. Rather, the picture *conveys information*, the *referent* of which is a house. That is, the house is the `*referent-of` the `*information` that is `*conveyed-by` the picture.

Consider `*temporal-object`. Such objects *represent* the temporal aspect of events; hence they are `*representational-objects`. They were introduced for reasons similar to those for introducing `*2d-areas` containing `*2d-objects`, such as corners. `*temporal-objects` like `*present`, `*past` and `*future` contain other temporal-objects called `*moments` and `*events`. They are used to analyze the meanings of terms like *later, now* and *for now*. `*moments` are temporally part of any `*temporal-object`, but they also have `*moments` as parts.[7] Also, `*past`, `*present` and `*future` are

---

[7]This commits us to `*moments` being indefinitely divisible. In the present domain, this is not a problem. However, one could put a stop to the indefinite divisibility of `*temporal-objects` by introducing `*temporal-points` as the parts of `*moments`. Then `*temporal-points` would be atomic `*temporal-objects`.

represented as *temporal-objects analogous to the way *2d-areas are represented as *2d-objects. And *past, *present and *future have as parts *moments that can be related by *temporal-relations such as *before and *after.[8]

Given present distinctions, the word *later* can then be analyzed as a *moment that is temporally part of the *future, the word *now* as a *moment temporally part of the *present and the phrase *for now* as a duration starting in the *present and extending to a moment in the *future.

A full sense of the function of the KBMT-89 concept lexicon requires the introduction of other components and processes with which it interacts. Some of these key components will be introduced in chapters 4 through 7. Now, however, it is best to introduce a representational device that relies on the concept lexicon, namely the interlingua text.

2.2   The Interlingua Text

The use of world knowledge is widely and correctly perceived as the salient property of a knowledge-based machine translation system. Many researchers, however, do not proceed to a detailed discussion of the peculiarities of the use and representation of world knowledge in such systems. This leads to a number of misconceptions and inaccurate assessments regarding the amount and nature of research and development necessary for producing a large natural language processing system.

First, the relationship between the interlingua text (the results of a comprehensive analysis of an input text) and the concept lexicon is typically not well understood, and the important differences between the two not well appreciated— with respect either to the nature of their elements or to the differences in the knowledge representation languages used for their specification.

Second, uncertainty prevails over the status and utility of a *speech situation* or the pragmatic knowledge encoded or inferable from the source language text. The pragmatic aspects of a source language text are an indispensable component of its overall meaning. It was undertaken to represent this kind of information in the KBMT-89 ILTs and to realize it in the project's target languages. In what follows, we discuss the types of knowledge covered by KBMT-89.

---

[8]KBMT-89 does not—indeed cannot—handle sets. Again, this is not a problem in the present domain.

2.2.1 Varieties of World Knowledge in a Knowledge-Based MT System

The concept lexicon, we will recall, contains an ontological model that provides uniform definitions of basic categories (such as objects, event-types, relations, properties, and episodes) used as building blocks for descriptions of particular domains. This world model is relatively static and organized as a multiply inter-connected network of ontological concepts.

An interlingua text is a representation of actual events in the world, as reported in a source language text. ILTs can be represented as networks of event- and state-tokens, complete with their participants, connected by a number of causal, temporal, spatial and other propositional links. These event-tokens, or *episodes*, are indexed through their corresponding ontological types. We do not produce the representations of these actual events, states and so forth on the fly. The main device in this process is the *instantiation* of tokens of appropriate concept types from the concept lexicon. Thus, the representation of the meaning of a text is understood as creating an episode. The participant roles in the episodes can be either instantiations of object- and event-types in the ontology or references to already existing named instances (such as *IBM* or *The Lyceum* or *Hank's Computer Shack*), permanently stored in a non-ontological part of the domain model. In principle, however, the episodes are relatively much more dynamic than the ontology—they are "forgotten" as well as merged with other episodes in memory. The distinctions among the various types of world knowledge that must be used in a comprehensive natural language processing (NLP) system are discussed in Nirenburg et al. 1991, and will not be reviewed further here.

2.2.2 Integration of Discourse and Propositional Knowledge

It is common, and perhaps epistemologically required, for scientific research to focus on a particular facet of a complex problem, either theory- or application-oriented, often to the comparative neglect of other, equally important problems. Natural language processing is, of course, no exception. Thus, specific projects have been devoted to components of an NLP system such as the design of knowl-edge representation languages in which to describe the ontology of an application (sub)world (e.g., Wilensky 1984; Brachman and Schmolze 1985); languages to describe events that take place during the use of a knowledge-based system (e.g., Kolodner 1984); and languages that help capture textual peculiarities such as co-hesion forces, characteristics of participants in the speech situation and thematic information (e.g., Tucker et al. 1986).

Other types of projects have used one or more knowledge representation language to acquire actual compendia of knowledge, namely, describing the ontologies of application (sub)worlds (e.g., Lenat et al. 1985; Hobbs 1986); collecting caches of events in an application (sub)world (e.g., Ashley and Rissland 1988; compare Ashley, forthcoming); describing the discourse/pragmatic structure of texts or dialogues (e.g., Grosz and Sidner 1985); and writing lexicons that connect lexical units of a natural language with elements of the forementioned ontologies, histories and structures (e.g., Nirenburg and Raskin 1987a).

Still another family of projects has involved the design of control structures for computer programs that, making use of this knowledge, translated natural language inputs into representations in the above artificial languages or vice versa (e.g., Fass 1986a, b; Jacobs 1985).

An important point is that, even while these tasks are universally recognized as extremely complex, the extent of meaning extraction and manipulation in application-oriented NLP has been typically limited. Some systems limit themselves to syntactic analysis only. Others add the analysis of "logical form." Those dealing with pragmatic/discourse-related issues are typically miniature systems designed specifically to test certain pragmatic/discourse hypotheses.

The relatively shallow and/or fragmented approach to natural language understanding was justified not only by the task's complexity but also by the supposed requirements of certain applications. One example is the transfer-based machine translation systems of the 1970s. But note also the relatively shallow requirements for the semantic description of input into many natural language generation systems (see Marcus 1987 for a critique of lexical selection in current systems). At the same time, some systems (e.g., McKeown 1985) attend to the discourse structure of the input. Some are even coupled with a separate discourse manager in a particular application (compare the Counselor project at the University of Massachusetts [e.g., Pustejovsky 1987]). This approach may be attributable in part to the nature of typical system environments, namely, natural language front-ends to various databases or other dialogue systems. With other applications, generation will have to attend more closely to all types of meaning. There are, however, a number of applications in which progress depends on a simultaneous use of more kinds of knowledge than before; specifically, progress depends on integrating the propositional and nonpropositional knowledge about concept types, concept tokens and text units.

2.2.3   Representative Classes of Discourse Knowledge

Knowledge requirements for knowledge-based machine translation are usually perceived as involving representations of propositional knowledge, similar to the ones described previously. However, to ensure adequate levels of understanding of input texts, it is necessary to extract and overtly represent nonpropositional *pragmatic* and *discourse* meaning about concept instances. Pragmatic meaning is usually understood as pertaining to the attitudes of the speaker/hearer to the set of uttered propositions. Discourse meaning reflects the (language-dependent) rules of combining separate utterances into coherent texts.

Problems whose solutions depend, in whole or in part, on nonpropositional knowledge are not esoteric but quite pervasive in meaning analysis. These problems include referential ambiguity, thematic structure of text, understanding of indirect speech acts and interpretation of discourse cohesion markers, such as *moreover* or *in any case*.

2.2.4   Combining Concept Tokens into Networks

This subsection is devoted to a discussion of the ILT syntax. Unlike a natural language text, an interlingua text is not linear. It is a potentially very complex network of interlingua units of sentence size, linked by cohesion markers. An interlingua text is represented as a frame that serves as an index for the interlingua clauses constituting the text. ILT clauses are represented as frames. The ILT clause is the place where event instances (tokens) are put into their modal, discourse and speech-situation context. Event- and object-tokens that appear in ILTs are produced by obtaining tokens of the appropriate concept types in the domain model and augmenting them with various property values identified during source-language text analysis in translation. It follows that the slots whose values express a component of contextual propositional meaning (e.g., negation) or any type of nonpropositional meaning (including discourse meaning) appear only in ILT frames for event- and object-tokens, not in the domain model.

Every token of an interlingua concept stands in the *is-token-of* relationship to its corresponding type. The frame for a type and the frame for a corresponding token are, however, not identical in either structure or semantics, even though they share some slot names. There are, of course, regular correspondences between units of the concept lexicon and ILTs. Property values in concept tokens are typically elements or subsets of data types listed as ontological constraints in the corresponding slots of the concept lexicon. Thus, as already noted, the `color` property slot in the concept lexicon frame for *flower* can be occupied by a list

`<white yellow blue red purple ...>`. But the ILT frame `rose21`, which is a token of a subclass of the class *flower*, will have the value `red` as the contents of its `color` slot.

The nonpropositional knowledge derived from the natural language input is overtly represented in interlingua text. Interlingua sentences, clauses and events carry this information. The overt representation of interlingua text units, not just as a sequence of events, is one of the technical innovations of the KBMT-89 project. Note that for representing nonpropositional relations (such as discourse or focus), we use the same knowledge structures as those traditionally used for representing the propositional content of natural language input.

The formalism used for representing ILTs is a kind of semantic network. The types of nodes in this network include

- ILT *clauses*, which are nodes that represent the combined propositional and nonpropositional meanings of a "unit" utterance; the representations of a proposition, a speech act and a focus value are combined at this level. Natural language sentences are syntactically defined entities and can contain more than one clause.

- ILT *propositions*, which typically represent the meaning of an action or a state; modality and aspect are specified in this node.

- ILT *roles*, which typically represent a conceptual object connected to a proposition through a well-defined case link.

The links in this semantic network are of the following kinds:

- *Role relations* (`agent`, `theme`, etc.), which connect roles to propositions;

- *Temporal relations*, which introduce a partial ordering of the temporal values of propositions and speech acts;

- *Causal relations* (causality and enablement), which are defined on propositions. These mark certain preconditions and effects that have been mentioned elliptically in the source language text (in a machine translation generator) or have been mentioned explicitly in the text plan (in interface-supporting generators);

- *Discourse cohesion relations*, which are defined on clauses and represent the rhetorical structure of the text to be generated; and

- *Focus-related links* (given and new), which connect a clause node with some of its component nodes.

Computer programs require formal symbolic representations of these networks. However, for human inspection it is desirable to be able to represent the networks graphically. The design of new graphics editors continues as a focus of post-KBMT-89 research.

2.2.5 Interlingua Text and the Concept of Microtheories

Significant progress has been made recently in natural language processing with respect to the theories of syntax. Semantic and pragmatic phenomena traditionally have been less amenable to computational analysis. It does not seem likely, then, that an integrated semantic/pragmatic theory that covers all lexical and compositional phenomena, as well as the various pragmatic considerations, will be formulated in the near future. This assessment becomes even more plausible if one recognizes the need to provide heuristics for automatic recognition of the multiple meaning facets of natural language texts. At the same time, linguistics has accumulated a significant body of knowledge about the various semantically laden phenomena in natural languages.

The foregoing suggests that one of the more productive ways of building a comprehensive computational model of human language understanding and generation behavior would be to develop a large number of *microtheories*. Each would treat a particular linguistic phenomenon in a particular language or group of languages and then provide a computational architecture that, in turn, would integrate the operation of all the modules. Thus, one can envisage microtheories of time, modality, speech act, causality and so forth.

In the rest of this chapter, we will illustrate how an integrated representation scheme such as our ILT can be used to capture the phenomena belonging to the various microtheories. The structure of the interlingua text described here is a superset of the actual ILT used in KBMT-89. In this project, certain ILT frames, slots and fillers will not be used because the constraints on the application render such microtheories spurious. For instance, in KBMT-89 there has been no need for the text frame, since we are working with single sentences; there seem to be no sentences with modality "desirable"; and the information about focus is not used to its maximum capacity. In addition, some of the linguistic microtheories have not yet been developed sufficiently to allow computational treatment. Therefore, some simplifications occur in the KBMT-89 representations: only a subset of the quantifiers is actually used, and symbolic rather than numerical values have been

assumed for most of the attributes and intensifiers. The specification that follows
can be used as the semantic and pragmatic representation component in machine
translation and general NLP systems that process multisentential text and require
a finer-grained description than the one found sufficient for our research.

2.2.6   Meaning and Representation

In this subsection we present some of the decisions made with regard to the
representation of natural language meaning components. The components to be
mentioned are clauses, propositions and roles, speech acts, quantification, modality
and discourse cohesion. Some are relatively undeveloped but are included to give
a sense of the approach. (For illustrations of others, such as space and time, see
Nirenburg et al. 1987a.)

First we consider ILT *clauses*. The clause representations have the following
structure:

```
clause ::= ((id <symbol>)
            (proposition <event-token>)
            (modality modality-set)
            (speech-act speech-act)
            (focus
             [(scope text | clause+ | proposition+ | role+)
              (given text | clause+ | proposition+ | role+)
              (new text | clause+ | proposition+ | role+))]*
            (discourse-relation discourse-expr))
```

Here, the focus slot refers to the thematic structure of a text component. Its
scope subslot is needed to determine the "background" against which given and
new information are determined. In some cases, there could be more than one
focus nucleus inside one (usually compound) sentence, as in (2.5).

(2.5)   When it comes to work, nobody beats him, but when it comes to relax-
           ation, Jack could learn something from Fred.

One plausible analysis of the thematic structure of this sentence would be that
there are two focus nuclei, corresponding to the two coordinate clauses, with both
the subordinate clauses serving as values of given and both main clauses as values
of new. Note that other analyses are possible. (A more complete microtheory of
focus will involve nested focus scopes and a taxonomy of given and new values.)
Thus, another treatment of the thematic structure of this text would involve four
focus nuclei, corresponding to each clause; the distribution of the values of given
and new are presented in table 2.1.

SCOPE	GIVEN	NEW
Clause1	[undefined]	*work*
Clause2	*beats him*	*nobody*
Clause3	[undefined]	*relaxation*
Clause4	*learn*	*from Fred*

Table 2.1: **Distribution of focus values for coordinate clauses.**

All *propositions* are tokens of events or properties (subsuming states). All roles are tokens of objects, events or properties. Property values listed in their corresponding type frames in the concept lexicon serve as default value ranges for the `proposition` and `role` slots, unless concrete values are listed in the proposition. Thus, if the concept lexicon frame for `*rose` has the slot `(color (value pink white red yellow))`, this range will be assumed as default for the instance `rose25`, unless the frame for it will explicitly include a slot like `(color (value white))`. The ILT formalism as such does not preclude the substitution of values from outside the ranges specified in the concept lexicon—for instance, having `(color (value blue))` in the prior example. The decision to allow this should be made depending on whether the analysis module in the system is expected to process metonymy and metaphor.

Following is the structure of proposition slots in an ILT:

```
proposition ::= ((id <symbol>)
                (is-token-of event-type | property-type)
                (property value)*
                (proposition-quantifier p-quantifier-set)
                (temporal-relation temporal-expr)
                (spatial-relation spatial-expr)
                (subworld computer-world | medicine-world | ...)
                (aspect
                    (phase begin | begin-end | end)
                    (duration <positive-real> | indefinite)
                    (iteration (times <integer>) | (lap <integer>)))
                (role-list (role-type role*))
```

And this is the structure of roles and role-types:

```
role ::= ((id <symbol>)
          (referent <symbol>)
          (description
            (is-token-of object | property)
            (property value)*
            (role-quantifier r-quantifier-set)
            (subworld computer-world | medicine-world | ...)
            (set-count integer))

role-type ::= agent | theme | patient | source |
              instrument | destination | ...
```

The value of subworld effectively works as a "view" mechanism that allows a knowledge-based machine translation system to use only the part of the concept lexicon that actually describes the current domain, while having additional domain descriptions in the same lexicon. Note that markers such as this constituted the first (and often only) semantic constraints used in earlier MT systems for word sense disambiguation.

The aspectual properties of events are factored out of the basic set of concept lexicon events. For each event-type used as the head of a proposition we determine the three aspectual properties *phase, duration* and *iteration*. This approach helps keep in check the number of primitive concepts in the concept lexicon. The aspect microtheory we are using in the ILT was developed by Pustejovsky (1988) and was restructured in computational terms, as described in Nirenburg and Pustejovsky 1988.

The taxonomy of *speech acts* is underdeveloped in this microtheory. The reason is not the difficulty of defining additional types of speech acts but rather the difficulty in formulating heuristic rules that would allow the analyzer to distinguish between, say, a promise and a threat. The value of the time of the speech act contributes to the representation of the meaning of tense in the source language sentence. Here follows the structure of speech acts in ILTs:

```
speech-act ::= (speech-act
                 (type statement | definition | request-info |
                     request-action)
                 (direct? yes | no)
                 (speaker object)
                 (hearer object)
                 (time temporal-expr)
                 (space spatial-expr))
```

And here is the *quantification* microtheory:

```
r-quantifier-set ::= n, 0 < n < 1
```

Here, the value '0.8' means "most"; '1' means "all" or "each"; '0' means "no"; and '0.2' means "few." One direction of improvement for quantification will take into account the concept of argumentative scales (e.g., Ducrot 1980; compare Defrise 1989), which would allow us to distinguish between (a) and (b) in (2.6) (Defrise and Nirenburg 1989).

(2.6)   a. I have little money (— only $10).

       b. I have a little money (— almost $10).

Even though the numerical values for the quantifiers *little* and *a little* will be identical (e.g., 0.2), the meaning of the two phrases is quite different. Speaking from an application-oriented standpoint, however, having an involved theory of quantification is relatively much less important than one would be led to believe in a reading of recent semantic literature. So

```
p-quantifier-set ::= negation | universal | existential | ...
```

may be representable in the same manner as *r*-quantifiers: negation is '0', universal is '1', existential is any intermediate value ranging from "almost never" to "very seldom" to "seldom" to "sometimes" to "often" to "usually" to "almost always."

The microtheory of *modality* reflects the paucity of modal meanings in the sublanguage of computer hardware. If the system is to be used in a subworld rich in modal expressions, the microtheory would require a significant amount of improvement, especially with respect to heuristic rules. The structure is as follows:

```
modality-set ::= real | desirable | conditional |
                 probable | possible | necessary | ...
```

Discourse cohesion markers are used to represent nonpropositional relations among clauses and sentences. The following microtheory is based on Tucker et al. 1986. A number of other theories of discourse cohesion have been suggested (e.g., Grosz and Sidner 1985); such findings would need to be incorporated in any substantial extension of the KBMT-89 system or its domains. In the structure that follows, `condi` is used to avoid congruence with `conditional` in the modality set.

```
discourse-expr ::= (cohesion-marker clause clause)*

cohesion-marker ::= condi | expansion | similar |
                    generalization | contrastive |
                    digression | ...
```

2.2.7   A Sample ILT

The particular tasks of KBMT-89, as well as the current unavailability of certain microtheories, have constrained the use of the various constructs in the ILT. This is expected, as should be clear to anybody who has attempted to implement a theoretical construct as a component of a large AI-oriented software system.

Nevertheless, the prospects for such development are arguably bright. We can conclude this chapter with an example of an actual KBMT-89 ILT. The role of ILTs in the system is made plain in subsequent chapters.

For the sake of the example below, consider as input to analysis the Japanese and English sentences given in (2.7).

(2.7)   a. Kaku souti no setuzoku ga syuuryou si ta ra sisutemu yunitto to purin-taa no den-gen-suitti ga 'kiru' gawa ni natte iru koto okakunin-si te kudasai.

   b. Confirm that the power unit switches of the system unit and the printer are in the 'off' position when the connection of each device is complete.

The ILT that follows would serve as input to the KBMT-89 augmentor. Note below that a number of frame slots are included as indices (e.g., all the -id slots). Asterisks, recall, mark a reference to a concept from the domain model.

```
(make-frame clause1
    (ilt-type (value clause))
    (clauseid (value clause1))
    (propositionid (value proposition1))
    (discourse-cohesion-marker (value (conditional clause2)))
    (speechactid (value speech-act1)))

(make-frame proposition1
    (ilt-type (value proposition))
    (propositionid (value proposition1))
    (clauseid (value clause1))
    (aspect (value aspect1))
    (complete (value yes))
    (is-token-of (value *connect))
    (agent (value unknown))
    (theme (value role2))
```

```
      (time (value time1)))

(make-frame role2
   (ilt-type (value role))
   (clauseid (value clause1))
   (is-token-of (value *device))
   (r-quantifier (value universal))
   (reference (value definite)))

(make-frame aspect1
   (ilt-type (value aspect))
   (clauseid (value clause1))
   (phase (value end)))

(make-frame speech-act1
   (ilt-type (value speech-act))
   (speech-act (value statement))
   (direct? (value yes))
   (speaker (value author))
   (hearer (value reader))
   (time (value (before time1))))

(make-frame clause2
   (ilt-type (value clause))
   (clauseid (value clause2))
   (propositionid (value proposition2))
   (speechactid (value speech-act2)))

(make-frame proposition2
   (ilt-type (value proposition))
   (propositionid (value proposition2))
   (clauseid (value clause2))
   (aspect (value aspect2))
   (is-token-of (value *confirm))
   (agent (value role3))
   (theme (value clause3))
   (time (value (after time1))))

(make-frame role3
   (ilt-type (value role))
   (clauseid (value clause2))
   (is-token-of (value *reader))
   (reference (value definite)))

(make-frame aspect2
   (ilt-type (value aspect))
   (clauseid (value clause2))
   (phase (value end)))

(make-frame speech-act2
   (ilt-type (value speech-act))
   (speech-act (value command))
   (direct? (value yes))
   (speaker (value author)))
```

```
        (hearer (value reader))
        (time (value (before time1))))

(make-frame clause3
    (ilt-type (value clause))
    (clauseid (value clause3))
    (propositionid (value proposition3))
    (speechactid (value speech-act3)))

(make-frame proposition3
    (ilt-type (value proposition))
    (propositionid (value proposition3))
    (clauseid (value clause3))
    (aspect (value aspect3))
    (is-token-of (value *discrete-position))
    (range (value off-position))
    (domain (value role4))
    (time (value (after time1))))

(make-frame role4
    (ilt-type (value role))
    (clauseid (value clause3))
    (is-token-of (value *set))
    (member (value *power-switch))
    (belongs-to (value role5)))

(make-frame role5
    (ilt-type (value role))
    (clauseid (value clause3))
    (is-token-of (value *set))
    (member (value *system-unit *printer))
    (type (value conjunction)))

(make-frame aspect3
    (ilt-type (value aspect))
    (clauseid (value clause3))
    (phase (value end)))

(make-frame speech-act3
    (ilt-type (value speech-act))
    (speech-act (value command))
    (direct? (value yes))
    (speaker (value author))
    (hearer (value reader))
    (time (value (before time1))))
```

Chapter 3

Syntactic Theory and Processing

■ LORI S. LEVIN

Knowledge about the world is at the core of a knowledge-based machine translation program. However, this knowledge cannot be extracted from a text unless we are clear about how languages encode it syntactically. This language-specific syntactic knowledge includes, for example, how a verb's arguments are distinguished from each other by case markings and word order and how tense and aspect are represented by auxiliary verbs and inflectional endings. So, this chapter describes the grammar formalism with which to represent language-specific syntactic knowledge.

Syntactic grammars are used for analysis and generation in KBMT-89. During analysis, the parser uses the grammar to build feature structures for source language sentences. The analysis mapping rules then map the feature structures onto frames in the concept lexicon or ontology. The resulting instantiated frames, which we call *parser output*, are in turn input to the augmentor, which produces an interlingua text. During generation, the generation mapping rules produce a feature structure from an interlingua text. This feature structure is then sent to the generator, which uses the generation grammar to produce a target language utterance. For ease of exposition, this chapter describes the grammar formalism as it is used in parsing. Differences between the analysis and generation formalisms are mentioned in chapter 4.

KBMT-89 employs a *unification-based* grammar formalism that has its roots in the theory of Lexical Functional Grammar described by Kaplan and Bresnan (1982).

We have also been influenced by work on other unification-based grammars, such as Kay 1985; Shieber 1986; and Pollard and Sag 1987. Still, our rules, output structures and organizational principles adhere most closely to those of LFG.

3.1   Two Types of Syntactic Structure

Each grammar rule consists of a context-free phrase structure rule and a set of equations. The context-free phrase structure rule describes a *constituent structure* (c-structure) and the equations describe a *functional structure* or *feature structure* (f-structure) (Kaplan and Bresnan 1982). In the grammar rule below, the context-free phrase structure rule describes a tree in which an S node immediately dominates an NP node and a VP node. The equations describe a feature structure associated with the S node. The first equation indicates that the feature structure for the S node is merged or *unified* with the feature structure for the VP node. The second equation indicates that the feature structure for the NP node is the subject in the feature structure for the S node.

```
(<S> --> (<NP>  <VP>)
((x0 = x2)
((x0 subj) = x1)))
```

The notation for writing syntactic rules will be described in detail in section 3.2, along with examples of how the notation is interpreted during parsing. The remainder of this section characterizes the types of information represented in c-structures and f-structures, describes the role of c-structure and f-structure in syntactic theory and motivates the utility of these structures in machine translation.

3.1.1   Constituent Structure

A c-structure is a tree that is generated by a context-free grammar. The nodes in the tree are labeled as parts of speech, such as N (noun) and V (verb), or as syntactic categories, such as NP (noun phrase) and VP (verb phrase). In English, the leaf nodes of the tree are words, but in Japanese the leaf nodes of trees are individual characters. Terminal nodes for Japanese are introduced by phrase structure rules, such as the one that follows. This rule produces a tree with a node labeled v5-dan dominating eight leaf nodes labeled t, o, r, i, n, o, z and o. (See chapter 4 for more information about parsing terminal strings in Japanese and for discussion of the choice of word-based parsing for English and character-based parsing for Japanese.)

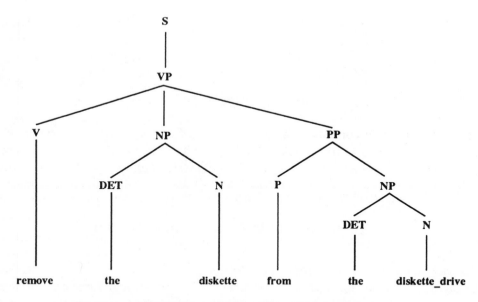

Figure 3.1: **Example of English constituent structure.**

```
(<v5-dan> <--> (t o r i n o z o)
 (((x0 root) = torinozoku))))
```

In LFG-based unification grammars, c-structures represent only surface word order and constituency. Therefore, there are no deep structures or rules that transform one c-structure into another; all possible sentence structures, including passive sentences and *wh*-questions, are generated by the phrase-structure rules, not by tree-to-tree transformations.

The interpretation of unexpressed but understood elements (such as the subject *you* in *turn on the computer*) and the grammatical role played by fronted *wh*-phrases are represented in f-structure or in the interlingua text. As a consequence, there is no need for empty leaf nodes in c-structure representing moved, deleted or understood elements.[1] (Chapter 4 contains more information about the interpretation of

---

[1]Kaplan and Bresnan (1982) present an analysis of long-distance dependencies that includes empty categories. However, the theory of functional uncertainty (Kaplan and Zaenen 1989) eliminates the need for empty categories in the treatment of long-distance dependencies. The KBMT-89 English grammar implements a modified slash-category strategy (Gazdar et al. 1985) without empty categories for resolving long-distance dependencies.

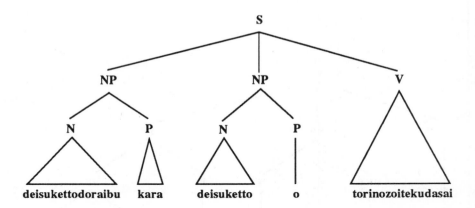

Figure 3.2: **Example of Japanese constituent structure.**

elements that are "missing" from c-structure.)

Figures 3.1 and 3.2 represent c-structures in English and Japanese for the sentence *Remove the diskette from the diskette drive* and its Japanese translation, *Deisukettodoraibu kara disuketto o torinozoite kudasai.*[2] The triangles in the Japanese tree represent the branching of the lexical categories into individual characters.

3.1.2   Feature Structures

Feature structures are sets of feature-value pairs. The features are usually grammatical functions, such as `subj` (subject) and `obj` (object), or names of grammatical features, such as `tense`, `number` and `person`. `root` is a special feature whose value (usually the citation form of a word) is associated with a *lexical mapping rule* (see chapters 5 and 6). This enables a lexical item to be mapped onto a concept.

Feature values can be atomic symbols or feature structures. For example, in the (simplified) Japanese f-structure that follows, the value of the `time` feature is the atom `present`, but the value of `obj` is an f-structure that consists of features and values. Inside the f-structure that is itself the value of the `obj` function, the feature `wh` has the value '-'. A feature's value can also be a disjunction of values

---

[2]Both trees are simplified from the actual English and Japanese grammars.

Note that *deisuketto* is the preferred transliteration of the Japanese word for "diskette" but that it sometimes is also rendered as `de-isuketto` in examples and traces. This is to facilitate mapping to kata-kana forms. *Kudasai* is the marker for moderate formality.

or a set of values.[3]

```
((ppadjunct ((part kara) (cat N) (root deisukettodoraibu)))
 (obj ((wh -) (case o) (cat N) (root deisuketto)))
 (causative -) (obj-case o) (subj-case ga) (passive -)
 (subcat trans) (formal +) (time present) (mood ((root imp)))
 (vtype v-5dan-ki) (cat V) (root torinozoku)))
```

Grammatical functions such as `subj` and `obj` as used here are quite different from "subject" and "object" as defined in traditional grammar books. In traditional grammars, "subject" might be defined as the actor or agent in a sentence, and "object" might be defined as something that is affected by the action. However, we follow LFG and Relational Grammar (Perlmutter 1983) in treating "subject" and "object" as purely syntactic categories. Membership in the categories is determined exclusively by syntactic behavior. Tests for subjecthood in the LFG framework are discussed by Andrews (1982); Mohanan (1982); Levin (1985); Zaenen (1987); and Mitamura (1989).

For the most part, our grammars draw from the set of functions in table 3.1, which is similar to that proposed by Bresnan (1982a). Each grammatical function name in the table is followed by a description and one or two sentences in which an italicized string exemplifies the function. The grammars of English and Japanese, as well as other languages, draw from this inventory of grammatical functions.

In contrast, grammatical features such as number and tense can vary a great deal from language to language. For example, some languages have singular, plural and dual nouns (Warlpiri), some have only singular and plural nouns (English) and some do not necessarily mark number on nouns at all (Japanese). There is also considerable variation in grammatical systems of case, tense and aspect. We have so far not enforced a universal inventory of grammatical features.

It is important to understand that f-structures represent grammatical functions and not "meanings." Two sentences that have the same meaning can have different f-structures if their grammatical functions are different. For example, *Someone turned off the computer* and *The computer was turned off* have different f-structures because *the computer* is direct object in the first sentence, but it is the subject in the second sentence. The similarity in meaning between these two sentences is represented by the interlingua text. In contrast, the sentences *Is the repairman fixing*

---

[3]In the KBMT-89 system, feature structures cannot be *reentrant*. That is, two features cannot share the same instance of the same value, although they can have values that appear identical. This is a result of the pseudounification algorithm. (See Tomita and Knight 1988 for details.)

FEATURE NAME	DESCRIPTION	EXAMPLE(S)
subj	subject	*An expansion unit* is attached. Do *you* have an expansion unit?
obj	object	Disconnect *the expansion unit cable* from the system unit.
obj2	second object	Chapter 3 gave you *a better* *understanding of how to* *handle diskettes.*
scomp *or* comp	complete sentential complement	Verify *that it is the* *diagnostics diskette.*
xcomp	sentential complement not containing a subj	The printer is prepared *to receive information.* The number should continue *to increase.*
obl-agent	agent of a passive sentence in oblique case	Your printer is also controlled *by program commands* *from the system unit.*
ppadjunct	any prepositional phrase	Get the diagnostics diskette *from the back of this manual.* Get the diagnostics diskette from the back *of this manual.*
advadjunct	adverb phrases that modify verbs	The printer should also work *well.* Operate your TV *normally.*
sadjunct	clauses that are not arguments of the main verb	Operate your TV normally *to verify color quality.* *If an expansion unit is attached,* set the Power switch to On.
modifier *or* xadjunct	modifier of a noun, including Japanese relative clauses	This is the *typematic* test. For *proper* operation, follow the procedure below.

Table 3.1: **Grammatical functions, with examples.**

the computer? The repairman is fixing the computer and *What is the repairman fixing?* have similar feature structures because they all have the same subject, verb and object (except that the object has been replaced by *what* in the third sentence).

Since all languages draw from the same inventory of grammatical functions, their f-structures can be very similar even if their c-structures are very different. We have already seen an example of a Japanese f-structure. Here is the (simplified) English f-structure for the sentence *Remove the diskette from the diskette drive*:

```
((obj
    ((case acc) (ref definite)
    (det ((root the) (ref definite)))
    (root tape) (person 3) (number singular)
    (count yes) (proper no)))
 (ppadjunct
   ((prep from) (ref definite)
    (det ((root the) (ref definite)))
    (root diskette drive) (person 3) (number singular)
    (count yes) (proper no) ))
 (valency trans) (mood imperative) (tense present) (form inf)
 (comp-type no) (root remove))
```

Notice that except for the language-specific grammatical features, the English and Japanese f-structures are the same. The `obj` is *diskette/deisuketto*, the `ppadjunct` is *diskette drive/deisukettodoraibu*, and the main verb of the sentence is *remove/torinozoku*.

Of course, English and Japanese sentences that mean the same thing will not always have such similar f-structures; the f-structures of an English sentence and a corresponding Japanese sentence will only be similar if they have the same grammatical functions. The English and Japanese sentences that follow will map onto the same interlingua text. However, the grammatical functions represented in f-structure will be different. The English f-structure will have *there* as the `subj`, *cable* as the `obj`, and *attached to the printer* as the `xcomp` of *is*. The Japanese f-structure will have *keeburu* (cable) as the `subj` and *purintaa ni tuiteiru* (attached to the printer) as the `xadjunct` of *keeburu* (cable).

(3.1)   There is a cable attached to the printer.

(3.2)   Purintaa ni   tuiteiru keeburu ga   arimasu
         printer particle attached cable   particle exists
         Literally, "The cable attached to the printer exists."

3.1.3   F-Structures in Machine Translation and Linguistic Theory

The KBMT-89 grammar formalism is quite general and could, for example, be used to build something closely resembling instantiated ontological frames directly—that is, without the intermediate stage of grammatical functions. However, the LFG design of f-structures containing grammatical functions was adopted for reasons of modularity, ease of formulating rules and cross-linguistic generality. In this section, we describe the motivation for f-structures in linguistic theory and their utility in machine translation.

The importance of f-structures in syntactic theory is that they allow us to talk about a grammatical function such as subj without referring to its various possible case markings, agreement patterns and structural positions. As a result, many cross-linguistic generalizations can be described more easily in terms of f-structures than c-structures, and even language-specific rules are more easily stated in terms of f-structures in languages with free word order. Phenomena that are more cleanly treated in terms of f-structures include interpretation of unexpressed subjects of nonfinite clauses (Simpson and Bresnan 1982; Bresnan 1982a; Mohanan 1983), syntactic constraints on pronoun reference (Bresnan et al. 1987; Dalrymple 1989) and some aspects of ellipsis (Levin 1982). This argument for f-structures in syntactic theory is equally valid in machine translation. The rules for handling these phenomena would be less elegant and would vary more from language to language if they were formulated in terms of c-structure or ontological frames.

F-structure also plays a significant role as the intermediate stage in the two-step mapping from surface constituents to predicate argument relations. This is important in linguistic theory because, although there are salient cross-linguistic generalizations in the mapping from c-structure to grammatical functions (Bresnan 1982a, 1982b; Mohanan 1982) and salient cross-linguistic generalizations in the mapping from grammatical functions to argument positions (Bresnan 1989; Levin 1987), the mapping directly from c-structure positions to argument positions does not reveal significant insights into the nature of human language.

In KBMT-89, f-structures constitute the input to mapping rules that produce instantiated frames. It is more convenient to map to the interlingua texts from f-structure than from c-structure for a number of reasons. Sometimes, for instance, more than one c-structure maps onto substantially the same f-structure. If we mapped from the c-structure, we would have to write more mapping rules. However, if we map from the f-structure, our mapping rules for different languages will be more alike. This allows us to take advantage of principles of linguistic theory and lexical semantics in the organization of mapping rules (Mitamura 1989). In short, a messy problem—mapping from c-structure to instantiated frames—is divided into two manageable modules, a mapping from c-structure to f-structure and a mapping from f-structure to frames.

A third role of f-structure in syntactic theory, as well as machine translation, is to store features of words (e.g., number, person and tense) to be matched against features of other words; this is used to handle such phenomena as agreement, case marking and verbal morphology. As mentioned above, KBMT-89 grammars do not conform to any particular theory of these phenomena, but unification-based formalisms have been found to be ideal for implementing them.

To summarize, certain constructs of syntactic theory have proven to be practical for machine translation as well. These include (i) constituent structure representations of word order and constituency, (ii) feature structure representations of grammatical functions and morphological features and (iii) mappings specified in the lexical entries of phrasal heads for linking grammatical functions and the semantic roles of their arguments.

3.2 Unification: Building F-Structures during Parsing

In what follows we present an informal introduction to some details of the KBMT-89 grammar formalism and how it is interpreted during parsing.[4] This is not intended to describe the implementation of the parser but rather to describe input and output from the point of view of a grammar writer.[5]

Before tracing the construction of an f-structure, in section 3.3, we will present three prerequisites: the correspondence between c-structure nodes and f-structures, the notation for referring to parts of f-structures and a simple description of unification.

3.2.1 C-Structures and Their Corresponding F-Structures

In LFG-based unification grammars, context-free phrase structure rules are supplemented with equations (see rules 1-4 following) that invoke the process of unification and result in the building of f-structures. The basis for the equations is that each daughter node has a corresponding f-structure, which are combined to form the f-structure for the mother node. In addition, the equations check constraints and add feature-value pairs to f-structures.

---

[4]Similar grammar formalisms have been developed for LFG (Kaplan and Bresnan 1982) and PATR-II (Shieber 1986).

[5]For another introduction to the use of unification in writing grammars, see Westcoat 1987.

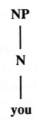

```
((root you) (person 2))
```

Figure 3.3: **F-structure for an NP node.**

In the sentence *You have a computer*, the first NP node corresponds to the f-structure, `((root you) (person 2))`. This information comes from the lexical entry of the word *you*.

The f-structure corresponding to the VP *have a computer* contains information about the root and tense of the main verb; it also incorporates the f-structure of an NP as the value of the `obj` function. This is illustrated in figure 3.4.

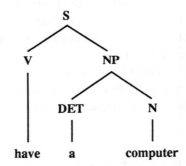

```
((root have)
 (tense present)
 (obj ((determiner ((reference indefinite)))
       (root computer) (number sg) (person 3))))
```

Figure 3.4: **F-structure for a VP.**

When an NP and VP are combined by rule 1 to form an S, the f-structure for the S consists of the VP's f-structure with the NP's f-structure inserted as the value of the `subj` feature, as shown in figure 3.5.

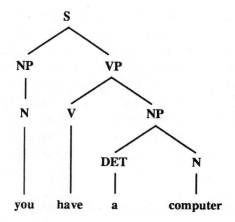

```
((subj ((root you) (person 2)))
 (root have) (tense present)
 (obj ((determiner ((reference indefinite)))
       (root computer) (number sg) (person 3))))
```

Figure 3.5: An f-structure containing information from S and VP.

Rule 1:

```
(<S> <== (<NP>   <VP>)
((x0 = x2)
((x0 subj) = x1)))
```

3.2.2   Names of F-Structures

In the KBMT-89 grammar formalism, the variables x0, x1, x2, x3 and so
forth take f-structures as their values. In what follows, we describe briefly how to
use these variables to refer to parts of f-structures. As an example, assume that x0
is bound to this f-structure:

```
x0 ((subj ((root you) (person 2)))
    (root have) (tense pres)
    (obj ((determiner ((reference indefinite)))
          (root computer) (number sg) (person 3))))
```

Because the entire f-structure is bound to the variable x0, we can simply call
the structure 'x0'. The sub-f-structure, ((root you) (person 2)), is not

bound to a variable. However, since it is the value of the `subj` function in `x0`, we can call it '`(x0 subj)`'. In general, `(xn f)`, where `xn` is a variable bound to an f-structure and `f` is a feature in `xn`, refers to the value of the feature `f` in `xn`.

To refer to the atom 'you', start by finding the value of `subj` in `x0`, `((root you) (person 2))`, and then find the value of `root` therein. We would write this as `(x0 subj root)`. In general, '`(xn f1 f2)`' means "find the value of `f1` in `xn` and then find the value of `f2` inside of that." Expressions of the form `(xn f1 f2)` are called *path names* and can be arbitrarily long (e.g., `(xn f1 f2 f3 f4 f5 f6)`), but in practice we rarely have need for path names of length greater than 3.

3.2.3 An Informal Characterization of Unification

Unification is an operation that combines information from two f-structures, provided that they do not contain conflicting information. The following informal description of unification should help illustrate the workings of the grammar formalism.[6]

To attempt to unify two feature structures, `x1` and `x2`, written `(x1 ⊔ x2)`:

- If `x1` and `x2` are both atomic and are the same entity, then `x1 ⊔ x2` is that entity: `sg ⊔ sg = sg`.

- If `x1` and `x2` are atomic but are not the same, then unification fails: `sg ⊔ pl = fail`.

- If `x1` is atomic and `x2` is not atomic, or vice versa, unification fails.

- If `x1` and `x2` are nonatomic f-structures, then their unification is an f-structure whose features are the union of their features, and the value of a feature `f` is `(x1 f) ⊔ (x2 f)`. That is, the value of a feature `f` in the unification `(x1 ⊔ x2)` is the value of `f` in `x1` unified with the value of `f` in `x2`. (If `f` has no value in an f-structure `xn`, then `(xn f) = []` or an empty f-structure, which is an identity element for unification.) Thus:

  (a) `((num sg) (pers 3)) ⊔ ((case nom) (gend masc)) =`
       `((num sg) (pers 3) (case nom) (gend masc))`

  (b) `((num sg) (pers 3)) ⊔ ((case nom) (num sg)) =`
       `((num sg) (pers 3) (case nom))`

---

[6]A similar algorithm is described by Kaplan and Bresnan (1982). For more details about the pseudounification algorithm implemented in KBMT-89, see Tomita and Knight 1988.

(c) `((num sg) (pers 3)) ⊔ ((case nom) (num pl)) = fail`

(d) `((subj ((num sg) (pers 3))) (root see) (obj ((root mouse))))`
`⊔ ((subj ((root cat) (def +))) (obj ((num sg)(pers 3))))=`
`((subj ((root cat) (def +) (num sg) (pers 3)))`
`(root see) (obj ((num sg) (pers 3) (root mouse))))`

- An empty feature structure is an identity element for unification:

  (a) `sg ⊔ [] = sg`

  (b) `((num sg) (pers 3)) ⊔ [] = ((num sg) (pers 3))`

3.2.4 Building F-Structures during Parsing

We are now ready to trace a sample parse of *A message appears on the screen.* The steps of the parse are described informally, as they appear to a grammar writer using the parser. (A description of source language analysis in KBMT-89 is given in chapter 7.)

Each grammar rule consists of a context-free phrase structure rule followed by a list of equations. In the first rule below, $x0$, $x1$ and $x2$ are variables bound to f-structures. $x0$ is the f-structure corresponding to the S node; $x1$ is the f-structure corresponding to the NP node; and $x2$ is the f-structure corresponding to the VP node. In general, $x0$ is bound to the f-structure corresponding to the node on the left-hand side of the arrow; $x1$ is bound to the f-structure corresponding to the first element on the right of the arrow; $x2$ is bound to the f-structure corresponding to the second element on the right; and so on. Recall also that $(xn\ f)$ refers to the value of feature f in xn.

The symbol '=' in an equation may be understood to mean:

1. Find the f-structures named by each side of the equation;

2. Unify them; and

3. Replace the f-structure named by the left-hand side of the equation with the result of unification.[7]

---

[7]This operation differs from other versions of pseudounification and from full unification. In the former, both sides of the equation are replaced by separate but indistinguishable copies of the results of unification. In the latter, the f-structures named by the left- and right-hand sides of the equation are replaced by a single instance of the result of unification.

Replacing only the left-hand side with the result of unification has consequences for the grammar writer: Output of the parse can be altered by changing the order of equations within a rule or by switching the right- and left-hand sides of an equation.

By way of illustration, the following, somewhat simplified, rules would be used in parsing the sentence *A message appears on the screen.* (Rule 1 was used in an earlier example.)

Rule 1

```
(<S> <== (<NP>  <VP>)
((x0 = x2)
((x0 subj) = x1)))
```

Rule 2

```
(<VP> <== (<V>  <PP>)
((x0 = x1)
((x0 ppadjunct) = x2)))
```

Rule 3

```
(<PP> <== (<P> <NP>)
((x0 = x2)
((x0 preposition) = (x1 root))))
```

Rule 4

```
(<NP> <== (<DET> <N>)
((x0 = x2)
((x0 determiner) = x1)))
```

In addition to the f-structures described by these rules, each word in the analysis lexicon carries a feature structure. When a word is attached to a node in the c-structure tree, the word's feature structure becomes the feature structure of the node.

Because the KBMT-89 parser builds c-structures from left to right, it will begin to operate with the word *a* in the sample sentence at hand. The word has this f-structure:

```
((number singular) (reference indefinite))
```

The word *a* will be attached to a det (determiner) node and its f-structure will become the determiner's f-structure. The next word is *message*, which has this f-structure:

```
((root message) (number singular) (person 3))
```

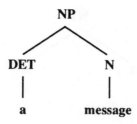

```
x0 []
x1 ((num  sg) (ref indef))
x2 ((root message) (num sg) (pers 3))
```

Figure 3.6: **C-structure and initial f-structures for** *a message.*

This will become the f-structure for an N node when *message* is attached.

Now that there is a determiner and a noun, they can be combined into a noun phrase using rule 4. In this rule, x0 is the f-structure for the NP, which is currently empty; x1 is the f-structure for the det node, which is the f-structure from the lexical entry of *a*; and x2 is the f-structure for the N node, which is the f-structure from the lexical entry *message*. Figure 3.6 shows the c-structure for *a message* and f-structures x0, x1 and x2 before unification.

The first equation, x0 = x2, causes x0 to unify with x2. After unification, x0 is replaced with the result of that unification. The following f-structures result:

```
x0 ((root message) (number singular) (person 3))
x1 ((number singular) (reference indefinite))
```

The next equation, (x0 determiner) = x1, unifies the value of x0's determiner feature with x1. Since x0 does not yet have a determiner feature, the expression (x0 determiner) refers to an empty f-structure. So, x1 will be unified with an empty f-structure. The result is ((number singular) (reference indefinite)). After unification, (x0 determiner) is replaced with the result of unification. At this point, (x0 determiner) has a value that is the result of the unification with x1. Here is what x0, x1 and x2 now look like:

```
x0 ((determiner ((number singular) (reference indefinite)))
    (root message) (number singular) (person 3))
x1 ((number singular) (reference indefinite))
x2 ((root message) (number singular) (person 3))
```

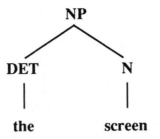

```
x0 []
x1 ((ref def))
x2 ((root screen) (num sg) (pers 3))
```

Figure 3.7: **C-structure and initial f-structures for** *the screen.*

The next word, *appears,* has the following f-structure, which becomes the f-structure of the V node to which *appears* is attached.

```
((root  appear) (tense present))
```

The next words to be parsed are *on the screen.* Their f-structures become the f-structures for the P, det and N nodes to which they attach.

```
((root  on))
((reference definite))
((root screen) (number singular) (person 3))
```

Rule 4, which expands NP into det and N, also applies in parsing *the screen.*

The c-structure for *the screen,* and initial f-structures for x0, x1 and x2 before unification, are given in figure 3.7. Just before *the* and *screen* are combined into an NP using rule 4, the f-structure for *the* is x1, the f-structure for *screen* is x2 and the f-structure for the entire NP is x0. Note that x0 is currently empty.

The equations associated with rule 4 trigger the unification of x0 with x2, replacing x0 with the result of unification, and (x0 determiner) with x1, replacing (x0 determiner) with the result of unification.

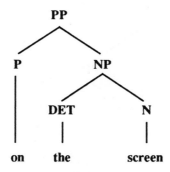

```
x0 []
x1 ((root on))
x2 ((determiner ((reference  definite)))
    (root screen) (number singular) (person 3))
```

Figure 3.8: C-structure and initial f-structures for *on the screen.*

```
x0 ((determiner  ((reference  definite)))
    (root screen) (number singular) (person 3))
x1 ((reference definite))
x2 ((root screen) (num sg) (pers 3))
```

Next, the preposition and NP can be combined into a PP using rule 3. The f-structure for *on* is x1 and the f-structure for the NP that was just built is x2. x0, currently empty, is the f-structure corresponding to the PP node.

Figure 3.8 shows the c-structure for *on the screen* and the f-structures x0, x1 and x2 before unification. Rule 3's first equation unifies x0 and x2, and x0 is replaced with the result of unification.

```
x0 ((determiner ((reference  definite)))
    (root screen) (number singular) (person 3))
x2 ((determiner ((reference  definite)))
    (root screen) (number singular) (person 3))
```

The second equation unifies (x0 preposition) with (x1 root). Since (x0 preposition) is currently undefined, its value is the empty f-structure []. The value of (x1 root) is on. So, on is unified with [], and (x0 preposition) is replaced with the results. The effect of this unification is that a preposition feature is added to x0 with the same value as (x1 root):

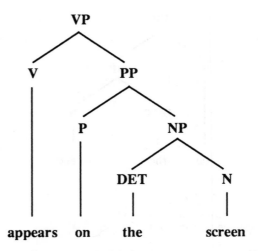

```
x0 []
x1 ((root appear) (tense present))
x2  ((preposition on)
     (determiner  ((reference definite)))
     (root screen) (number singular) (person 3))
```

Figure 3.9: C-structure and initial f-structures for *appears on the screen.*

```
x0 ((preposition on) (determiner ((reference definite)))
    (root screen) (number singular) (person 3))
x1 ((root on))
```

Now the PP and V can be combined into a VP using rule 2. In this rule, x0 is the f-structure for the VP, x1 is the f-structure for V and x2 is the f-structure for PP. Figure 3.9 shows the c-structure for *appears on the screen*, as well as the f-structures x0, x1 and x2 before unification. The first equation in the VP rule unifies x0 with x1:

```
x0   ((root appear) (tense present))
x1   ((root appear) (tense present))
```

The next equation unifies x2 with (x0 ppadjunct), which in turn is replaced with the result of unification.

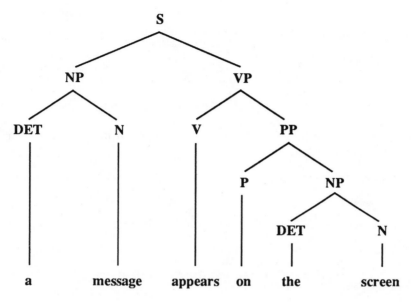

```
x0[]
x1 ((determiner ((number singular)
                 (reference indefinite))))
    (root message) (number singular) (person 3))
x2 ((ppadjunct ((preposition on)
                (determiner ((reference definite)))
                (root screen) (number singular)\\
                (person 3)))
    (root appear) (tense preson))
```

Figure 3.10: **C-structure and initial f-structures for** *a message appears on the screen.*

```
x0 ((ppadjunct ((preposition on)
               (determiner ((reference  definite)))
               (root screen) (number singular) (person 3)))
    (root appear) (tense present))
x2 ((preposition on) (determiner ((reference definite)))
    (root screen) (number singular) (person 3))
```

Finally, rule 1 puts NP and VP together to form an S. In this rule, x0 is the f-structure for S, x1 is the f-structure for NP and x2 is the f-structure for VP. The c-structure for *A message appears on the screen* and the f-structures for x0, x1 and x2 before unification are given in figure 3.10.

As should now be clear, the first equation in this rule unifies x0 and x2:

```
x0 ((ppadjunct ((preposition on) (determiner ((reference definite)))
                (root screen) (number sg) (person 3)))
   (root appear) (tense present))
x2 ((ppadjunct ((preposition on) (determiner ((reference definite)))
                (root screen) (number singular) (person 3)))
   (root appear) (tense present))
```

The second equation unifies x1 with (x0 subj), resulting in these f-structures:

```
x0 ((ppadjunct ((preposition on) (determiner ((reference definite)))
                (root screen) (number singular) (person 3)))
   (root appear) (tense present)
   (subj ((determiner ((number singular) (reference indefinite)))
          (root message) (number singular) (person 3))))
x1 ((determiner ((number singular) (reference indefinite)))
   (root message) (number singular) (person 3))
x2 ((ppadjunct ((preposition on) (determiner ((reference definite)))
                (root screen) (number singular) (person 3)))
   (root appear) (tense present))
```

Finally, the value of x0 is returned for the parse.

3.2.5   Constraining Grammatical Features

During parsing and generation, it is sometimes necessary to rule out sentences containing conflicting inflectional features. For example, we might want the parser to fail while parsing *a messages* or *messages appears on the screen*; we certainly do not want to generate these phrases.

We can ensure compatibility of inflectional features by adding equations to rules and lexical entries. The KBMT-89 noun phrase rule, for example, will need one additional equation requiring that the f-structures of the determiner and noun have the same value for number:[8]

```
(<NP> <== (<DET> <N>)
((x0 = x2)
((x1 number) = (x2 number)))
((x0 det) = x1)
```

---

[8]This is an instance of the sort noted earlier, in which exchanging (x1 number) = (x2 number) for (x2 number) = (x1 number) can change the f-structure produced. The f-structure would also vary depending on the order of the equations in this example.

Now consider how this rule will apply to *a messages*. When the rule fires, x1 will be the f-structure associated with the determiner *a*, and x2 will be the f-structure associated with the noun *messages*:

```
x1 ((number singular) (reference indefinite))
x2 ((root message) (number plural) (person 3))
```

The equation ((x1 number) = (x2 number)) requires that the value of the number feature in x1 be unified with the value of the number feature in x2, but this unification will fail, causing the parse to fail.

The parse of *messages appears on the screen* will also fail because of unification failure. In this case, we must add information to the feature structure for the word *appears*. The additional information concerns the number and person of the subject of *appears* in grammatical sentences:

```
((root appear) (tense present)
 (subj ((number singular) (person 3))))
```

The f-structure for *appears on the screen*, taking this new information into account, is the following:

```
((ppadjunct ((preposition on)
             (determiner ((reference  definite)))
             (root screen) (number singular) (person 3)))
 (root appear) (tense present)
 (subj ((number singular) (person 3))))
```

When rule 1 for building an S is invoked, the f-structure will be bound to x2. The first equation in the S rule unifies x0, which is empty at this point, with x2. After unification, x0 will be identical to the f-structure.

The second equation in the S rule unifies the value of (x0 subj) with x1. The value of (x0 subj) is ((number singular) (person 3)) and the value for x1 in the sentence *messages appears on the screen* is ((root message) (number plural) (person 3)). Unification of these two f-structures will fail because they contain different values for the number feature. In this way, the grammar formalism and unification store and check grammatical features in f-structure, to ensure compatibility. Additional mechanisms for constraining f-structures are described in chapter 4.

3.2.6   F-Structures and Mapping Rules

F-structures are input to mapping rules, which produce instantiated ontological frames (parser output).   In the earlier example, mapping rules associated with the words *message* and *screen* map them onto instances of the concepts `*text-group` and `*full-screen-configuration`.   Mapping rules for *appear* indicate that an instance of the concept `*see` should be created, that the frame corresponding to the `subj` of *appear* in f-structure should map onto the `theme` slot of `*see`, and that the frame corresponding to a `ppadjunct` with the preposition *to* should map onto the `goal` slot. The result is an instance of `*see` with `*text-group` filling the `theme` slot and `*full-screen-configuration` filling the `goal` slot.   Mapping rules are described in detail in chapters 5 and 6 and the mapping rule interpreter is described in chapter 7.

It is important to note that different f-structures can map onto the same frame. For example, the f-structure for the active sentence *Someone serviced the computer* is associated with a mapping rule that maps the `obj` of *service* (in this case, *the computer*) into the `theme` slot of `*to-service`, whereas the passive sentence *The computer was serviced* is associated with a mapping rule that puts the `subj` of *was serviced* into the `theme` slot of `*to-service`.   The f-structures and mapping rules are different, but they both result in the `*to-service` frame with *computer* mapped onto the `theme` slot.

Since c-structures are not accessed in the construction of the parser output, it is important for f-structures to encode all information that will be relevant for translation.   In chapter 4 we discuss the issue of designing f-structures to be compatible with the mapping rules and other components of the system.

Chapter 4

Grammars in Analysis and Generation

■ LORI LEVIN, TERUKO MITAMURA, DONNA M. GATES AND
KOICHI TAKEDA

A grammar is a set of formal rules. A parser uses the rules to build structures for sentences, and a generator uses them to construct sentences from syntactic structures. This chapter presents selected parts of the KBMT-89 English and Japanese grammars and describes aspects of their development. In addition to the primary task of capturing linguistic generalizations about data from the corpus, development of the grammars required (i) determining which phenomena should be handled by the grammar and which by some other component of the system, (ii) designing syntactic structures (output of analysis and input to generation) so the parser and generator interacted properly with other components of the system and (iii) deciding which grammatical sentences to cover and which ungrammatical sentences to exclude. Many of these decisions involved trade-offs between linguistic accuracy and efficiency or practicality of implementation.

The first section of this chapter briefly describes the process of grammar writing, taking these issues into account. The next three sections contain examples of the treatment of some key constructions in the English and Japanese grammars, highlighting wherever possible the motivations for design decisions. The final section emphasizes the generation grammars and includes a discussion of bidirectionality. The purpose of the presentation is not only to describe the grammars but also to show how linguistic accuracy and practical engineering were combined to achieve optimal instruments for a small sample of actual text. The presentation is not intended to be complete but rather to give a sense of the kinds of decisions that were made during implementation. Decisions made for the English component are emphasized.

We seek a middle ground in terms of readers' linguistic expertise. Some concepts are explained at a basic level, while others unavoidably refer to issues in syntactic theory accessible to those with backgrounds in linguistics.

4.1 Designing a Grammar

4.1.1 Identifying Linguistic Generalizations

The first task in writing a grammar is to identify linguistic patterns, or *generalizations*, in the corpus. A grammar that reflects these generalizations will be more modular, more robust and more easily modified. Linguistic generalizations are descriptive statements about data, such as "yes-no questions in English start with an auxiliary verb followed by the subject" and "English sentences are negated by placing *not* or a contracted form of *not* after the first auxiliary verb."

When linguists say a grammar captures generalizations, they mean that it factors out common components of different linguistic patterns so that the same fact is not accounted for in more than one place in the grammar. For example, in the KBMT-89 grammar, the word *works* carries the information that its subject must be a third-person singular noun phrase, as in *This computer works well*. In the sentence *Which computer do you think works well*, the words *computer* and *works* must agree in number even though they are separated by several words. (One can tell that they agree in number because *which computers do you think works well* is ungrammatical.) This is an instance of a *wh*-question in which the *wh*-phrase, *which computer*, plays the role of the subject of *works*. Once we determine that *which computer* functions thus, we know that the subject of the word *works* must be third-person singular. This is the same information that was used in *This computer works well*. This is considered to be a good solution because the apparently difficult problem of agreement with a remote phrase is handled modularly by two simpler mechanisms, one that determines the role played by a fronted *wh*-phrase and one that enforces agreement between a verb and its subject. Furthermore, we say that we have captured the generalization that a verb agrees with its subject. This is so for the following reason: Even though the two sentences (*This computer works well* and *Which computer do you think works well*) are very different in structure, a single mechanism for subject-verb agreement works for both of them. A grammar that does not capture this generalization might say that the word *works* requires either a third-person singular noun immediately to its left or, if there is no noun to its left, a third-person singular *wh*-phrase at the front of the sentence. This does not capture the generalization because it involves two different statements of agreement for two different constructions.

In general, grammars that capture generalizations are upwardly compatible. That is, even if the grammar is not very detailed and does not have very wide coverage of data, it will be easy to update to accommodate additional data when it becomes necessary.

In well-studied languages such as English, generalizations about common linguistic structures, as well as analyses that adequately capture these generalizations, are easily found in numerous books and articles (e.g., the grammar by Quirk et al. [1985] and most any book of basic syntax). However, writing a grammar for a language that is not well studied will require the discovery of generalizations through text analysis.

4.1.2 The Scope of the Grammar

Since a knowledge-based machine translation system contains many components in addition to the syntactic grammar, it is necessary to decide which phenomena to cover in the syntactic part of the system and which to cover in some other component. In KBMT-89, the other components in question are the mapping rules, the augmentor and the ontology.

A simple example of this type of decision may be found in the treatment of discourse connectives such as *because, however* and *even though*. The rules for parsing in KBMT-89's English grammar simply store these markers in the syntactic feature structure; but the discourse relationships between clauses (e.g., cause and effect) are determined by the mapping rules and the augmentor.

A major decision about the scope of the grammar concerns the filling of slots in the concept lexicon frames. Since the grammar formalism can produce any output consisting of features and values, it could be made to produce semantic frames consisting of concepts and slots, instead of syntactic feature structures consisting of grammatical functions and inflectional features. This might be desirable for fairly small applications, but for a large system an approach using syntactic feature structures is more modular, readable and extendable, and it allows one to take advantage of cross-linguistic generalizations, as described in the previous chapter.

Some decisions about the scope of the grammar are imposed by parsing algorithms and mapping rules. For example, the construction known in syntactic theory as "control" —such as determining that *he* is the subject of *to expect to like the movie* and *to like the movie* in *he seems to expect to like the movie*—is usually implemented in unification-based grammars as structure sharing between the main clause and embedded clause subjects (Bresnan 1982a). However, it is difficult in a pseudounification grammar to implement structure sharing for arbitrarily deep embedding in the control construction (e.g., *he seems to appear to tend to expect to . . . service the computer*). As a result, the best way to implement control in KBMT-89 is in the mapping rules rather than in the syntactic grammar.[1]

4.1.3   The Content and Structure of Feature Structures

In addition to characterizing the set of sentences that the parser will accept or generate, the grammar also determines the contents of feature structures that are the output of parsing or the input to sentence generation. The hierarchical organization of feature structures (that is, are they embedded or flat? which phrase structure node corresponds to the head of each feature structure?) as well as the choice of features (for example, `subj` instead of `NP`) are important aspects of system design. Feature structures must fill several requirements as syntactic structures and as input to and output from other system components.

Feature structures must be designed for modular syntactic processing and for

---

[1]In fact, there is no structure sharing in pseudounification. Constructions that would require structure sharing in full-unification grammars must be implemented with copying in pseudounification grammars. To understand the differences in writing grammars for control constructions in full- and pseudounification grammars, consider the sentence *He seems to appear to tend to expect to service the computer*. When a full-unification grammar running in a bottom-up parser encounters the control construction *expect to service the computer*, it will note that the subject of *expect* and the subject of *service* share the same structure. At this point in the parse, nothing is known about that structure except that it is shared. As the parser moves up the tree, the grammar indicates that the subject of *expect* is shared with the subject of *tend*, which in turn is shared with the subject of *appear*. When the parser reaches the top clause, the grammar indicates that the subject of *seem* is shared with the subject of *appear*, and that this structure is the feature structure for the NP *he*. This feature structure automatically fills the subject structure for all lower verbs because all of the subject structures are shared.

When a bottom-up parser using a pseudounification grammar encounters the control construction *expect to service the computer*, it can only copy information from the subject of *service* to the subject of *expect* because there is no structure sharing. At this point in the parse, however, there is no information to copy. When the parser reaches the top clause, it can copy the feature structure for *he* from the subject of *seem* to the subject of *appear*, but that feature structure will not automatically be copied into the subject structures of the lower verbs. Therefore, the feature structure that is produced for the sentence does not indicate that *he* is the subject of *tend*, *expect* or *service*.

supporting the writing of grammars that capture syntactic generalizations. It was argued in chapter 3 that feature structures containing grammatical functions are adequate in this respect. In addition to supporting modularity and well-structured grammars, feature structures must also sometimes be engineered for efficient syntactic processing by including features to help reduce ambiguity and eliminate extra parses. Examples of features that contribute to increased efficiency of parsing are discussed later in this chapter.

As the input to analysis mapping rules, feature structures must contain all information needed for the rules to produce an appropriate frame representation of the sentence. Further, this information must be structured in a way that the mapping rules can use. For example, the mapping rule interpreter is able to map a syntactic head of a feature structure only onto the semantic head of a frame and to map syntactic non-heads only onto fillers of slots in frames. This requires the grammar to be written so that the syntactic head of each feature structure corresponds to its semantic head. Semantic structures are determined by the design of the concept lexicon, which is independent of the syntax of individual languages. Therefore, some syntactic structures cannot be used for syntactic processing of a language in isolation.

The ontology and ILTs also influence the choice of syntactic features. For example, the features `near` and `definite` in the representation of the English demonstratives *this* and *that*, the features `possibility` and `necessity` in the representation of English modals and the feature `pre-vp-adv` (indicating that an adverb comes before the verb rather than after it) are motivated by ILT design.

4.1.4   Undergeneration

The KBMT-89 English grammar covers fairly complex sentences, such as those in (4.1), as well as many sentences that contain domain-specific syntactic constructions and punctuation having to do with numbered lists, instructions and titles of chapters and sections, such as those in (4.2).

(4.1)   a. The keyboard, which is the primary input to the system, attaches to the system unit with a six-foot coiled cable.

      b. When the expansion unit is installed, the fixed disk drive and fixed disk adapter from the system unit are installed in the expansion unit.

(4.2)   a. If the responses are not correct, go to Section 2, "Problem Determination Procedures."

b. The "IBM Personal Computer BASIC" message will appear.

c. Did you get an 1820 error message?

d. WARNING: Always roll the forms ahead.

e. 6. To change the Top of Page Setting, repeat the procedure in steps 1-5.

f. Set the power switch on the system unit to ON.

g. Continue with "System Cabling."

h. YES — Go to "Diagnostic Testing."

However, it does not handle common elliptical constructions such as verb-phrase deletion (*I haven't turned on the computer, but I will*) and deletion of the copula as found in newspaper headlines (*Computer smashed by angry user*). Nor does it handle the full range of English comparative (or comparative-like) constructions (e.g, *as many . . . as . . . , too many . . . to . . . , so many . . . that . . .*) or many other syntactic constructions. As a result, the KBMT-89 system will not parse many sentence types that are common in other types of texts.

These constructions were not included in the English grammar simply because they did not occur in the project corpora. But, even for the sake of completeness, it is not always possible or desirable to have the grammar cover every possible grammatical construction. One problem is that many parsers, including that used in KBMT-89, become quite slow when grammars contain more rules because they must attempt to apply more rules in order to find the appropriate ones for each sentence being parsed. Another problem is that if semantic constraints are not strong enough, the parser can produce extra parses that are structurally well formed but semantically corrupt.

The strategy employed throughout the KBMT-89 project was to avoid implementing complex linguistic mechanisms if they were not called for by the corpus data. Much simpler mechanisms that covered only slightly more than what was in the corpus were implemented. However, care was always taken to capture linguistic generalizations so that the grammars could be extended to cover larger corpora without being completely rewritten.

4.1.5   Overgeneration

There are also reasons to allow the parsing grammar to "overgenerate," that is, to accept sentences that are not grammatical. In unification-based grammars, constraints on phenomena such as agreement, case marking and correct verb forms are implemented by unification of features. Unification of the features will succeed for grammatical sentences and fail for ungrammatical sentences. Adding many of these unifications to the grammar could make it unreadable, hard to maintain and slow, and could unreasonably require the user to enter completely grammatical text. For these reasons, it might be desirable to eliminate some constraints and allow the grammar to accept some ill-formed input.

However, constraints are needed not only to identify ungrammatical sentences. They also eliminate certain paths in the parsing of grammatical sentences. To eliminate the constraints, therefore, is to allow the parser to traverse incorrect paths farther, increasing parsing time. Example (4.3) shows one possible effect of removing constraints on subject-verb agreement and determiner-noun agreement. The bracketing in (4.3b) indicates an incorrect path that will be followed up to the word *is* before failing. If agreement constraints are enforced, the incorrect path will fail much earlier, on the word *computer*. The correct parse of the sentence is shown in (4.3c).

(4.3)   a. That computers running obsolete operating systems are useless is obvious.

   b. [s [NP [DET that] [N computers] [VP running obsolete operating systems]] [VP are useless]] is obvious.

   c. [s [s̄ [COMP that]
         [s [NP [N computers] [VP running obsolete operating systems]]
            [VP are useless]]]
      [VP is obvious.]]

Removing constraints also results in some extra parses of grammatical sentences. For example, without subject-verb agreement, the two sentences in (4.4) will each have two parses, whereas they are both unambiguous if subject-verb agreement is enforced.

(4.4)   a. A computer with a tape drive and a hard disk is in the carton.

   b. A computer with a tape drive and a hard disk are in the carton.

It should be obvious from the preceding discussion that writing a grammar involves juggling several considerations. It follows that there is no uniquely correct grammar or feature structure for a given sentence. Instead, the grammar writer must tailor the syntactic structures to the needs of the system. The idea of an all-purpose, off-the-shelf grammar is overoptimistic because (i) the sublanguage that the grammar must handle varies from domain to domain and from application to application (e.g., natural language interfaces, grammar checking, translation and computer-assisted language instruction), and rules for specialized syntactic constructions might or might not be required; (ii) the output of the grammar is the input to other components of the system, and that output will have to vary to suit the needs of the other components; (iii) different applications will tolerate different degrees of overgeneration and undergeneration; and (iv) different parsers require different grammar formalisms or grammar-writing languages, which may require the rules to be written differently. In short, while there might be a core grammar that is transferable to other applications, much of the grammar must be designed specifically for each application. The following sections describe selected parts of KBMT-89's English and Japanese grammars, concentrating on design issues specific to the system.

4.2   Basic English Sentence Structure

4.2.1   Heads and Projections

Following the $\overline{X}$ theory of phrase structure (Jackendoff 1977), it is assumed that a phrase consists of a head surrounded by layers of specifiers, modifiers and complements. Each layer is called a "projection." In an NP (noun phrase), the N is the head, the specifiers are typically determiners, the modifiers are typically adjectives and the complements are typically PPs (prepositional phrases) or embedded sentences. So in the NP *the new input to the system*, *input* is the head noun, *the* is a specifier, *new* is a modifier and *to the system* is a complement. In a VP (verb phrase), the V is the head, and the direct object, indirect object, some prepositional phrases and some embedded clauses are complements.

Embedded syntactic projections are important in syntactic theory and application. This internal structure is necessary for input to certain types of semantic interpretation (items that are more closely related to the head tend to be in the lower layers) and for some syntactic rules, such as coordination, that identify each projection as a discrete unit (see section 4.2.4.1). In addition, having projections contributes to the organization and readability of the grammar: Without them we would need a separate grammar rule for every combination of specifiers, modifiers and complements.

In the KBMT-89 English grammar, the primary purpose of projections is readability and organization of the grammar. Because KBMT-89 semantic structures do not distinguish arguments that are semantically close to the head of the phrase from adjuncts that are semantically distant, there is no need to distinguish between them in syntactic structures. Coordinate structures in the English corpus do not call for a very complex projection structure. Therefore, the internal structure of noun phrases and verb phrases described in the following subsections differs from customary linguistic descriptions. This illustrates a method of culling general strategies from linguistic theory, while omitting or changing details that are not necessary or expedient for the system under development.

4.2.2 Noun Phrases

It is useful to separate English NPs into two groups. Most NPs, which we will call the *basic NPs*, fall into the first group. These are common types of NPs that can be found in almost any corpus of English sentences. The second set, which contains *nonbasic NPs*, is smaller and contains NPs that either are not typical or are domain specific and would not ordinarily be found in English texts.

The following is a list of the context-free rules that characterize basic NPs in the KBMT-89 English grammar. There are four projections of N. An N1 is a noun or compound noun with recursively adjoined adjectives, cardinal numbers or participial phrases (such as *program defined variable* or *IBM supported program language*). An N2 is an N1 with a determiner or possessive NP. An N3 is an N2 with prepositional phrases, relative clauses or reduced relative clauses adjoined recursively. An NP is an N3 with a quantifier phrase. Figure 4.1 gives a graphic representation of these projections.

```
COMPOUND-N --> N
COMPOUND-N --> N COMPOUND-N

N1 --> COMPOUND-N
N1 --> ADJP N1
N1 --> CARDINAL-NUM N1
N1 --> PARTICIPLEP N1

N2 --> N1
N2 --> DET N1
N2 --> POSS N1

N3 --> N2
```

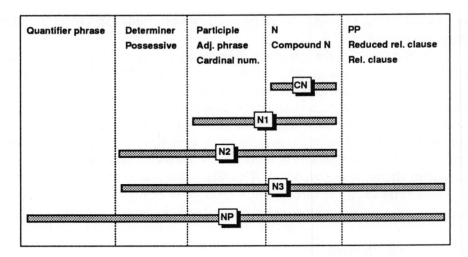

Figure 4.1: **Representation of basic NP projections.**

```
N3 --> N3 PP
N3 --> N3 RELATIVE-CLAUSE
N3 --> N3 REDUCED-REL
N3 --> PRONOUN

NP --> N3
NP --> QP N3
```

Example (4.5) lists some of the basic NPs that can be parsed with the KBMT-89 English grammar.

(4.5) keyboards
       new keyboards
       three keyboards
       IBM designed keyboards
       three new IBM designed keyboards
       those three new IBM designed keyboards
       those three new IBM designed keyboards on the table
       those three new IBM designed keyboards which you bought
       those three new IBM designed keyboards purchased by you
       those three new IBM designed keyboards in the box which are typematic
       all of those three new IBM designed keyboards in the box which are
           typematic

The English grammar also contains rules for the following nonbasic NPs, among others:

(4.6)   a six-foot coiled cable
          the procedure below
          damaging your diskettes
          how to handle diskettes
          step 6
          steps 1-5
          key number 9
          "System Cabling"
          the "IBM Personal Computer Basic" message
          Section 2, "Problem Determination Procedures"
          Disk A
          the word RETURN
          On

It will be well to present a feature structure for the following noun phrase:

(4.7)   all of your 5 new computer keyboards with a numeric keypad in the
          packing material.

The components of the feature structure serve various functions. Some supply information needed by the mapping rules, others are used to enforce syntactic or morphological constraints and some help reduce ambiguity during parsing. Put differently, the contents of the feature structure are motivated not by the grammar alone but also by the morphological processor, the mapping rules and the concept lexicon.

```
((quantifier ((root all) (of-req -)))
 (root keyboard) (ref definite)
 (NP-justified +)
 (count yes) (person 3) (number plural)
 (proper no) (meas-unit no)
 (ppadjunct
  (*multiple*
   ((prep in) (ref definite) (det ((root the) (ref definite)))
    (root packing_material) (person 3) (number singular) (count yes)
    (proper no) (meas-unit no))
   ((prep with) (ref indefinite)
    (det ((root a) (ref indefinite) (number singular))) (count yes)
    (root numeric_keypad) (person 3) (number singular) (proper no)
    (meas-unit no)))))
 (possessive
  ((root pro) (pro +) (person 2) (number (*or* singular plural))
```

```
   (case poss)))
(quantity ((root 5) (value 5)))
(modifiers ((root new)))
(pre-nom-noun
 ((root computer) (number singular) (person 3) (count yes)
  (proper no) (meas-unit no))))
```

This feature structure represents a reading in which the keyboards have numeric keypads and the keyboards are in the packing material. The reading in which the numeric keypads are in the packing material has a different feature structure, which is not shown here. `*multiple*` indicates that the value of `ppadjunct` is a set rather than a single value. This set contains the feature structures for the phrases *with a numeric keypad* and *in the packing material*. The different semantic functions of the prepositional phrases are not identified in the syntactic structure. Mapping rules map them onto the correct slots based on whether the preposition (`(prep with)` or `(prep in)`) can be a marker of the slot and whether the concepts corresponding to `(root numeric_keypad)` and `(root packing_material)` satisfy the semantic restrictions on the slots they are mapped onto.

`(proper no)` says the noun is not a proper noun. This feature is used by the English morphology program in building the run-time lexicon; for instance, this program does not build plural lexical entries for nouns with the feature (`proper yes`). The feature is also used by the syntactic grammar to allow common nouns, but not proper nouns, to take modifiers and determiners.

The syntactic grammar does not enforce the distinction between count and mass nouns. Hence, the morphology program that produces the run-time lexicon uses the feature `count` to avoid producing unnecessary lexical entries. Thus, plural entries are not produced for mass nouns (`(count no)`) such as *information*.

`NP-justified` means that `NP` is the lowest projection of `N` that covers the phrase *all of your five new computer keyboards with a numeric keypad in the packing material*. The `NP-justified` feature, along with the features `N2-justified` and `N3-justified`, is used as part of a strategy to avoid extra parses of coordinate structures. Without these features, a phrase such as *the monitor and the keyboard* might have the following parses:

(4.8)   a. [NP [N3 [N2 [N2 the monitor] and [N2 the keyboard]]]]

          b. [NP [N3 [N3 [N2 the monitor]] and [N3 [N2 the keyboard]]]]

          c. [NP [NP [N3 [N2 the monitor]]] and [NP [N3 [N2 the keyboard]]]]

The strategy is to choose the parse that has coordination at the lowest projection of N, in this case (4.8a). In order to do this, we assign the feature-value pair (N2-justified +) to *the monitor*, indicating that *N2* is the lowest projection of N that can dominate *the monitor*. (NP-justified +) in the feature structure given earlier indicates that the noun phrase *all of your five new computer keyboards with a numeric keypad in the packing material* could occur as one conjunct in a coordinate structure such as that in (4.8c). Notice that this strategy for avoiding extra parses is implemented in the grammar rather than in the parsing algorithm.

Next, (meas-unit no) is also used to prevent extra parses. Only nouns that have the feature (meas-unit yes) can occur in prenominal quantifier phrases (QP). This will ensure that *five glasses of water*, for example, has the structure in (4.9a), whereas *five pictures of someone* has only the structure in (4.9b).

(4.9)   a. [NP [QP five glasses of] water]

   b. [NP five pictures [PP of someone]]

There are two noun-noun compounds in the noun phrase in (4.7): *computer keyboard* and *packing material*. The latter is treated as one lexical item with (root packing_material), and the former is treated as two lexical items— (root keyboard) and (pre-nom-noun ((root computer))). This reflects decisions that were made in the domain model. *Packing material* corresponds to the concept *packing_material in the ontology, but *computer keyboard* corresponds to the concept *keyboard with the part-of slot filled with *computer. In general, when the noun-noun compound corresponds to a single concept, it is treated as one item in the lexicon; when it corresponds to two concepts, with one filling a slot in the other, it is treated as two items in the lexicon. Note that the adjective-noun combination *numeric keypad* is treated as a single lexical item.

Information about definiteness provides important semantic information about a sentence. The KBMT-89 mapping rules pick up the feature ref with values definite or indefinite and transmit this to the ILT.

The numeral '5' appears in the feature structure above as (quantity ((root 5) (value 5))). The word *five* would have appeared as (quantity ((root five) (value 5))).

Any lexical item that is involved in a lexical mapping rule must have the root feature. Lexical mapping rules map the value of the root feature onto a frame in the domain model.

Finally, the features person and number are relevant to meaning as well as to syntactic processes such as agreement. In the KBMT-89 corpus, morphologically plural forms correspond to semantically plural concepts.

4.2.2.1   NP Rules and Structures

In addition to the grammatical noun phrases listed in examples (4.5) and (4.6), the English grammar will accept ungrammatical noun phrases with incorrect word order, such as *a box on the table of diskettes.*

This overacceptance of ungrammatical sentences can be prevented structurally by making use of projections of N. For example, the relevant linguistic generalization about ordering of PPs, as expressed in commonly accepted syntactic treatments of NP, is that PPs that are semantically closer to the head (arguments of N) will precede PPs that are semantically less close (adjuncts of NP) (see Radford 1988, especially 177ff, and references therein). This ordering can be enforced syntactically by attaching some PPs as sisters to N inside N1 and attaching other PPs at higher projections. Such an analysis of PPs within NPs thus represents the distinction between arguments (semantically closer) and adjuncts (semantically less close), as well as enforcing ordering restrictions on types of PPs.

For the sake of rule simplicity, it was decided in KBMT-89 not to enforce ordering restrictions on PPs and prenominal modifiers in the analysis grammar and, consequently, to allow the parser to accept ungrammatical NPs. It is not necessary for grammar rules to distinguish between argument and adjunct PPs because this distinction is not made in the concept lexicon or in the mapping rules.

In contrast to the analysis phase of translation, in which the grammar may accept ungrammatical sentences, the generation phase must produce only grammatical sentences. The ordering of prepositional phrases is performed by the generation mapping rules. These rules determine the order in the f-structure, which will then determine the phrases' positions in the sentence.

Constituent structures in KBMT-89 differ from commonly accepted treatments of NP in other ways as well. For example, DET (determiner) is always lower in the tree than PP. The relative scope of DET and PP in constituent structure is less important than it would seem because the entire structure is flattened in f-structure, so that all of the specifiers, modifiers and complements of N are at the same level. (The need for a flat f-structure for NPs is partly motivated by the desired ILT and by limitations on the power of mapping rules.) Constituency does play an important role in coordination since only constituents can be conjoined. The phrase structure rules given earlier, although nonstandard by purely linguistic criteria, provide all of the constituents that are needed to accommodate all coordinate NPs in the KBMT-89 English corpus.

4.2.2.2 Compound Nouns

Compound nouns in the KBMT-89 corpus can be up to six nouns long (e.g., *IBM color display problem determination procedure*). When there are more than two nouns, different groupings become possible. For example, in the correct analysis of *printer power switch* and *IBM color display*, the last two nouns are grouped together and modified by the first one: [printer [power switch]], [IBM [color display]]. But in *game control adapter*, the first two nouns are grouped together and modify the third: [[game control] adapter]. It is not practical to test all possible noun groupings.

The grammar assigns right-branching constituent structures to all noun-noun compounds. These right-branching trees correspond to flat feature structures headed by the last noun, with all previous nouns in a list that is the value of pre-nom-noun. This feature structure corresponds to a "flat" semantic grouping in which each noun modifies the final one. This works in many cases and is adjusted by creating new dictionary entries in cases in which it does not work. For example, in [IBM [color display]], *IBM* fills the manufactured-by slot of the concept *monitor, and *color* causes the chromality slot of *monitor to be filled with the value multi-color. However, this analysis of noun-noun compounds is incorrect for [[game control] adapter]. It would be wrong to say that *game* and *control* both fill slots of the concept *adapter. Instead, we want an analysis in which *game control* is one unit that fills the adapts-for slot in *adapter. To solve this problem, *game control* was added to the dictionary as a single lexical item that fills the adapts-for slot with the value *analog-cursor-control. In general, to avoid the potential ambiguity of allowing all possible branchings of compounds, the KBMT-89 grammar allows only one constituent structure for each compound. Where this constituent structure is incorrect, some components of the compound are added to the lexicon to force the compound into the only allowable structure.

4.2.3 Verb Phrases

4.2.3.1 Syntactic Subcategorization

The term *subcategorization* refers to the identification of subcategories of verbs that occur in different syntactic contexts. For example, intransitive verbs such as *arrive* occur with a subject and possibly some prepositional phrases; transitive verbs like *find* and *omit* occur with a subject and an object; and bitransitive verbs like *give* can occur with a subject and two objects (*give someone something*). There are many other subcategories of English verbs that occur with various combinations of objects, prepositional phrases, clausal complements and predicative complements.

In the KBMT-89 English lexicon, subcategorization is represented by two features, `valency` and `comp-type`. The value of the `valency` feature determines how many noun phrases occur with a verb, and the value of `comp-type` determines what type of clausal and predicative complements occur. The English grammar does not distinguish between prepositional phrases that are arguments of verbs and prepositional phrases that are adjuncts.[2] There are, therefore, no features indicating subcategorization for prepositional phrases.

The value of `valency` can be `trans,` `intrans` or `bitrans`. A value of `trans` means that the verb must occur with a direct object, `bitrans` means that the verb must occur with two objects and `intrans` means that the verb cannot occur with an object.

Various grammar rules that expand VPs contain constraints that check the value of the `valency` feature. These constraints will, for example, prevent the parser from using the rule (`<VP>` `<==>` `<V>`) if the verb has `valency` `trans` or `bitrans` and prevent it from using the rule (`<VP>` `<==>` (`<V>` `<NP>`)) if the verb has `valency` `intrans`. This helps increase parsing speed by eliminating faulty hypotheses as early as possible.

Clausal and predicative complements in the KBMT-89 English grammar appear in feature structures as the values of the features `npcomp`, `apcomp`, `scomp` and `xcomp`. The following are examples of these types of complements.

- `npcomp` — nominal complement, a non-object post-verbal NP:
  They made him president.

---

[2]It is much simpler not to distinguish between argument and adjunct prepositional phrases in the syntactic component of the system. One source of difficulty is that tests for distinguishing arguments from adjuncts do not always yield clear results, and it is, therefore, not possible to identify with certainty that any given prepositional phrase is an argument or an adjunct. Another source of difficulty is that prepositional phrase arguments are often optional. Furthermore, there are many rules of lexical semantics that add prepositional phrase arguments, resulting in several subcategorization frames for many verbs.

It not only was simpler to ignore the distinction between argument and adjunct prepositional phrases, it was unnecessary to make such a distinction. In KBMT-89, the mapping rules assign syntactic prepositional phrases to semantic slots. To do this, the mapping rule must take into account the identity of the preposition and the semantic class of the verb that governs it—but it is not necessary to know whether the prepositional phrase is an argument or an adjunct. Different syntactic behavior by argument and adjunct prepositional phrases (as, for instance, regarding word order) was also unimportant because we did not want to enforce fine distinctions in grammaticality.

- apcomp — an adjectival complement:
    They made him happy.

- scomp — a sentential complement:
    Verify that the power switch is off.
    Determine why the power switch is off.

- xcomp — a verb phrase complement:
    Use the test to verify the result.
    It continued running.
    Have the display serviced.
    Watch the characters change.

The grammar uses the feature comp-type to represent subcategorization for these types of complements. The feature has nine values: no (the verb can occur without a complement), wh (embedded wh-question), NP (noun phrase complement), AP (adjective phrase complement), inf-S (infinitival sentence complement), S (full sentential complement), vpbar (infinitival VP complement with *to*), pstprt (past participle VP complement), prsprt (present participle VP complement) and VP (infinitival VP complement without *to*). So, (comp-type X) means that the verb can, but need not, occur with comp-type X.

In unrestricted text, each verb can belong to many subcategories and undergo many productive rules that alter subcategorization. (An extensive list of such rules is contained in B. Levin 1989.) The KBMT-89 lexicon and grammar allow only for the subcategories that occur in the project corpora. (See section 4.3.2, "Japanese Case Markers and Grammatical Functions.")

4.2.3.2 Auxiliary Verbs

The English analysis grammar strictly enforces sequencing conditions on auxiliary verbs and verb forms. It captures the following basic facts about English auxiliary verbs (Chomsky 1957).

- There can be at most four auxiliary verbs in a clause: at most one modal verb, at most one instance of have, and at most two instances of be (e.g., *the diskette will have been being removed*; *the diskette has been removed*; *the diskette will be removed*; *you will remove the diskette*; *you have removed the diskette*; *you are removing the diskette*; *the diskette is being removed*).

- The auxiliary verbs must be in the order modal have be-progressive be-passive.

- Morphological restrictions: The verb after a `modal` must be a base form; the verb after `have` must be a past participle; the verb after the first `be` must be a present participle; and the verb after the second `be` must be passive.

- The first auxiliary verb must be past or present tense (not a participle or infinitive) and must agree with the subject in number and person.

The English auxiliary system provides an interesting example of conflicting requirements of the syntactic and semantic components of the system. The syntactic class of auxiliary verbs (identified by their behavior in *yes/no* questions and negated sentences) is not the same as the semantic class of verbs that add temporal, aspectual and modal information to a sentence. The relevant class of auxiliary verbs identified by syntactic tests includes only *have*, *be* and the modal verbs. However, the relevant semantic class includes aspectual verbs like *start*, *stop* and *continue*, as well as some verb sequences like *be going to* and *have got to*.

The implementation of auxiliary verbs in the KBMT-89 English grammar was dictated by the semantic components of the system (the ILT, ontology and mapping rule interpreter) and by the capabilities of pseudounification. In the ontology, verbs that add temporal, aspectual and modal information to sentences are not heads of frames; they appear as features in the ILT. The KBMT-89 mapping rule interpreter therefore required them not to be syntactic heads in feature structures, because syntactic heads could only be mapped onto semantic heads. Furthermore, the usual implementation of auxiliary verbs in Lexical Functional Grammar (Kaplan and Bresnan 1982, 206) treats auxiliary verbs as heads of verb phrases, taking main verbs or other auxiliary verbs as their complements. This involves using control (unification of a subject or object with the subject of the complement) to indicate that the subject of the auxiliary verb is also its complement's subject. However, as was explained earlier, control is difficult to implement with pseudounification.

The rules for auxiliary verbs are shown here as a realistically complex example of the grammar formalism and as a realistic example of how ideal syntactic analyses must sometimes be modified to meet the requirements of other system components. The rules are indexed with numerals that correspond to immediately subsequent annotations.

```
(<AUXP> <==> (<AUX>)                              ; (1)
     (
          ((x0 tense) = (x1 tense))
          ((x0 negation) = (x1 negation))
          ((x0 auxiliary) > x1)                   ; (2)
          ((x0 aux1) = x1)                        ; (3)
```

```
            ((x0 auxn) = x1)                          ; (4)
      ))

(<AUXP> <==> (<AUXP> <AUX>)

            (.......
              (*OR* (((x1 auxn modality) =c +) ; (5)
                     ((x2 form) = inf)
                     (x0 = x1))
                    (((x1 auxn root) = have)     ; (6)
                     ((x2 passive) = -)
                     ((x2 form) = pastpart)
                     (x0 = x1)
                     ((x0 perfective) = +))
                    (((x1 auxn root) = be)       ; (7)
                     ((x2 form) =c prespart)
                     (x0 = x1)
                     ((x0 progressive) = +)))
              ((x0 auxiliary) > x2)                ; (8)
              ((x0 auxn) <= x2)                    ; (9)
    ))

(<V2> <==> (<AUXP> <V-A>)                                  ; (10)
              ((*OR* (((x1 auxn root) =c be)
                      (*OR* (((x2 passive) =c +)
                             ((x2 form) =c pastpart)
                             (x0 = x2)
                             ((x0 passive) = +))
                            (((x2 form) = prespart)
                             (x0 = x2)
                             ((x0 progressive) = + ))))
                     (((x1 auxn root) =c have)        ; (11)
                      ((x2 passive) = -)
                      ((x1 passive) = -)
                      ((x2 form) =c pastpart)
                      (x0 = x2)
                      ((x0 perfective) = +))
                     (((x1 auxn modality) =c +)       ; (12)
                      ((x2 form) =c inf)
                      (x0 = x2))
                     (((x1 auxn do-support) =c +)     ; (13)
                      ((x2 form) =c inf)
                      (x0 = x2)))
              ((x0 auxiliary) = (x1 auxiliary))       ; (14)
              ((x0 aux1) = (x1 aux1))
              (*OR* (((x1 progressive) = *defined*)  ; (15)
                     ((x0 progressive) = (x1 progressive)))
                    (((x1 progressive) = *undefined*)))
              (*OR* (((x1 perfective) = *defined*)
                     ((x0 perfective) = (x1 perfective)))
                    (((x1 perfective) = *undefined*)))
              ((x0 do-support) = (x1 do-support))
              ((x0 conditional) = (x1 conditional))
              ((x0 tense) = (x1 tense))
```

```
                          ((x0 possibility) = (x1 possibility))
                          ((x0 ability) = (x1 ability))
                          ((x0 necessity) = (x1 necessity))
                          ((x0 negation) = (x1 negation))
                          ((x0 advadjunct) > (x1 advadjunct))
                          ((x0 adv-conj) = (x1 adv-conj))
        ))
```

1. This rule will pick up the first auxiliary verb. The `tense` and `negation` of the first auxiliary verb determine the tense and negation of the sentence. The first two equations here pass those features up one level.

2. Append the auxiliary verb to the `auxiliary` register.

3. `aux1` contains the first auxiliary verb. This will eventually be used in subject-verb agreement.

4. `auxn` holds the last auxiliary verb. This will be overwritten as subsequent auxiliary verbs are encountered. `auxn` will eventually be used to determine the morphological form of the main verb.

5. This rule adds an auxiliary verb (`aux`) to the `auxp` that has been built so far. The first set of equations here determines if the last auxiliary verb in `auxp` is a modal. If so, `aux` must be an infinitive.

6. If the last auxiliary verb in `auxp` is *have*, `aux` must be a past participle, but not passive.

7. If the last auxiliary verb in `auxp` is *be*, then `aux` must be a present participle.

8. Append `aux` to the `auxiliary` register.

9. Replace the old value of `auxn` with `aux`.

10. This rule combines the auxiliary phrase built by the previous two rules with the main verb. The first set of equations applies when the last auxiliary verb is *be*. In this case, the main verb can be a present participle or passive.

11. If the last auxiliary verb was *have*, the main verb must be a past participle, but not passive.

12. If the last auxiliary verb was a modal, the main verb must be infinitive.

13. If the last auxiliary verb was *do*, the main verb must be infinitive.

14. Pass `auxiliary` and `aux1` up one level in the f-structure. `aux1` must be passed up because it is used in checking subject-verb agreement.

15. Pass several features of the `auxp` up one level. These are promoted because the tense and modality of the `auxp` determine the tense and modality of the sentence.

The grammar of auxiliary verbs also handles phrases such as those in (4.10) with *not* and adverbs following auxiliary verbs.

(4.10)   a. will not beep

   b. has also been serviced

4.2.3.3   Projections of V

Basic verb phrases in the KBMT-89 corpus consist of a verb with some combination of the following: adverbs, particles, noun phrase objects and second objects, prepositional phrases (not distinguishing arguments from adjuncts), predicative complements and clausal complements.

To avoid writing a separate verb phrase rule for each possible combination of arguments and adjuncts, a series of binary or ternary branching projections of V was implemented. The rules are designed for efficiency (for example, reducing the number of parses) and maintainability—each type of complement or adjunct appears on the right-hand side of exactly one rule. However, the rules are lax with respect to word order. In the most recent version of the KBMT-89 English grammar, the rules for core verb phrases allow the word orders summarized in the following regular expression. NP is associated with the function `obj`, `obj2` or `npcomp`; PP is associated with the function `oblique` or `ppcomp`; AP is associated with the function `apcomp`; VP and VP' are associated with the function `xcomp`; and S' is associated with the function `scomp`. Subcategorization constraints in the form of equations prevent the appearance of more than one `scomp`, `xcomp`, `ppcomp` or `apcomp`.

```
<ADVP>* (<AUXP>) <V> (<PARTICLE>) (<NP>) (<NP>)
{<ADVP> | <PP> | (<NOT>) <ADJ> | <VP> | <VPBAR> | <SBAR> | <EMB-WH>}*
```

Following is the context-free part of each of the core verb-phrase rules. Notice that the English rules are like the Japanese rules described later in that some complements and adjuncts are added recursively in binary-branching trees. However, the English rules impose some word order constraints at nonrecursive inner layers.

```
<V1> <==> (<V>)
<V1> <==> (<V> <PARTICLE>)
<V2> <==> (<V1>)
<V2> <==> (<V1> <NP>)
<V2> <==> (<V1> <NP> <PARTICLE>)
<V2> <==> (<V1> <NP> <NP>)
<V2> <==> (<V2> <ADJ>)
<V2> <==> (<V2> <NOT> <ADJ>)
<V2> <==> (<V2> <VP>)
<V2> <==> (<V2> <PP>)
<V2> <==> (<V2> <PP>)
<V2> <==> (<V2> <ADVP>)
<V2> <==> (<V2> <SBAR>)
<V2> <==> (<V2> <VPBAR>)
<V2> <==> (<V2> <EMB-WH>)
<VP> <==> (<V2>)
<VP> <==> (<AUXP> <V2>)
<VP> <==> (<ADVP> <VP>)
```

4.2.4   Other Constructions in English Grammar

In this section we very briefly summarize the English grammar's treatment of co-ordination, relative clauses, passive sentences and constructions with unexpressed subjects.

4.2.4.1   Coordination

Following is a catalog of types of coordinate structures, with examples found in the KBMT-89 English corpus. Coordination in Japanese is treated similarly.

- Conjoined NPs: *the printer power switch* and *the system unit power switch*

- Conjoined Ns: the *printer* and *cable*

- Conjoined compounds: the *fixed disk drive* and *fixed disk adapter*

- Conjoined VPs: *push in on the adjustable leg handles* and *turn them to the desired tilt position.*

- Conjoined Vs: have *installed* and *arranged* your IBM Personal Computer XT

- Conjoined Ss: *Your commands to the system can then be entered through the keyboard* and *the system responses will be displayed.*

- Conjoined PPs: *out of paper* or *near the end*

- Conjoined adjectives: The *proper* and *improper* use of diskettes

To illustrate the treatment of coordination in the grammar, the remainder of this section presents rules and feature structures for coordinate NPs, Ss and VPs.

Coordinate NP

The following example shows the c-structure and f-structure of a conjoined NP, *the system unit and the printer*. Although the individual conjuncts, *the system unit* and *the printer*, are NPs, the lowest projection of N that dominates a string consisting of a determiner and a (compound) noun is N2. Therefore, as explained previously in the discussion of the feature NP-justified, these phrases are conjoined at the N2 level. The following are among the rules used to process the phrase *the system unit and the printer*:

```
(<N2> <== (<N2-coord> <conjunction> <N2>)
          (...
           (x0 = x1)
           ((x0 conjuncts) > x3)
           ((x0 conjunction) = (x2 root))))

(<N2-coord> <== (<N2>)
          (...
           ((x0 conjuncts) = x1)))
```

The resulting f-structure is as follows:

```
((conjuncts  (*multiple* ((root printer) ...)
                         ((root system_unit) ...))))
 ...
(conjunction and))
```

Note that conjuncts contains a list of all conjuncts. The mapping rule interpreter picks up the content of conjuncts and maps it into semantic parser output (see the discussion in chapter 7).

The append operator '>', used in place of an equal sign in equations, allows multiple values to be attached to a feature in the f-structure. The list of multiple values is marked with `*multiple*` in f-structure.

Coordinate Sentences

When sentences are conjoined, the entire f-structure is a `*multiple*` followed by a list of conjoined sentences. Thus, for the following sentence,

(4.11)   Connect the cable to the system unit and turn it on.

the (abbreviated) syntactic f-structure is as follows:

```
(*multiple*
   ((root connect)
    (conjunction and)
    (subj ((root pro) (person 2) (number singular)))
    (obj ((root cable) (det ((root the)..)) ...))
    (ppadjunct ((root system_unit) (prep to)..))
    ...)
   ((root turn_on)
    (conjunction and)
    (subj ((root pro) (person 2) (number singular)))
    (obj ((root pro) (person 3) (number singular)))
    ...))
```

Coordinate VP

A coordinate VP such as *appears and increases to 9* is also represented as a `*multiple*`.

```
(*multiple*
   ((root increase)
    (conjunction and)
    (ppadjunct ((root 9) (person 3) (number singular) (prep to) ...))
    ...)
   (
   ((root appear)
    (conjunction and)
    ...)))
```

When an S node is built by combining this VP with a subject, the subject is inserted into each f-structure in the `*multiple*`. The result of this is the following f-structure, which has a `subj` in each conjunct even though the subject only appeared once in the input. In fact, this could be the f-structure for *the number 0 appears and the number 0 increases to 9* as well as *the number 0 appears and increases to 9*.

```
(*multiple*
   ((root increase)
    (conjunction and)
    (subj ((root number) (post-nom-mod ((root 0))) ...))
    (ppadjunct ((root 9) (person 3) (number singular) (prep to) ...))
    ...)
   (
   ((root appear)
    (conjunction and)
    (subj ((root number) (post-nom-mod ((root 0))) ...))
    ...)))
```

4.2.4.2 Relative Clauses

A relative clause contains a *gap* that can be filled by a *filler*. The relative clauses in (4.12a-d) are typical of those found in the corpus. The gaps in these relative clauses, indicated by underscores, are in the positions of subject, object, object of a preposition, and locative adjunct. To produce a complete ILT for a relative clause, we must identify where the gap is and what fills it. That is, when *the computer which you bought* is parsed, we need to identify that the gap is the object of *bought* and that *the computer* fills the gap.

(4.12) a. Remove the shipping cardboard *which ____ is inserted inside.*

   b. The following are examples of error messages *you may receive ____* and the probable reasons for the messages.

   c. If you have saved the original cartons and packing material *that your IBM Personal Computer units were shipped in ____* use them to pack your units.

   d. By short distance, we mean any distance *where trucking is not involved ____*

In the KBMT-89 English corpus, as in most actual corpora, the relative clauses that occur are much less complex than the "interesting" cases discussed by syntacticians. In particular, there are no *long distance* gaps—namely, gaps that are embedded at least one finite or nonfinite clause below the filler, as in *the computer that you were told to turn on ____* and *the computer that you thought you broke ____*.

In the English corpus of 150 sentences used in the KBMT-89 project, all gaps were in subject position, as in (4.12a). However, the grammar rules accommodate gaps in object position and prepositional object position as well. Participial clauses (also known as reduced relative clauses), as in *the amount of memory installed in your system*, are by far the most common type of clausal modifier of a noun. These are parsed by a different set of rules, as was shown earlier in the discussion of NP rules.

Relative clauses with gaps in subject position are parsed as VP s by the following annotated rule:

```
(<N3> <==> (<N3> <RP> <VP>)                                  ; (1)
            (((x1 root) =c (*not* pro))
             ...
             ((x3 gap) = subj)
             ((x3 subj root) =  GAP)                         ; (2)
             ((x1 anim) = (x2 rel-anim))                     ; (3)
              (*OR* ...                                      ; (4)
                    (((x3 aux1) = *defined*)
                     ((x3 aux1 modality) = -)
                     (*OR* (((x3 tense) =c present))
                           (((x3 tense) =c past)
                            ((x3 aux1 root) =c be)))
                     ((x3 aux1 person) =c 3)
                     (*OR* (((x1 conjunction) = *undefined*)
                            ((x1 number) = (x3 aux1 number)))
      ...)
    ))
             ((x3 rel-pro) = x2)                             ; (5)
             ((x3 mood) = bound)
             (x0 = x1)                                       ; (6)
             ((x0 rel-adjunct) = x3)))                       ; (7)
```

1. This rule describes phrases with an N3 followed by a relative pronoun (RP above), such as *which, that* or *who* followed by a VP.

2. Since VP is not an S, it does not have a subject (that is to say, English VPs do not contain subjects). A subject feature with the value ((root gap)) is added to its f-structure. A gap feature with value subj is also added to its f-structure.

3. Make sure the relative pronoun agrees in animacy with the object that is being modified. For example, if the relative pronoun is *who*, N3 must be human.

4. Ensure that N3 agrees in number and person with VP. The rule will accept *the cable which is attached to the keyboard* but not *the cable which are attached to your keyboard.*

5. Add the relative pronoun to VP's f-structure as the value of the feature
   `rel-pro`.

6. Unify the entire N3 (i.e., the left-hand side of the rule) with its head, N3.

7. Attach the relative clause as the value of the feature `rel-adjunct`.

To illustrate, the f-structure for *the disk which is inserted* will appear thus:

```
X0 =

(det ((root the) (ref definite)))
(ref definite)
 (person 3)
 (number singular)
 (count yes)
 (root disk)
 (rel-adjunct
         ((rel-pro ((root which) (rel-anim -)))
          (subj ((root gap)))
          (root insert)
          (passive +)
          (tense present)
          (mood bound)
          (aux1 ((root be) (person 3) (number singular) ...))
          (auxiliaries ((root be) (person 3) (number singular) ...))
          ...)))
```

The strategy for identifying gaps in object position is also straightforward. A
verb phrase containing no noun phrases must contain either an intransitive verb
or a transitive verb with an object gap. Similarly, a PP that consists only of a
preposition can be analyzed as containing a gap.

```
(<V2> <==> (<V1>)
 ( ...
    (*OR* (((x1 valency) =c trans)
           (x0 = x1)
           ((x0 gap) = obj))
          (((x1 valency) =c intrans)
           (x0 = x1)
           ((x0 gap) = *undefined*)))))

(<PP> <==> (<P>)
  (((x0 gap) = P-obj)
   ...))
```

Object and prepositional object gaps are filled by the following rule. This rule
is used in parsing noun phrases like *the computer that you bought _____; and the*

material your computer was packed in _____ The gaps will be filled by the feature structures of *the computer* and *the material*. In this rule, DEC is a declarative sentence.

```
(<N3> <==> (<N3> <RP> <DEC>)
  (...
   (*OR* ...
        (((x3 gap) =c obj)
         ((x3 valency) =c trans)
         ((x3 obj) = x1))
        (((x3 gap) =c P-OBJ)
         ...
         ((x3 P-obj) = x1)
         ((x3 ppadjunct) > (x3 P-obj))))...))
```

The implementation of rules for parsing relative clauses was based on the principle of capturing linguistic generalizations, but it does not include complex machinery (such as a complete implementation of slash categories [Gazdar et al. 1985]) that is not needed for the corpus.

4.2.4.3 Passivization

As pointed out in chapter 3, active sentences and corresponding sentences have different constituent structures and different feature structures. The meaning similarity between active and passive sentences is captured by mapping corresponding active and passive feature structures onto the same parser output.

Passive verbs are created during morphological processing. For each English verb with the feature-value pair (valency trans) in the lexicon, the morphology rules create another lexical entry with the feature-value pairs (valency intrans) and (passive +).

An active verb with (valency trans) will occur only in verb phrases with direct objects, such as *remove the diskette*, and the passive verb will occur only in verb phrases without direct objects, as in *the diskette is removed from the diskette drive*.

In Japanese, the feature (passive +) is added when a passive morpheme is parsed in the morphological rules (see section 4.3.1 below for a discussion of Japanese morphological rules). Case assignment rules for passive structures are applied after all morphological rules are parsed.

4.2.5 Unexpressed Subjects

In addition to constructions involving conjoined verb phrases and relative clauses with subject gaps, there are two other constructions in the corpus—control and imperatives—involving verb phrases whose subjects are understood but not overtly expressed.

As mentioned earlier, control, the interpretation of unexpressed subjects of non-finite clauses, cannot be implemented as a syntactic rule using pseudounification. Instead, one of the feature-value pairs (subj *subj-controlled*) or (subj *obj-controlled*) is added to the feature structure of the clause that is missing a subject.

In the course of parsing, the feature structure for the passive participle *serviced* in (4.13a) will get the feature-value pair (subj *obj-controlled*), indicating that the *system unit*, the object of *have*, is the subject of *serviced*. The feature structure for the infinitive *to work* will get the feature structure (subj *subj-controlled*) to indicate that the subject of *work* is *the computer*, the subject of *seem*.

(4.13) a. Have the system unit serviced.

  b. The computer seems to work.

The actual insertion of the feature structures of *system unit* and *computer* into the subj slots of *serviced* and *work* is carried out by a separate program that was written after KBMT-89 was first demonstrated.

Feature structures for imperative sentences (e.g., *Install the printer*) do not contain grammatical function subj at all. Instead, the mapping rules for verbs check for the feature-value pair (mood imperative) in the syntactic feature structure. If it is present, the concept *reader is inserted into the semantic slot that the value of subj would have mapped onto if it had been present.

4.3 Japanese Word Order

Japanese word order is relatively free. Although the normal order is SOV, any noun phrase in the same clause can appear anywhere as long as the verb comes at the end.[3] So, if there are four noun phrases in a clause, they can be ordered 24 different ways. The grammar can be written recursively, eliminating the need to write 24 different rules for all possible word orderings. The recursive rules may be represented as follows:

---

[3]In spoken Japanese, a verb sometimes comes before a noun phrase, which appears as an afterthought. For example: *tuketekudasai denki o* ("turn on, the light") instead of the normal order, *denki o tuketekudasai* ("turn on the light").

```
(<S> <--> (<V>)
     ((x0 = x1)))

(<S> <--> (<NP> <S>)
     (((x2 subj-case) = *defined*)
      ((x2 subj-case) = (x1 case))
      (x0 = x2)
      ((x0 subj) = x1)))

(<S> <--> (<NP> <S>)
     (((x2 obj-case) = *defined*)
      ((x2 obj-case) = (x1 case))
      (x0 = x2)
      ((x0 obj) = x1)))

(<S> <--> (<NP> <S>)
     (((x2 obj2-case) = *defined*)
      ((x2 obj2-case) = (x1 case))
      (x0 = x2)
      ((x0 obj2) = x1)))
```

These rules cover three noun phrases (subject, object and object2) and a verb. They are used to parse the different noun phrases made possible by various word orderings.

4.3.1 Japanese Morphological Rules

Morphological differences between Japanese and English suggest an opportunity for examining the grammars' handling of various phenomena. (English morphological rules are discussed in chapter 7.)

Unlike English grammar rules, the Japanese grammar rules are character-based and operate on transliterations of kana-kanji ideograms rather than words. Taking advantage of this feature, morphological rules can be written in the same formalism as syntactic rules. Affixation of a word can be handled by writing a context-free phrase structure rule. For example, complex verb forms can include causative morphemes, passive morphemes, various aspectual markers and tense. These morphemes are not stored in a lexicon, but they are introduced by rules in the course of parsing. Morphological information in the form of an assignment equation is contributed to the f-structure.

Consider this input string:

(4.14)   okikae   sase   rare   ta
             replace caus   pass   past
             "[I] was forced to replace [it]"

The following is the lexical entry rule for *okikaeru* ("to replace"). In general, the verb stem is parsed by the lexical entry rule for that verb, and the equation in the lexical entry rule assigns a dictionary form of the verb to the root function. A lexical entry rule may also contain some additional information, such as subcategorization for verbs.

```
(<v-1dan> <--> (o k i k a e)
       (((x0 cat) = V)
        ((x0 subcat) = trans)
        ((x0 root) = okikaeru)))
```

Now examine the following morphological rules:[4]

```
(<v-1dan> <--> (<v-1dan> s a s e)
        (((x1 passive) = *undefined*)
         ((x1 tense) = *undefined*)
         ((x1 causative) = *undefined*)
         (x0 = x1)
         ((x0 causative) = +)))

(<v-1dan> <--> (<v-1dan> r a r e)
        (((x1 tense) = *undefined*)
         ((x1 passive) = *undefined*)
         (x0 = x1)
         ((x0 passive) = +)))

(<v-1dan> <--> (<v-1dan> t a)
        (((x1 tense) = *undefined*)
         (x0 = x1)
         ((x0 tense) = past)))
```

Armed with these morphological rules and the previous lexical entry rule, the following verb forms are transparent to the parser:

(4.15)   a. *okikae*
             replace-past

         b. *okikaesaseta*
             replace-caus-past

         c. *okikaerareta*
             replace-pass-past

---

[4]Here, *defined* indicates that the left-hand side of the equation must have a value; *undefined* indicates that it must not.

      d. *okikaesaserareta*
      replace-caus-pass-past

However, the following ungrammatical verb forms cannot be parsed:

(4.16)   a.**okikaeraresaseta*
       replace-pass-caus-past

       b.**okikaetasaserare*
       replace-past-caus-pass

       c.**okikaetararesase*
       replace-past-pass-caus

       d.**okikaeraretasase*
       replace-pass-past-caus

       e.**okikaesasetarare*
       replace-caus-past-pass

       f.**okikaeraresase*
       replace-pass-caus

       g.**okikaetarare*
       replace-past-pass

       h.**okikaetasase*
       replace-past-caus

As we can see in the preceding morphological rules, equations containing `*undefined*` and `*defined*` are convenient devices for preventing a rule from applying at an undesirable point. Because there is no need to write a separate entry for each verb form, morphological rules reduce the number of rules required in the grammar.

Note further that lexical entry rules can be written for each member of a word's inflectional paradigm, thus avoiding the use of morphological rules. Alternatively, lexical entry rules can contain only root forms, and morphological rules may be used to define all instances of affixation.

4.3.2   Japanese Case Markers and Grammatical Functions

Japanese noun phrases are marked by case markers such as *ga* and *ni*; these play an important role in determining grammatical functions such as subject and object. Case markers do not stand in a one-to-one correspondence with grammatical functions. The nouns marked by the same case markers can embody different grammatical functions, depending on associated verbs. For example, the verb *torinozoku* ("remove") usually takes *ga* for a subject marker and *o* for an object marker, as in *Yuuzaa ga deisuketto o torinozota* ("The user removed the diskette"). On the other hand, to take a different kind of example, the verb *oriru* ("disembark") usually takes *ga* for a subject marker and *o* for an oblique locative marker, as in *Taro ga basu o orita* ("Taro got off the bus"). Furthermore, the same verb would take different case markers depending on the type of morpheme attached to the verb. When the verb *torinozoku* has the morpheme *-tai* ("want"), then the verb can take either *ga* or *o* for an object marker. Therefore one would say, *deisuketto ga torinozokitai baai* ("in case (you) want to remove the diskette").

Since case markers are determined by verb forms, features are used to test the verb forms and assign case markers for each grammatical function. When a noun phrase is parsed, a case marker for the noun must agree with the case assigned in the verb. In the following sample case-assignment rules, subcat is equivalent to valency in the English grammar.

```
(<V1> <--> (<V>)
    (((x1 subcat) =c trans) ((x1 passive) = -) ((x1 causative) = -)
     (x0 = x1)
     ((x0 subj-case) = ga) ((x0 obj-case) = o)))

(<V1> <--> (<V>)
    (((x1 subcat) =c trans2) ((x1 passive) = -) ((x1 causative) = -)
     (x0 = x1)
     ((x0 subj-case) = ga) ((x0 obj-case) = ni)))

(<V1> <--> (<V>)
    (((x1 subcat) =c intrans) ((x1 passive) = -) ((x1 causative) = -)
     (x0 = x1)
     ((x0 subj-case) = ga)))

(<V1> <--> (<V>)
    (((x1 subcat) =c bitrans) ((x1 passive) = -) ((x1 causative) = -)
     (x0 = x1)
     ((x0 subj-case) = ga) ((x0 obj-case) = o)
     ((x0 obj2-case) = ni)))

(<V1> <--> (<V>)
    (((x1 subcat) =c stat) ((x1 passive) = -) ((x1 causative) = -)
     (x0 = x1)
```

```
          ((x0 subj-case) = ga) ((x0 obj-case) = ga)))

(<V1> <--> (<V>)
    (((x1 subcat) =c inv) ((x1 passive) = -) ((x1 causative) = -)
     (x0 = x1)
     ((x0 subj-case) = (*or* ga ni))
     ((x0 obj-case) = ga)))

(<V1> <--> (<V>)
    (((x1 subcat) =c trans) ((x1 tai) =c +) ((x1 passive) = -)
     ((x1 causative) = -)
     (x0 = x1)
     ((x0 subj-case) = ga) ((x0 obj-case) = ga)))
```

4.4   Generation Grammars

The KBMT-89 grammars are used in analysis to produce source language f-structures and in the generation phase to produce target language strings. They may be understood as reverse or mirror images of each other. Indeed, the Japanese analysis grammar was designed to be bidirectional.

However, some rules that simplify a grammar can be used for either analysis or generation but not for both. The English generation grammar was designed from the outset with that principle in mind; on the other hand, bidirectionality is theoretically challenging.

Clearly, both approaches have advantages and disadvantages, and decisions have involved trade-offs. For instance, bidirectionality eliminates the need to write separate grammars but requires increased attention to rule ordering. The question of which approach is more efficient has not been explicitly addressed; it might provide impetus for future research. At any rate, the formal aspects of the Japanese grammar are described in section 4.5.

The generation grammars serve as the knowledge sources for the language generator. The GENKIT system (Tomita and Nyberg 1988) uses this knowledge to build a grammatical string or sentence from an f-structure. Such f-structures are produced from ILTs by applying generation mapping rules after the lexical selection process has been completed. The production of f-structures from ILTs is described in chapter 9, where an introduction to GENKIT is found.

The approach embodied in the English generation grammar rules is based on the same phrase-structure framework that was used to build the analysis grammar. The generation grammar is designed to process an f-structure by decomposing it into smaller f-structures such that each substructure corresponds to a phrase-structure category. This is the opposite of the process by which the analysis grammar builds up a large f-structure from smaller f-structures corresponding to phrase-structure categories.

4.4.1 Ordering of Equations within Rules

Equations are ordered differently in the generation grammars than in the analysis grammars to allow f-structures to be disassembled rather than built. As one might expect, the general pattern is that the order of the generation equations is the reverse of the order of the analysis equations. The contrast will be illustrated shortly.

An analysis rule for creating an f-structure by parsing a declarative sentence looks like this:

```
(<DEC> <== (<NP> <VP>)
   ((x0 = x2)
    ((x0 subj) = x1)))
```

This rule builds the following f-structure:

```
((subj ((root computer) (ref definite) (number singular)))
 (root turn_off) (passive +)))
```

Then the following generation rule takes the above f-structure as input to the generation grammar's version of the declarative sentence rule, in which <DEC> is x0, <NP> is x1 and <VP> is x2.

```
(<DEC> ==> (<NP> <VP>)
   ((x1 == (x0 subj))
    (x2 = x0)))
```

This rule builds two English phrases, given here with their corresponding f-structures:

(4.17)   a. the computer

```
        <NP> = ((root computer) (ref definite) (number singular))
```

   b. is turned off

```
        <VP> = ((root turn_off) (passive +))
```

The LISP strings that are generated from these f-structures are combined to create the sentence *The computer is turned off.*

4.4.2   Rule Ordering

Since analysis returns all possible parses for any given input string, it is not necessary to order the phrase-structure rules within the data file. In generation, however, this is not the case. Phrase-structure rules that have identical left-hand sides are generally ordered according to a set of principles adopted to generate correct strings efficiently.

The generator is designed so that it does not need to consume the entire input f-structure in order to succeed. This feature allows information that may be extraneous to the creation of a grammatical sentence in the target language to be present in the input f-structure. Once the generator has succeeded in constructing a grammatical output, it will stop. The generator's definition of a grammatical output is determined by the rules in the generation grammar. The generator tries the rules in the order in which they occur in the grammar, and higher-level rules call lower-level rules. Thus, if a higher-level rule is fired and succeeds, the generator will produce a string and then stop, even if a substantial amount of f-structure remains to be consumed.

Given this state of affairs, the first principle governing rule ordering is to consume as much as possible of the input f-structure. In other words, the goal is to realize as much of a string as possible. To accomplish this, rules are arranged in the data file in the order of most complex right-hand sides to simplest right-hand sides. Complexity is generally a function of the number of right-hand nodes.[5] Following are two sample phrase structure rules for generation:

```
x0 = ((det ((root the))) (root computer) (number singular))

(<N2> ==> (<DET> <N1>)
          ((x1 == (x0 det))
           (x2 = x0)))
```

---

[5]The complexity of the right-hand nodes may be in some cases be hidden. Consider (i.a) and (ii) below. These <NP> rules appear to be equal in complexity in that they have an equal number of right-hand nodes. Now note (i.b) and (i.c), the possible right-hand sides of (i.a)'s right-hand side. In (i.b), <POSS-NP> would consist of an <NP> followed by a possessive marker (either an apostrophe or an apostrophe followed by an 's'); or in (i.c) it would consist of a possessive pronoun. On the other hand, both <DET> and <N> in (ii) are terminal nodes.

```
  i.  a. (<NP> ==> (<POSS-NP> <N>) ...)
      b. (<POSS-NP> ==> (<NP> <POSS-MARKER>) ...)
      c. (<POSS-NP> ==> (<POSS-PRO>) ...)
 ii.  (<NP> ==> (<DET> <N>) ...)
```

```
(<N2> ==> (<N1>)
          ((x1 = x0)))
```

These rules are ordered so that the more complex rule is tried before the simpler. The first rule, if fired with the f-structure input given, will produce the string *the computer*. The second rule will produce *computer* but will not consume the part of the f-structure that contains the determiner *the*. Either rule can succeed with the input given, so whichever rule is fired first will produce output. This success will cause the generator to stop looking for an <N2> rule and proceed to the next step indicated by the grammar.

When a lower-level rule (that is, a rule called by another rule) is used and succeeds, it creates a substring that forms part of the output. The grammar continues generating such substrings until a complete sentence or NP is formed.[6]

4.5 Bidirectionality

As noted earlier, the Japanese analysis grammar is designed to be bidirectional. We can now present this idea formally and in greater detail.

Wedekind (1988) proved that an LFG grammar G parses a sentence s with a resulting f-structure f if and only if s is generated by a derivation of G, starting from an f associated with a start symbol. Since the KBMT-89 grammar formalism is based on LFG, the property also holds for our grammar if:

- The well-formedness of f-structures is satisfied;

- Destructive operations are recoverable (see item 3f in the algorithm below); and

- For each grammar rule, there is no equation including $x\text{-}j$ after an equation of form $(x\text{-}i = x\text{-}j)$.

Takeda (1989) gives a further discussion of these conditions. He shows that a general unification grammar (a set of context-free rules, each of which is associated with a set of equations) has the property of being bidirectional.

---

[6]If the initial f-structure represented only an NP, there would be a higher-level rule that would fire and create an NP as its output. Since this NP-only rule has a simple right-hand side, it appears in the rule ordering *after* those rules that call for some combination of NPs and VPs.

Now bidirectionality may be understood as a function on grammars such that for each analysis grammar rule of the form

(<X> ← (<Y1> ... <Yn>)
  (equation-1 ... equation-k))

there is a corresponding rule in the generation grammar

(<X> → (<Y1> ... <Yn>)
  (equation-1′ ... equation-k′))

For any valid set of *n* f-structures { *f1*, ... , *fn* } for *<Y1>*, ... , *<Yn>* that satisfies the analysis grammar rule and defines the resulting f-structure *f0* for *<X>*, the generation grammar will also define the set of f-structures { *f1*, ... , *fn* } for *<Y1>*, ... , *<Yn>*, given the f-structure *f0*. For KBMT-89, a basic algorithm was written to create a generation grammar from a given analysis grammar. The algorithm is presented here:[7]

1. Input: An analysis grammar consisting of *n* rules. Let each subset of *k* rules with the same left-hand side be *r* = {*r-1, r-2, ... , r-k*}.

2. For each *r* and for each *r-i (i=1, ... , k)*, apply (3) to obtain the generation rule *g* = {*g-1, g-2, ... , g-k*} .

3. Let *r-i* have *m* equations *e-1, e-2, ... , e-m*. Then, *g-i* consists of *m* equations *e-m′, ... , e-2′, e-1′*, where

   (a) *e-j′* is *(path =c atom)* iff *e-j* is *(path =c atom)*

   (b) *e-j′* is *((path =c atom) (path = *remove*))* iff *e-j* is *(path = atom)*

   (c) *e-j′* is *(path = *defined*)* iff *e-j* is *(path = *defined*)*

   (d) *e-j′* is *(path = *undefined*)* iff *e-j* is *(path = *undefined*)*

   (e) *e-j′* is *(path2 == path1)*, a removal, iff *e-j* is *(path1 = path2)*

   (f) *e-j′* is *(path-1 = (f-1 path-0)) ... (path-p = (f-p path-0))* iff *e-j* is *(path-0 = (f path-p ... path-p))*, where *f* is a user-defined function in the analysis grammar, and *f-1, ... , f-p* are inverse functions to recover f-structures of *path-1, ... , path-p* from that of *path-0*.

---

[7]Since one can always have an equivalent set of disjunction-free rules for any rule with disjunctions, it is assumed that the input analysis grammar has no disjunctions; there is no resulting loss of generality.

(g) Otherwise, *e-j´* cannot be defined, and the input grammar does not satisfy the requirements of bidirectionality.

4. Generate a set of rules *g* as a generation grammar.

Although it is possible to create a generation grammar automatically from an analysis grammar using the above algorithm (except for inverse functions in (3f)), the KBMT-89 Japanese generation grammar was modified by hand to improve its performance. This modification consisted in adding equations such as (path = *undefined*) and (path = (*not* atom)). This roughly corresponds to the rule-ordering strategy in the English generation grammar.

An example of such an equation is ((x1 cat) = N) for a rule NP -> N. This is the case because no f-structure without (cat N) will succeed later in generation. It can be easily shown that the number of possible f-structure pairs (*f1*, *f2*) that can be unified to become a given f-structure *f* is exponentially many in terms of the size of *f*. Hence a naïve generation algorithm with backtracking may take an exponential time until it can successfully generate a sentence for a particular f-structure as input. Modifying the generation grammar by adding equations is therefore crucial.

There are several other differences between the analysis and generation grammars. They can be stated briefly:

- Terminal symbols are implemented using hash tables in the generation grammar.

- The order of rules is important in the generation grammar because only the first answer is sought by the system.

- Those rules that generate stylistically poor sentences are removed.

As a result, the generation grammar's coverage was narrowed. However, the broad coverage of the analysis grammar could be retained in the generation grammar, although this would require weighing the trade-offs mentioned earlier.

Let us consider a functional illustration of the Japanese generation grammar. The following f-structure is the input for the sentence *Tenkii no 9 wo osite kudasai* ("Press 9 on the numeric keypad"):

```
((time ((root present))) (mood ((root imp)))
 (obj
  ((wh -) (case o)
   (xadjunct ((cop ((form no))) (cat N) (root tenkii)))
   (root 9)))
 (causative -) (obj-case o) (subj-case ga) (passive -) (subcat trans)
 (formal +) (vtype V-5dan-s) (cat V) (root osu))
```

With this as input to the final phase, the generator can produce the output sentence. In what follows, we constrain a large trace by showing only the rules that applied successfully. The rules are annotated line by line.

```
sentence --> S                  ;Time, mood values verified.
 S --> XP S                     ;Object case filler identified and
                                ;   causative, passive values verified.
   XP --> NP <obj-case>         ;NP, object-case marker identified.
     NP --> NP <cop> NP         ;Head NP and modifier NP are identified.
       NP --> N                 ;Modifier NP examined as a noun.
         N --> tenkii           ;Modifier noun is generated.
       NP --> N                 ;Head NP is examined as a noun.
         N --> <integer>        ;Head noun identified as an integer.
           <integer> --> 9      ;Integer 9 is generated.
   S --> VP                     ;VP is examined.
     VP --> V <kudasai>         ;Inflection rules are examined.
       V --> <v-mizen> <te>
         <v-mizen> --> <v-root> <si>
           <v-root> --> o       ;Root form is identified.
```

Next, the character string of each terminal symbol is concatenated in sequence. This produces the final output:

```
TENKII NO 9 WO OSITE KUDASAI
```

Chapter 5

Analysis Lexicons

■ Teruko Mitamura, Donna M. Gates, Lori Levin, Marion Kee, Margalit Zabludowski, Dawn Haberlach and Koichi Takeda

5.1 Introduction and Overview

This chapter describes the form and function of a key knowledge source for knowledge-based machine translation, namely, the lexicons for natural language analysis. Generally, the analysis lexicons for English and for Japanese are computationally similar. In what follows we attempt to convey this air of generality. To be sure, there remain differences, and we try to capture some of these where most appropriate in language-specific examples.

An analysis lexicon is a dictionary, indexed by word and by part of speech, that contains the syntactic information, mapping rules and semantic data required for semantic parsing. During the parser's loading phase, an analysis lexicon is built up from declarative knowledge sources for each language. We usually refer to the final form of the lexicon as the *dictionary* for that language. When a word is encountered in the input, the run-time parser consults the dictionary and retrieves the features and mappings associated with that word.

The English and Japanese analysis lexicon entries generally include the following parts: a word, its category, its inflection, its root form, and its associated

syntactic features and mapping rules. A top-level outline for an entry is given below in Backus-Naur Form (BNF), followed by an informal explanation of the terms
and their origins. A more detailed BNF specification for lexicon entries appears in
the following section.

```
<analysis-lexicon-entry> ::=
    (<word>
          <category>
        ?<inflection>
        ?<infl-form>
        ?<root>
        ?<features>
        ?<mapping>)
```

The dictionary for each language is created from several knowledge sources: a
base lexicon for each word category in the language, the syntactic feature hierarchy
for each category, the morphological and mapping rules for that language and the
concept lexicon entries. We refer to the process of building an analysis lexicon as
expansion, because it begins with the base lexicon and adds to it information from
the other knowledge sources. The format of the entries is the same throughout
this process. During expansion, most existing entries will have more information
added; and a new entry will be created for each morphological variation on the
basic or root form of the word.

The base lexicon is the original source of the values for <category>,
<word>, <inflection>, <features> and <mapping>, as given in the
example above. The <category> of the word indicates a part of speech, such as
V for verb or N for noun. If the same word has more than one category, separate
entries are created. The <inflection> consists of an inflectional type, such
as past or present, and its form (e.g. "saw" or "see"). Information about
any irregular forms in the word's inflection appears here; it will override the default, which is to assume that all the word's forms have regular morphology. The
syntactic features (<features>) are used during syntactic parsing and include
number, agreement and valency category.

Valency refers to the argument structure of a predicate, most typically a verb
or a de-verbal noun. A verb usually corresponds to a proposition, which has
certain roles associated with it. The roles usually correspond to noun phrases,
prepositional phrases or clauses; these appear in the syntax as arguments to the
verb (for instance, as the verb's subject or object). However, a role is sometimes
filled with an understood or tacit reference that is not syntactically realized. For
example, the English verb *move* corresponds to a proposition having the following

roles: agent, for the actor doing the moving; theme, for the object being moved; source, for the location being moved from; and goal, for the location being moved to. All of these may be syntactically realized, as in (5.1a).

(5.1)   a. John moved the book from the chair to the table.

   b. John moved the book.

   c.*John put the book from the chair to the table.

   d. John put the book on the table.

   e.*John put the book.

The arguments corresponding to the source and goal roles may be left out of the sentence (as in (5.1b)), but fillers for those roles will still be understood to exist, even if they are not specified.

Now consider the English verb *put*, which corresponds to the same propositional structure. This verb will not allow the syntactic realization of the source role, as a comparison of (5.1c) and (5.1d) reveals. Neither will it allow the deletion of the argument corresponding to the goal role, as in (5.1e). Despite their semantic similarities, *put* and *move* have different valencies. Generally, the valency of a verb signifies those semantic roles that may be filled by actual syntactic arguments to the verb, and the permissible lexical categories and features of these arguments (e.g., whether they may be nouns or prepositional phrases).

In the base lexicon, the parts of the entry represented by <features> and <mapping> contain either a pointer to default information in a separate hierarchy (see following), or information specific to the individual entry, or both. In the case of <features>, specific information will override the default for any given feature; in the case of <mapping>, specific information will simply be added to the default information.

Before expansion, <word> is the citation form of a word. During expansion, separate entries are created for each inflected form that can be derived from the citation form. In these entries, <word> will be an inflected form. For example, the base lexical entry contains a <word> such as remove; after expansion, there will be three additional entries: removes, removed and removing.

The function of the mapping rules is to unite the concept lexicon's frame definitions for a particular domain with the syntactic rules for a given language. There are two kinds of mapping rules for a particular word: lexical mapping rules and structural mapping rules. The former map a word onto a head concept or a slot of a concept. The structural mapping rules map a syntactic slot of an f-structure, such as subject or object, onto a semantic slot in a concept (such as agent or theme).[1]

Syntactic features and structural mapping rules can be defined in an analysis lexicon entry either locally (using `local`) or nonlocally (using `class`). The first of these is an information holder for "word specific" syntactic features and mapping rules. The second contains a pointer to a general structure in which common information can be stored. These general structures for the syntactic features and for the structural mapping rules are called the *syntactic feature hierarchy* and the *structural mapping hierarchy*, respectively. The analysis lexicon inherits information from these hierarchies through the pointers contained in the individual entries.

5.2   Structure of the Lexicon Entries

In the course of analysis lexicon expansion, `<infl-form>` and `<root>` will be added to those entries that are created by the morphology package during expansion. The Japanese analysis lexicon does not need to be expanded, because the morphological derivation is performed by the grammar. The English morphological functions are described in the next section. Also, because Japanese features are incorporated into the grammar, they are not contained in the Japanese analysis lexicon. Furthermore, the mapping rules are language dependent—some verbs, for instance, are transitive in one of the languages but transitive and intransitive in the other—and so the mapping rule hierarchies were created separately. As a result, inheritances may differ between languages even as particular words will correspond to the same concept. This will be seen shortly in the different analysis lexicon entries for *remove* and *torinozoku*.

A more detailed representation of an analysis lexicon entry is as follows:

```
(<word>
        (cat <cat>)
      ?(<infl>   {+ (<infl-type> <form>)} )
      ?(<inflectional-form> <infl-type>)
      ?(root <value>)
      ?(features
            ?(class {+ <class-name-feat>})
            {* (local {+ (<feature>   <value>)} )}
            ?(all-features <f-structure>) )
```

---

[1]An explanation of the mapping rules appears below. The function of the mapping rule interpreter is described in chapter 7.

```
?(mapping
    ?(class {+ <class-name-map>})
    {*
     (local
       ?(sem-test {+ <sem-test>})
       ?(test {+ <syn-test>})
       {+ {(head <sem-head> {* <slot-value-pair> }) |
           (embed <slot-value-pair>) |
           (slot {+ <structural-mapping>} )}}) })
```

So, the entry for *remove* in an expanded English analysis lexicon appears thus:

```
("remove"
       (cat V)
       (conj-form infinitive)
       (features
           (class default-verb-feat)
           (all-features (*or*
                           ((form inf) (valency trans) (comp-type no)
                            (root remove))
                           ((person (*or* 1 2 3)) (number plural)
                            (tense present) (form finite) (valency trans)
                            (comp-type no) (root remove))
                           ((person (*or* 1 2)) (number singular)
                            (tense present) (form finite) (valency trans)
                            (comp-type no) (root remove)))))
       (mapping
           (local
               (head (remove)))
           (local
               (slot (source = (ppadjunct (prep = from)))))
           (class cb-th-verb-map)))
```

In the structural mapping rule, which begins in this example with `mapping`, the line (`class cb-th-verb-map`) indicates that the rule applies to verbs with `caused-by` and `theme` slots; examples are *remove* and *control* (see section 5.7.)

The expanded Japanese analysis lexicon entry for *torinozoku* ("remove") is constituted as shown in the following. *Torinozoku* inherits mapping rules from the `agent-theme-map` class. The mapping rule classes are different for English and Japanese because they reflect classes of verbs that undergo the same valency alternations and the same syntactic-to-semantic mappings within each language but are mapped differently in English and Japanese (Mitamura 1989).

```
("torinozoku"
     (cat V)
         (mapping
             (local
                 (head (remove)))
             (class agent-theme-map)))
```

5.3   Notation

The notational conventions for an analysis lexicon entry are presented in this subsection. A BNF-like specification is used to show how entries are structured, but it should be understood that this specification is intended as a human-readable convenience. The actual entries in the system are built up using the notation that results when the following BNF specifications are fully expanded.

- Miscellaneous characters (cf. table 1.1)

  ? = [optionality] 0 or 1

  {+ } = 1 or more

  {* } = 0 or more { | } = disjunction

  * = name of concept

  ; = comments

  & = atomic value

- `<word>` expands to a word represented as a LISP string. It corresponds to a terminal input string in a word-based syntactic grammar, but it is not used as a terminal string in character-based parsing. However, in both character-based and word-based parsing, `<word>` serves as an index into a hash table that contains pointers to lexical entries and is, by default, the value of `root`. `<word>` can be a LISP string containing spaces, such as `"shipping cardboard"`, in which case the `root` is a symbol with underscores substituted for the spaces (e.g., `shipping_cardboard`).

- `<category>` expands to (cat `<cat>`).

- `<cat>` expands to the syntactic category of a word. The name of the category of a word is the same as the category name used in the syntactic grammar and the concept lexicon. The category names for English are n, v, adj, adv, p, det, conjunct and so forth.

- `<inflection>` is found only in the base lexicon. It consists of (`<infl>` {+(`<infl-type>` `<form>`)}). This can be used for making irregular forms of verbs (e.g. *begin, began* and *begun*) or preventing the plural morphology rule from applying to mass nouns (e.g., *knowledge*). Further,

  - `<infl>` expands to {infl | conj | decl}.

- `<infl-type>` expands to the name of an inflectional category, such as `past` or `pastpart` for a verb and `singular` or `plural` for a noun.

- `<form>` expands to an inflected form of the root word represented as a LISP string. During expansion, the morphology rules will use the `<form>` instead of generating a regular form for `<infl-type>`.

During the expansion phase, the morphology package checks for `<inflection>` and uses any information it contains instead of the default morphological expansion. `<inflection>` can apply to verbs, adverbs, nouns, adjectives and so forth, depending on the language.

• `<infl-form>` expands to (`<inflectional-form>` `<infl-type>`) and `<inflectional-form>` expands to {`infl-form` | `conj-form` | `decl-form`}. It is created when the analysis lexicon is expanded and indicates an entry's inflection type. All inflected entries contain this information. If `<infl-form>` appears in a base lexicon entry, the entry passes directly into the dictionary, unchanged from its base lexicon form. Alternative plural forms of nouns are marked in this manner. For instance, with the word *matrix* we allow not only *matrixes* but *matrices* as well. Since *matrixes* follows a regular rule, *matrices* is entered in the lexicon separately, as follows:

```
("matrices" (cat N)
            (root matrix)
            (infl-form plural)
            (features (class default-noun-feat))
            (mapping (class object-map))))
```

Other examples of `<infl-type>` are `past`, `pastpart`, `prespart`,`3sg` and so forth. The names of the `infl-types` are based on the names of the morphology rules used for the given language (see section 5.4 on English inflectional morphology).

• `<root>` expands to (`root` `<value>`). This is created during expansion if the expanded form is not the citation form of the word. For example, the base lexicon contains an entry with `<word>` = `"see"`. The expanded lexicon will contain an entry with `<word>` = `"seen"` and `<root>` = (`root see`). It will also contain an entry with `<word>` = `"see"` and no `<root>` because `"see"` is the citation form and (`root see`) can be derived automatically.

In some cases the `<root>` is not created during expansion but is entered into the base entry directly. For instance, the sentence *Turn the computer on* contains a verb particle construction with the verb *turn*. In the lexical entry for this verb-particle combination, `<word>` is `"turn"` because `<word>` is the input to morphological expansion and only *turn* needs to be inflected. However, `<root>` is (`root turn_on`), because `<root>` serves as an index into the concept lexicon via lexical mapping rules and so must distinguish the sense of *turn* in *turn on* from other senses of *turn*.

- `<features>` expands to (`features ?<class-feat> {* <local -feat>} ?<all-features>`). Here, `<features>` are syntactic features. These can be defined either locally in `<local-feat>` or nonlocally in `<class-feat>`. `<features>` will not appear in either the base or the expanded lexicon for entries that have no syntactic features, such as adverbs and most prepositions in English.

- `<local-feat>`. This designates locally specified features and expands to (`local {+ (<feature> <value>)}`). Following is an example in which `valency` and `abbr` are feature names and `ditrans` and `+` are values:

  ```
  (local   (valency ditrans)
           (abbr +))
  ```

- `<feature>` The name of a feature.

- `<value>` The value of a named feature.

- `<class-feat>` expands to (`class {+ <class-name-feat>}`); this points to nonlocally specified feature-value pairs.

- `<class-name-feat>` expands to the name of a syntactic feature class. Such a class specifies feature-value pairs that are inherited by members of that class. If a feature is not specified locally in a lexical entry but appears in the `class` specified for that entry, then the expanded version of the entry will inherit the feature and its associated value from its `class`.

- `<all-features>` expands to (`all-features <f-structure>`). This information is added to an entry when the morphological expansion and syntactic feature class inheritance are performed by the system. An entry that has not undergone morphological expansion will not contain `<all-features>` (e.g., adverbs and prepositions in English).

- `<f-structure>` expands to the parser's internal representation of the f-structure representing an entry's syntactic features. It is created during expansion and includes all features that were added by the morphological rules and inherited from the syntactic feature classes as well as the local features. `<f-structure>` does not include information from any of the mapping rules associated with the entry. The primary reason for including this f-structure is to enable the grammar writer to check the postexpansion features of an entry at a glance; this can be very helpful in debugging grammars.

- `<mapping>` expands to (`mapping ?<class-map> {*<local -map>}`). This is where all mapping rule information for a lexical entry is stored. Mappings can be defined either locally or nonlocally. `<mapping>` will not appear in either the base or expanded lexicon for entries that have no mapping rules, such as English prepositions and Japanese case markers.

- `<class-map>` expands to (`class {+ <class-name-map>}`). This simply specifies the notation used to reference one or more classes of structural mapping rules.

- `<class-name-map>`. This expands to the name of a structural mapping rule class. Mapping rule classes are used to store structural mapping rules in an inheritance hierarchy (similar to the syntactic feature hierarchy previously described). Structural mapping rules are explained later under `<structural-mapping>`.

- `<local-map>` expands to (`local {+<map>} ?<map-test>`). Local mapping rules are used for lexical mapping as well as structural mapping. Local mappings are specific to the entry in which they appear; they add information to the inherited mappings but cannot override inherited information.

- `<map>` expands to {`<lexical-map> | <structural-map>`}. This distinction corresponds to the organization of mapping rules into two broad categories, namely, lexical and structural.

- `<lexical-map>` expands to {`<headed-lexical-map>`|`<embedded -lexical-map>`} . These are the two basic types of lexical mapping rules.

- `<headed-lexical-map>` expands to (head `<sem-head>`{*`<slot -value-pair>`}). Head is used for lexical mapping in which a `<word>` maps onto the head of a concept. The `<slot-value-pair>` is used for adding finer-grained distinctions than concept names alone will allow.

- `<embedded-lexical-map>` expands to (embed `<slot-value- pair>`). This is used for lexical mappings in which a `<word>` maps onto a slot and a concept.

- `<slot-value-pair>` expands to (`<sem-slot>` `<sem-value>`). This is used to assign a value to a slot.

- `<sem-slot>` expands to the name of a slot in a concept lexicon entry.

- `<sem-value>` expands to an ontological value. An ontological value is a concept or a value-set element in the concept lexicon.

- `<structural-map>` expands to (slot {+ `<structural-map- ping>`}). If an entry has more than one structural mapping, slot is used to group them.

- `<structural-mapping>` expands to a rule of the form: (`<sem-slot>` = {`<syn-slot>` | (`<syn-slot>` {+ `<syn-test>`})}). Structural mappings associate syntactic functions with semantic relations. Some examples of structural mappings include (agent = subj), (theme = obj) and (goal = (ppadjunct (prep = to))).

- `<syn-slot>` expands to the name of a slot in the syntactic grammar.

- `<map-test>` expands to ?`<sem-map-test>` ?`<syn-map-test>`. These respectively correspond to semantic and syntactic tests. The tests determine whether the system will apply the mapping rules within their local.

- `<sem-map-test>` expands to (sem-test {+ `<sem-test>`}). This tests semantic constraints on rule application.

- `<sem-test>` expands to `(<sem-slot> <sem-value>)`. Here the slots will be relation names and the values will be ontological values. It is unified with the semantic structure being built; if unification fails, none of the mapping rules inside the `local` where the test is located will be applied.

- `<syn-map-test>` expands to `(test {+ <syn-test>})`. This tests syntactic constraints on rule application.

- `<syn-test>` expands to `(<syn-slot> = <syn-value>)`. This test is unified with the syntactic f-structure being built; if the unification fails, none of the mapping rules inside the `local` where the test is located will be applied. An example is the test for a passive feature structure: `(passive = +)`.

- `<syn-value>` expands to a syntactic feature value.

5.4 English Inflectional Morphology

Instead of storing all inflected forms of English nouns and verbs in the analysis lexicon, we store only the singular forms of nouns and the infinitival forms of verbs. Morphological rules expand this base lexicon by generating all of the inflected forms of nouns and verbs.

The morphological rules for English do two things: they add and delete characters to produce inflected words, each having its own lexical entry, and they add syntactic features to the new entries so the entries can be used with the English analysis grammar.

The input to the morphological rules is a file containing lexical entries for uninflected nouns and verbs. Each lexical entry includes syntactic features that are common to all inflected forms of the given word. The following is an example of a lexical entry for an uninflected noun before expansion:

```
("diskette" (cat N)
         (features (local (count yes) (person 3) (meas-unit no)
                          (proper no) (root diskette)))
         (mapping (class object-map)))
```

The rules that strip characters from and add suffixes to words are written in a notation similar to that of phonological rules in linguistics. The rules for each allomorph of a morpheme are mutually exclusive, so that only one rule should be able to fire on any given lexeme. In the following example of a morphological rule that forms plural nouns, the lines are indexed with numbers that correspond to enumerated comments in the subsequent text. The first line of the rule gives the part of speech and the inflectional form.[2]

```
(N plural
    (("" <-> "s" / NOT-SIBILANTorOorY _ #)       ; (1)
     ("" <-> "es" /  SIBILANTorO _ #)             ; (2)
     ("y" <-> "ys" / V _ #)                        ; (3)
     ("y" <-> "ies" / C _ #)                       ; (4)
     irregular)                                    ; (5)
    (((x0 number) = plural)                        ; (6)
     ((x0 person) = 3)                             ; (7)
     ((x0 count) = yes))) )                        ; (8)
```

The rule says that nouns become plural in the following ways:

1. If the last letter in the word is not a sibilant ('s', 'x', 'sh', 'ch' or 'z'), not 'o' and not 'y', then add 's' to the lexeme, as in *computer* → *computers* and *diskette* → *diskettes*.

2. If the last letter is a sibilant or 'o', then add 'es', as in *switch* → *switches*, *loss* → *losses* and *potato* → *potatoes*.

3. If the lexeme ends in 'y' and is preceded by a vowel, add 's'. (Actually, the program strips the 'y' off and adds 'ys'.) Thus, *key* → *keys*.

4. If the lexeme ends in 'y' preceded by a consonant, change the 'y' to 'ies': *memory* → *memories*.

5. If the lexical unit is marked as irregular, do not strip or add anything. Instead, get the plural form from the `infl` or `conj` slot of the uninflected word. For example, the analysis lexicon entry for *mouse* shows that the plural form is *mice*: `("mouse" (cat N) (conj (plural "mice"))...)`. Hence, *mouse* → *mice*.

---

[2]Note in the rule that `V` is a variable that represents the set of English vowels; `C` represents the English consonants; `SIBILANTorO` represents the set of sibilants and the vowel 'o'; and `NOT-SIBILANTorOorY` represents the set of alphabetical characters excluding the sibilants and 'o' and 'y'.

These suffixation rules are accompanied by a list of equations. The final lexical entry for plural forms will include the results of applying these equations, in addition to the features contained in the original, uninflected lexical entry.

The equations serve two purposes. First, they add syntactic information about the inflected form of the word. This information is used in the analysis grammar. For instance, the morphological rule that produces plural nouns also adds information about the noun's number; this information is used for checking subject-verb agreement in the grammar. Second, the equations can prevent incorrect forms from being generated. Such errors can occur when the equations introduced by the morphology rule contain information that conflicts with information in the original, uninflected lexical entry.

The equations are the same as those used in the analysis grammars,[3] and any operator used in the analysis grammar can also be used in these morphology rules. (One can think of X0 as the `feature-structure` found in the lexical entry of a word.)

The three equations in the rule under consideration do the following:

6. Unify (`number plural`) with the feature structure of the lexeme. Given that the lexical entry will not yet contain number information, this equation will add the feature-value pair to the feature structure.

7. Unify (`person 3`) with the feature structure of the lexeme.

8. Unify (`count yes`) with the feature structure of the lexeme. This feature is already in the unaugmented lexical entry of each noun. This unification will fail for mass nouns. That is, the unification will prevent a noun with the feature (`count no`) from becoming pluralized, as in *knowledge* → **knowledges*.

Now we can display the result of a morphological expansion for a noun:

```
("diskette" (cat N)
         (features (local (count yes) (person 3) (meas-unit no)
                          (proper no)  (root diskette)))
         (mapping (class object-map)))
("diskettes" (cat N) (root diskette)
         (features (local (count yes) (person 3) (meas-unit no)
                          (proper no)  (root diskette) (number plural)))
         (mapping (class object-map)))
```

---

[3]The equations are discussed in chapter 4.

Passivization is a product of the morphology rules. Verbs are expanded by morphological rules, and all of their forms (infinitive, third-person singular present tense, present participle, past participle and past tense) are placed in the analysis lexicon. The morphological rules produce two past-participial lexical entries for each transitive verb. One contains the features of the original uninflected entry; the other has the feature (passive +) and (valency intrans) instead of the original (valency trans). So, a verb entry before expansion is as follows:

```
("erase" (cat V)
        (features  (local (comp-type no)
                          (valency trans))))
```

After expansion it is:

```
("erase" (cat V)
   (conj-form infinitive)
   (features
       (class default-verb-feat)
       (all-features (*or*
                          ((form inf) (valency trans) (comp-type no)
                           (root erase))
                          ((person (*or* 1 2 3)) (number plural)
                           (tense present) (form finite) (valency trans)
                           (comp-type no) (root erase))
                          ((person (*or* 1 2)) (number singular)
                           (tense present) (form finite) (valency trans)
                           (comp-type no) (root erase))))))
```

And the expansion for past participles (nonpassive and passive) is:

```
("erased" (cat V)
    (root erase)
    (conj-form pastpart)
    (features
        (class default-verb-feat)
        (all-features (*or*
                          ((passive -) (valency trans) (form pastpart)
                           (comp-type no) (root erase))
                          ((valency intrans) (passive +)
                           (form pastpart) (comp-type no)
                           (root erase))))))
```

5.5   Lexical Mapping Rules

There are two types of rules that map between an input string and a concept: open-class lexical mapping rules and closed-class lexical mapping rules.

Open-class lexical items are defined to be nouns, verbs, adjectives and adverbs. All other parts of speech, such as prepositions, determiners and conjunctions, constitute the set of closed-class lexical items. However, some special items, such as phasal verbs (i.e., verbs of *phase* such as *begin, continue* and *end*); semifunctional verbs (*do, make, proceed*); and aspectual adverbs (*already, always, still*) are defined to be closed-class as well. Hence, the delineation between these two types of lexical items is determined by part of speech as well as by function.

The function of the lexical mapping rules is to unite an input word with a concept. Open-class rules are divided into those in which a word may be mapped onto a head of a concept and those in which a modifier may be mapped onto a semantic slot and a head of a concept.

In one such mapping, the English *remove* and the Japanese *torinozoku* represent the concept *remove. This is called *head mapping* and is illustrated in the following rule:

```
("torinozoku"
    (cat V)
        (mapping (local (head (*remove))))))
```

The second type of mapping occurs when a modifier maps onto a slot and a concept. This is called *embedded mapping*.[4] For example, the noun phrase *sisutemu yunitto no deisuketto doraibu no rebaa* ("the lever of the diskette drive of the system unit") contains modifiers, *sisutemu yunitto* ("system unit") and *deisuketto doraibu* ("diskette drive"), for a head noun *rebaa* ("lever"). The head noun concept is *lever, and *lever is a part of *diskette-drive. In turn, *diskette-drive is a part of *system-unit. Therefore, the following output is expected:[5]

```
[*lever
    (part-of [*diskette-drive
              (part-of [*system-unit])])]
```

---

[4]Headed and embedded mappings are further described in chapter 7.

[5]Compare the trace that appears as appendix B.

In order to map *system-unit onto the part-of slot in *diskette-drive, and *diskette-drive onto the part-of slot in the head noun concept *lever, the slots must be defined in the mapping rules for the modifier. Two embedded mapping rules define the mappings of the modifiers. This reduces the number of ambiguities, because the system does not attempt to map these modifiers onto all possible semantic slots in the head-noun concept.

The embedded mapping rules for *diskette-drive and *system-unit are:

```
("deisuketto doraibu"
   (cat N)
   (mapping (local (embed (part-of (*diskette-drive)))))))

("sisutemu yunitto"
   (cat N)
   (mapping (local (embed (part-of (*system-unit)))))))
```

In both headed and embedded mapping, some words map onto general concepts, which must be further specified to capture the meaning of a word as completely as possible. In these cases, a value can be assigned to a semantic slot to make the concept more specific. For example, the Japanese *akai* ("red") maps onto the concept *color. In that *color is a general concept for all colors, distinctions need to be made among all color terms, such as, in English, *red, yellow* or *blue*. The mapping of *akai* appears thus (with the ampersand signifying that the color term is an atomic value and the percent sign being a relic of implementation):

```
("akai"
   (cat ADJ)
   (mapping
      (local (head (*color (%attribute-range &red)))))))
```

For convenience, the lexical mapping rules can be written in the concept lexicon as well. The notation is slightly different from that of the analysis lexicon, but the lexical mapping rules in the concept lexicon are converted automatically into the analysis lexicon format during loading.

The format of the lexical mapping rules in the concept lexicon is shown below. The example is for a Japanese rule. In English, the mappings would be ehead and eembed.

```
(head-of-concept
   (jhead ((word (cat X)))
   (jhead ((word (cat X) (%slot-name &value)))
   (jembed ((word (cat X) (%slot-name *concept)))
   (jembed ((word (cat X) (%slot-name *value)))))))))
```

For a particular concept, the lexical mapping rule appears in the concept lexicon as:

```
(remove
   (jhead ((torinozoku (cat V)))))
```

And it appears in the analysis lexicon as follows:

```
("torinozoku"
   (cat V)
      (mapping (local (head (*remove))))))
```

Here and below, the rules for the concept and analysis lexicons are interpreted identically. Now consider a head mapping rule with value assignment, in the concept lexicon:

```
(color
      (jhead ((akai (cat ADJ) (%attribute-range &red)))))
```

and in the analysis lexicon:

```
("akai"
   (cat ADJ)
   (mapping
      (local (head (*color (%attribute-range &red))))))
```

Finally, an embedded mapping rule appears in the concept lexicon thus:

```
(system-unit
   (jembed ((sisutemuyunitto (cat N)
            (%part-of *system-unit)))))
```

and in the analysis lexicon:

```
("sisutemuyunitto"
   (cat N)
   (mapping (local (jembed (part-of (*system-unit))))))
```

5.6   Closed-Class Lexical Mapping

Closed-class lexical items are nonproductive sets of words with a small, finite number of members. They are sometimes called *function words* because they are generally nonreferential. As a rule, the number of closed-class items in a language does not increase. In other words, while one can coin new nouns and verbs, new prepositions or numerals are very seldom, if ever, created.

Analysis lexicon entries for closed-class items usually carry information about some properties of the concept tokens instantiated for the open-class words in the sentence. It follows that closed-class items do not usually map into domain concepts. (For this reason, some adverbs are treated as closed-class items.) In KBMT-89, however, abstract concepts were created in the concept lexicon for some closed-class items, thus treating them as regular open-class items. This course of action was adopted largely for ease of implementation. Some of the closed-class items are treated during syntactic parsing, and their contributions to the overall meaning representation of the sentence take the form of certain property-value pairs that are included in the representations of syntactic constituents. Other closed-class items add property-value pairs to the interlingua representations of the meanings of open-class items.

The emphasis in the description here is on the closed-class items from the project corpora (personal-computer instruction manuals). Treatment of additional closed-class items is illustrated whenever a solution for them could be found within the bounds of our computational architecture and knowledge-interaction constraints. In the several tables here, items and item classes not in the KBMT-89 corpora are marked with a '†'.

It should be stated quite prominently that the decisions made with respect to the closed-class items, especially quantifiers and determiners, are not always informed by the wealth of findings about them in the linguistic literature. Our decisions were very often determined by the size and nature of the corpora, by the necessary granularity of description and even by the constraints imposed by the formalisms and algorithms used in our computational implementation. The treatment of closed-class items should be improved by the creation or incorporation of more advanced (micro)theories of these phenomena (see chapter 2 for a discussion of microtheories).

In what follows we list a variety of English closed-class items and their feature-value pairs.

ITEM	FEATURE-VALUE PAIRS
a/an	(reference indefinite) (number singular)
some	(reference indefinite) (number plural)
the	(reference definite) (specific +)
this	(reference definite)(specific +)(number singular) (near +)
that	(reference definite)(specific +)(number singular) (near -)
these	(reference definite)(specific +)(number plural) (near +)
those	(reference definite)(specific +)(number plural) (near -)
any/any of	(specific -) (r-quantifier universal)
specific	(specific +)
either	(specific +) (dual +) (r-quantifier universal)
additional	(new +)
other	(new +)
further	(new +)
†another	(number singular) (new +)
same	(new -)
no	(r-quantifier negation)
†none	(r-quantifier negation)
†some of	(r-quantifier existential)
†a number of	(r-quantifier existential)
multiple	(r-quantifier existential)
a variety of	(r-quantifier existential)
several	(r-quantifier existential)
many	(r-quantifier existential)
†much	(r-quantifier existential)
all	(r-quantifier universal)
whole	(r-quantifier universal)
each	(r-quantifier universal)
every	(r-quantifier universal)
†few	(r-quantifier minority)
a little	(r-quantifier minority)
most	(r-quantifier majority)
approximately	(precision -)
about	(precision -)
†precisely	(precision +)
†exactly	(precision +)

Table 5.1: **Parsing features of demonstratives, determiners and quantifiers. Items marked with a '†' do not appear in the** KBMT-89 **corpora.**

Demonstratives, Determiners and Quantifiers

These items are treated at parsing stage. The features that they add to the parser results are given in table 5.1 (cf. the following discussion of pronouns).

Numerals

We have divided numerals into five groups, as shown in table 5.2.

ITEM	EXAMPLE
number bullets	**1.** *Turn on the power*
cardinal numerals	**three** *books*
measurement cardinals	*A* **six-foot** *cable*
virtual ordinals	*disk drive number* **1**
†ordinals	*a* second *time*.

Table 5.2: **Numerals and examples.**

When in a text the parser encounters numerals followed by periods, it places these in the field `number-bullet`, which is inserted unchanged into the interlingua text at the clausal level. Cardinals fill a quantity slot in the f-structure. This slot is mapped into the *cardinality* slot in the ILT. The measurement expressions in the corpus are hyphenated forms such as *128K-byte, six-foot* and so forth. The parser converts each such into two property-value pairs, as in:

```
((root foot)
 (quantity 6))
```

Future implementations should see the augmentor converting nonstandard units into our interlingua standard. Each type of measurement has a standard in the concept lexicon. For example, length is always converted into meters, volume into liters and so forth. The information is then placed in the `*conversion` frame appropriate to the units used in the input. In this way, we retain the original numerals and units and still have a standard by which to express slot restrictions. Depending on the target language, the generator can use either the original units or the standard units. The result of the conversion might appear in the ILT as the following:

```
(conversion-foot-meter
   (source-number 6)
   (source-units foot)
   (goal-number 1.83)
   (goal-units meter))
```

Virtual ordinals are placed in the syntactic f-structure field `post-nom-mod`
for "postnominal modifier." If the word *number* or any variation thereof occurs,
as in *disk drive number 1* , it is discarded. The root of the `post-nom-mod` field
is mapped into a value of the concept lexicon property `object-label`. This
strategy is also used to handle the identifying letter in phrases such as *disk drive A*.

Prepositions

Prepositions are included in a field within the f-structure for prepositional
phrases. No other semantic information is given, except in the case of the English
by: then one parse of the f-structure in which *by* is contained is labeled `obl-agent`
for "oblique agent," that is, for the "by" phrase in a passive construction.

Prepositional phrases occur as arguments and modifiers of nouns, verbs and
adjectives. These nouns, verbs and adjectives are associated with mapping rules
that map the f-structure representation of prepositional phrases onto slots in the
ontology. In English, each mapping rule consists of the mapping from the f-
structure slot `ppadjunct` to a semantic slot. A syntactic test makes sure that the
correct preposition is present. For example, the (abbreviated) mapping rule below
is associated with the verb *remove*. It says that a `ppadjunct` is mapped onto the
`source` slot if the feature-value pair `(prep from)` unifies with the f-structure
for the `ppadjunct`.

```
("remove"
        (cat V)
        ...
        (mapping
            (local
                (head (remove)))
            (local
                (slot (source = (ppadjunct (prep = from)))))
            (class cb-th-verb-map)))
```

Aspectual Adverbs

ITEM	FEATURE-VALUE PAIRS
always/every time	(literal-iteration always)
(once) again	(literal-iteration again)
usually/often/frequently	(literal-iteration frequent)
first	(phase begin)
†rarely	(literal-iteration rare)
once	(literal-iteration 1)
immediately	(phase begin)
yet/already	(phase end)
†never	(literal-iteration 0)

Table 5.3: **Aspectual adverbs and their feature-value pairs.**

Aspectual adverbs appear as f-structures that are the values of the feature `advadjunct`. For example, *yet* is represented as

```
(...
 (advadjunct ((root yet)))
 ...)
```

These adverbs carry an embedded head mapping rule. That is, each one indicates which slot it fills and which value fills the slot. Words of this class are listed in table 5.3 along with the slots and fillers they add to parser output.

Attitudinal Adverbs

These adverbs convey the speaker's attitude to a proposition. They appear in the f-structure as `advadjunct` and are divided into two classes: those that correspond semantically to the modal *might* and those that do not.

The former are processed by setting the `modality` feature to `possibility` in the ILT. The members of this class are *perhaps*, *maybe* and *possibly* (none of which appeared in the corpora).

All other attitudinal adverbs trigger the creation of an `attitude` feature at the clausal level of an ILT. Possible values are `negative`, `positive`, `probable`, `unexpected`, `only` and `finally`. These are presented in table 5.4.

ITEM	FEATURE-VALUE PAIRS
†unfortunately	(attitude negative)
†luckily	(attitude positive)
†probably	(attitude probable)
†particularly	(attitude unexpected)
†even	(attitude unexpected)
only	(attitude only)
†just	(attitude only)
at last	(attitude finally)
†finally	(attitude finally)

Table 5.4: **Attitudinal adverbs and their feature-value pairs.**

Embedded head mapping rules associated with attitudinal adverbs in the analysis lexicon specify the ILT feature-value pairs shown in table 5.4. For example, the following is part of the analysis lexicon entry for *only*.

```
("only" (cat reg-adv)
    (mapping
        (local
            (unhead (attitude only))))))
```

Discourse Cohesion Markers

English discourse cohesion markers are members of various parts of speech: subordinate conjunctions, adverbs, prepositions and *wh*-words. They appear in the ILT as values of the property discourse-cohesion-marker at the clausal level. Table 5.5 lists several English and Japanese discourse cohesion markers and their ILT values.

The following are examples of English discourse cohesion markers:

```
("here" (cat reg-adv)
        (features (local (conjadv +)))
        (mapping
          (local
            (unhead (discourse-cohesion-marker now)))))

("if" (cat subord-conj)
```

ENGLISH ITEM	JAPANESE ITEM	ILT VALUE
if	baai	conditional
when, every time	toki	when
while, as long as, at	aida	during
before	mae	before
immediately before, until	made	immediately-before
since	irai	since
to	tameni	purpose
so-that	tameni	for-purpose
after	ato	after
because	node, kara	cause
immediately after, once, then	sonogo	immediately-after
even though	temo	although
therefore	sitagate	therefore
however	sikasinagara	however
also, too, in addition	mata, nao	also
here, now, at this point	kokode, ima	now
hereafter	atoha	hereafter
in this case	konobaai	in-this-case
nevertheless	soredemo	nevertheless

Table 5.5: **Discourse cohesion markers and ILT values.**

```
(mapping
 (local
  (unhead (discourse-cohesion-marker conditional)))))
```

Modal Operators

Most modals would cause the parser to create the features `ability`, `necessity`, `conditional` and `possibility` with the values + or -.[6] The only exception to this is *will*, which sets the `tense` feature to `future`. These features appear in the f-structure and the semantic parser output.

The augmentor transforms the parser output for modals into a `modality` feature with the four values just given. The feature-value pair `(tense future)` is transformed into `(time (value (after time1)))` in the proposition

---

[6]*Will* and *should* are the only modals in the KBMT-89 corpus, hence the use of the subjunctive in this sentence.

frame, in which `time1` is the time of the speech act. Other features, such as `speech-act` and `direct?` in the `speech-act` frame, may also be set by the augmentor. The following are examples of the ILT representation of *will* and *should*. First, *will*:

```
(make-frame-old speech-act1
    (ilt-type (value speech-act))
    (speech-act (value assertion))
    (direct? (value yes))
    (speaker (value author))
    (hearer (value reader))
    (time (value time1)))
(make-frame-old proposition1
    ...
    (time (value (after time1)))))
```

Now, *should*:

```
(make-frame-old speech-act1
    (ilt-type (value speech-act))
    (speech-act (value command))
    (direct? (value no))
    (speaker (value author))
    (hearer (value reader))
    (time (value time1)))
(make-frame-old proposition1
    ...
    (time (value (after time1)))))
```

Pronouns

The f-structures record the syntactic features of pronouns along with the feature-value pair `(root pro)`. If the value for a certain feature is not determined, that feature is left out (e.g., number for *you*). Thus, the pronoun *it* will receive the following f-structure:

```
((root pro)
 (person 3)
 (number singular)
 (gender neuter)
 (human -))
```

Table 5.6 presents the English pronouns handled by KBMT-89.

Non-second-person nominative, objective, possessive and absolute possessive pronouns are mapped to `$pronoun$` with the embedded features `person`,

PRONOUN	VALUES
nominative	*I, you, he, she, it, we, they*
objective	*me, you, him, here, it, us, them*
possessive	*my, your, his, her, its, our, their*
absolute possessive	*mine, yours, his, hers, its, ours, theirs*
quantified pronouns	*everybody, everyone, everything, anything, something, nothing*
demonstratives	*this, that, these, those*

Table 5.6: **English pronouns.**

`gender`, `number` and `human`. Second person pronouns map to `*reader`. Here, `$pronoun$` is a frame that is not in the concept lexicon because it is designed to be replaced by a pointer to the frame that represents the pronoun's antecedent. The mapping rule interpreter allows it to fill a semantic slot but waives semantic constraints on the filler of the slot. In future implementations, the semantic constraints will be checked when the referent of the pronoun is determined. Demonstrative pronouns are mapped to `$pronoun$`, with the embedded features `number` and `near`.

Special Characters, Words and Symbols

Many strings are not easily classifiable according to the standard taxonomy of lexical categories. We have processed these special cases as shown in table 5.7. Note that "untranslated" in the table means that the string is carried through to the target language text without analysis or generation.

5.7 Structural Mapping Rules

The structural mapping rules map grammatical functions in the f-structure, such as subject and object, onto semantic roles in concept structures.[7] For example, the f-structure for the Japanese sentence

(5.2)   Deisuketto doraibu kara deisuketto o nukitotte kudasai
         "Remove the diskette from the diskette-drive"

---

[7]These and related rules are considered from the perspective of analysis in chapter 7.

ITEM	EXAMPLES	TREATMENT
Abbreviations	*TV, DOS, IBM*	Open-class nouns.
Keyboard names	*Caps Lock, Tab, Shift*	Open-class nouns.
Key responses	*A, B, RETURN*	Untranslated.
Special numerals	*0, 1, . . . , 9* (keyboard numbers), *6025013* (part number)	Untranslated.
Question responses	*yes, no*	Open-class nouns.
Screen-display responses	*pressed, released*	Untranslated.
Screen messages	*IBM Personal Computer BASIC*	Untranslated.
Variables, placeholders	*xxx (xxx will be either 400 or 500)*	Untranslated.

Table 5.7: **Special cases and their treatment.**

is as follows:

```
((time ((root present))) (mood ((root imp)))
 (ppadjunct
   ((part kara) (cat N) (root deisukettodoraibu)))
 (obj ((wh -) (case o) (cat N) (root deisuketto)))
 (causative -) (obj-case o) (subj-case ga) (passive -)
 (subcat trans) (formal +)
 (vtype v-5dan-r) (cat V) (root nukitoru))
```

This f-structure contains only syntactic information and must be mapped onto a semantic structure. The verb *nukitoru* subcategorizes for agent, theme and source. The subject maps onto agent; the syntactic object maps onto theme; and ppadjunct, with the particle *kara*, maps onto the source. Therefore, the structural mapping for this sentence would look like this:

```
(mapping
  (local (slot
          (agent = subj)
          (theme = obj)
          (source = (ppadjunct (part = kara)))))))
```

The following is the expected semantic parser output (not the ILT representation) for (5.2).

```
[*remove
  (mood imp)
  (passive -)
  (theme [*diskette])
  (source [*diskette-drive])
  (tense present)]
```

Because the same structural mapping can be used for other verbs of the same class, such as *hazusu* ("detach") and *nukitoru* ("remove"), these rules can be written once and stored in a mapping rule hierarchy. The `class` field in the `mapping` field of an analysis lexicon entry contains a pointer to a node in the mapping rule hierarchy. This enables the entry to inherit structural mapping rules from the hierarchy.

The KBMT-89 system makes use of a mapping rule hierarchy described in Mitamura 1989, which presents a full-fledged hierarchical model of interpretive mapping (including lexical and structural mapping rules). The core set of Japanese predicate frames described in the model can be extended through the addition of new lexical items in the hierarchy. Once the mapping hierarchy has been developed, lexical acquisition proceeds in a structured way, and the same basic hierarchy can be used in various domains. The proposed method for organizing interpretive mapping rules is language-independent and may be used to organize predicate frames for any language, but the hierarchies that result from applying the method are language-dependent.

The notation of the structural mapping rules in the mapping rule hierarchy is basically the same as that of the <mapping> field in the description of the analysis lexicon. The difference is that <mapping> in the hierarchy does not contain the lexical mapping; hence, there are no heads and embeds.

- <structural-mapping-rule> = (<class-name-map><mapping>).

- <class-name-map> = The name of a class for structural mapping rules, for example, perception-trans-map.

- <mapping> = {(mapping <class-map> | {+ <local-map>} ?<class-map>}).

- <class-map> = (class {+ <class-name-map>}).

- <local-map> = (local ?<syn-test> ?<sem-test> <syn-map>).

- `<syn-test>` = (test {+ `<syn-equation>`}).

- `<syn-equation>` = This is a syntactic equation; for example, (passive = +).

- `<sem-test>` = (sem-test {+ (`<sem-slot>` `<sem-value>`)}). This is a semantic slot-value pair that is unified with the parser output; for instance, (sem-test (agent *reader)).

- `<syn-map>` = (slot ({+ `<structural-mapping>`})). For instance,

```
(slot ((agent = subj)
       (theme = obj)
       (goal = (ppadjunct (prep = to)))))
```

- `<structural-mapping>` = (`<sem-slot>` = {(`<syn-slot>` {* `<syn-equation>`}) | `<syn-slot>`}). Examples:

```
(goal = (ppadjunct (prep = to)))
(agent = subj)
```

- `<syn-equation>` = (`<syn-slot>` = `<syn-value>`). For example, (prep = to).

- `<sem-slot>` = Name of semantic slot from concept lexicon entry.

- `<sem-value>` = A semantic value.

- `<syn-slot>` = Name of syntactic feature.

- `<syn-value>` = Syntactic structure value.

Now we can display the general structure of the structural mapping rules:

```
(<class-name-map>
    (mapping
       {(class {+ <class-name-map>})   |
         ?(class {+ <class-name-map>})
         {+ (local
             ?<syn-test>
             ?<sem-test>
              (slot {+ <structural-mapping>})})}}))
```

The following English example illustrates how these rules work. The structural mapping rule for the English verb *change* is

```
("change" (cat V)
   (mapping (local (slot
                   (goal = (ppadjunct (prep = to)))))
            (class c-i-verb-map)))
```

The verb belongs to the causative-inchoative verb class (`c-i-verb-map`). It can be intransitive, as in the English sentence *Therefore, even if you push the Kana key, the square on the screen will not change.* Because the subject NP (*the square*) is inanimate, it should be mapped to the semantic slot `theme`. The necessary mapping rule is inherited by *change* from the following:

```
(c-i-verb-map
   (mapping
      (local
         (test (passive = -) (valency = intrans))
         (slot (theme = subj)))
      (class cb-th-verb-map cb-tr-verb-map cb-tp-verb-map)))
```

Here, the last conjunct in the class listing refers to a "caused-by-theme-property" verb, that is, a verb that maps onto a concept that takes a `caused-by` slot and a `theme-property` slot. The syntactic `subj` maps to the semantic `caused-by` slot and the `obj` to the `theme-property` slot.

The verb *change*, because it is of the causative-inchoative class, can also be transitive, as in the English sentence *6. To change the Top of Page Setting, repeat the procedure in steps 1 - 5.* Here the object NP (*Top of Page setting*) is assigned to `theme`; there is no surface subject. The object NP maps to the `theme` semantic slot. The necessary rule is inherited from the following:

```
(cb-th-verb-map
   (mapping
      (local
         (test (passive = -) (valency = trans))
         (slot (caused-by = subj)
               (theme = obj)))
      (local
         (test (passive = +))
         (slot (caused-by = obl-agent)
               (theme = subj))
         (sem-test (focus theme)))
```

```
(local
    (test (passive = +))
    (slot (theme = subj))
    (sem-test (focus theme)
              (caused-by unknown)))
  (class ag-th-verb-map)))
```

5.8 Special Mapping Rules

Three mapping rule operators are invoked by single, double and triple equal signs in structural mapping rules. (In chapter 7 we describe the processes that these operators trigger in the mapping rule interpreter; the discussion here unavoidably covers some of the same material.) The operators differ depending on whether (i) semantic constraints are checked when semantic slots are filled, (ii) syntactic information is copied verbatim to parser output and (iii) a slot is created that does not exist in the ontology. In this section, we will illustrate typical usage of the mapping operators.

First, a *predefined slot mapping* rule is used in conjunction with embedded head mapping rules. A single equal sign identifies a predefined slot mapping. (Recall that single equal signs are also customarily used to map grammatical functions onto semantic slots, as with (agent = subj).) When a particular slot name is indicated in an embedded head mapping rule associated with a modifier, a *predefined-slot* mapping is required in the mapping rule of the head. This tells the mapping rule interpreter to examine the modifier's mapping rule to see what slot it fills in the concept corresponding to the head. For example, the mapping of *deisuketto doraibu no rebaa* ("the lever of the diskette drive") requires this operation. The *predefined-slot* mapping rule for *rebaa* indicates that its syntactic xadjunct will fill a slot in the concept that rebaa maps onto:

```
("rebaa"
    (mapping
        (local (slot
                   (*predefined-slot* = xadjunct)))))
```

However, the slot name is not specified. In order to find the slot name, we have to look at the embedded head mapping rule for *deisuketto doraibu*, which fills the part-of slot with the value *diskette-drive:

```
("deisuketto doraibu"
    (cat N)
        (mapping (local (embed (part-of (*diskette-drive)))))))
```

The second mapping rule operator is for *syntactic promotion*, instances of which contain a double equal sign. These typically map syntactic features that do not correspond to an independent lexical item. For example, tense or mood may be represented as `(tense present)` or `(mood imperative)`.[8] However, `present` and `imperative` are syntactic values that are associated not with any single lexeme but rather with a syntactic construction or a morphological form. The following are examples of syntactic promotion mapping rules.

```
(mapping (local (slot (mood == mood)
                      (tense == time)
                      (ability == ability)
                      (progressive == progressive)
                      (negation == negation)
                      (passive == passive)))))
```

The left-hand side of the double equal sign is a slot name that does not appear in the ontology but is added to the parser output as a result of applying the syntactic promotion mapping rule. The right side of the double equal sign is a syntactic feature. (In the earlier examples, most of the slot names happen to be identical to the syntactic feature names.) The double equal sign causes the mapping rule interpreter to create a slot with the name on the left-hand side and copy into it the value of the syntactic feature on the right-hand side. No semantic constraints are checked during this mapping. If the syntactic features `mood`, `time` and `passive` had the values `imperative`, `present` and '`-`', these mapping rules would produce the following parser output:

```
(mood imperative)
(tense present)
(passive -)
        ...
```

The third mapping rule operator, *unchecked semantic mapping*, contains a triple equal sign. The triple sign, like the double equal sign, causes the creation of a slot that is not contained in the ontology. Also, like the double equal sign, it prevents semantic constraints from being applied when the slot is filled. The following example illustrates a mapping rule for Japanese relative clauses. It causes a slot called `rel-clause` to be created in the parser output. The slot is filled by retrieving the value of the `xadjunct` feature in f-structure, provided that its head is a verb, and then finding its semantics. If the syntactic slot to the right of the

---

[8]Here, "mood" refers to the type of sentence parsed, e.g., declarative, imperative or interrogative.

three equal signs is `xadjunct` and if the category is V, then the slot can map onto `rel-clause`. Thus:

```
(mapping
   (local (slot
          (rel-clause === (xadjunct (cat = V))))))
```

The mapping of an integer would also use this notation when semantic restrictions are not required. Such a case is seen in the mapping to `number-bullet`, which is used for numerals followed by periods, as in enumerated lists.

Chapter 6

Generation Lexicons

■ Donna M. Gates, Rita McCardell, Koichi Takeda
and Sergei Nirenburg

The KBMT-89 generation lexicons and generation mapping rules are the knowledge sources used in generating syntactic f-structures from interlingua representations. The lexicons and mapping rules for English and Japanese are structurally the same and so, as in the previous chapter, the discussion following will attempt to convey this generality by using both English and Japanese examples.

The generation lexicons contain all open-class items that appear in the corpus. These lexicons are used in generation by the lexical selection module (see chapter 9) to determine for a target language the correct open-class lexical items (nouns, verbs, adjectives and adverbs) for a given interlingua text.

After an ILT has been processed by the lexical selection modual and open-class lexical items have been chosen, the generation mapping rules are applied. These rules are used for (i) selecting closed-class lexical items, (ii) mapping semantic roles in the ILT frame into grammatical functions in the f-structure and (iii) mapping speech act and propositional information into the appropriate syntactic feature structure representation. These rules are used in generation by the mapping rule interpretter.

145

6.1 Differences in Analysis and Generation Lexicons

The analysis and generation lexicons were developed independently by different research subgroups. This resulted not only in different formalisms for the lexicons and mapping rules but also in different solutions to similar problems.

The generation lexicon was designed for selecting the target language lexeme closest in meaning to the ILT representation. Thus it contains information that is not necessary in analysis, such as importance values associated with semantic features of words, as well as the subcategorization constraints based on thematic roles (rather than on grammatical functions) for verbs and nouns.

While the sets of structural mapping rules for both generation and analysis include rules for semantic-to-syntactic slot mappings, there are many differences in the rules for analysis and generation. First, generation mapping rules must be ordered. This ensures that modifiers are generated in the correct sequence and that rules for special cases apply before default rules.

Second, analysis mapping rules map from feature structures to parser output, which the augmentor then turns into an ILT by inserting `clause`, `proposition` and `speech-act` frames, as well as appropriate structures for representing passives, modals, declaratives, interrogatives, imperatives and so forth. Generation mapping rules, in contrast, map directly from ILT to feature structures.

Third, structural mapping rules in analysis are associated with lexical items, whereas structural mapping rules in generation are associated with ILT frames. Because of this, structural mapping rules are contained in the analysis lexicon but not in the generation lexicon.

Fourth, closed-class lexical items are contained in the analysis lexicon along with their lexical mapping rules, just like open-class lexical items. In generation, closed-class items are introduced into feature structures by mapping rules on the basis of features of the ILT. Thus, closed-class items are not contained in the generation lexicon.

In short, the generation lexicon specifies only open-class lexical mappings. Structural mapping rules, not contained in the generation lexicon, perform semantic-to-syntactic slot mappings, create closed-class lexical items and add to f-structures those features required to establish word order, voice and sentence type (e.g., declarative, interrogatory, imperative or exclamatory).

6.2 Generation Lexicon Entries

Generation lexicon entries represent the open-class words that are used to

```
GL-entry               :=   (make-frame-old <frame>)
<frame>                :=   <frame-name> <patterns>
<patterns>             :=   <meaning-pattern> <TL-pattern>*
<meaning-pattern>      :=   (is-token-of (value <CL-concept>))
                           (<relation> (value <value>))
                           (importance (<importance-value>))*
```
`<CL-concept>`   :=   **Any concept in the concept lexicon**
`<relation>`   :=   **Any relation from the concept lexicon**
`<value>`   :=   **Any concept or attribute (scale) value**
                                   in the concept lexicon
```
<importance-value>     :=   1 | 2 | ... | 10
<TL-pattern>           :=   <lexeme> <lex-info>
<lexeme>               :=   (lexeme (value <TL-lexical-unit>))
```
`<TL-lexical-unit>`   :=   **A word in the target language**
```
<lex-info>             :=   <syntactic-info>
                           <subcat-info>
                           <morph-info>
<syntactic-info>       :=   (syntactic-info (cat <category>)
                              <features>)
<category>             :=   N | V | ADJ | ADV
<features>             :=   (features (<feat-val>)*)
```
`<feat-val>`   :=   **A syntactic feature and its value**
`<subcat-info>`   :=   **Subcategorization constraints, e.g.,**
```
                              (?<required-roles> ?<optional-roles>)
<required-role>        :=   (req <thematic-role>+)
<optional-role>        :=   (opt <thematic-role>+)
```
`<thematic-role>`   :=   **Agent, theme, etc.**
```
<morph-info>           :=   (morphological-info ?<inflections>)
<inflections>          :=   (infl <infl-type>)
<infl-type>            :=   regular | irregular |(<form> <surface>)+
<form>                 :=   past | 3sg | prespart | pastpart
```
`<surface>`   :=   **An irregular form of a word**

Table 6.1: **BNF for generation lexicon entries.**

compose a sentence. Each entry contains information that is relevant to the lexical selection of a content word. Entries are defined as FRAMEKIT frames. They can be obtained automatically from lexical mapping rules contained in Ontos concepts. Additionally, valency of verbs, morphological information and subcategorization information are manually added to the entries. So, the entries minimally contain a frame name, the name of the concept from which the word is mapped, a meaning pattern (to be explained shortly), a lexeme, syntactic features and information about subcategorization. The BNF for complete generation lexicon entries is given in table 6.1. Generally, though, a generation lexicon entry has the following format:

```
(make-frame
        <frame-name>
        <meaning-pattern>
        <lexeme>
        <syntactic-info>
        <subcat-info>
        <morph-info>
)
```

The Japanese generation lexicon entry for *tyousetusuru* ("to adjust") is as follows. The first line gives the frame name, the second the concept name, the third the meaning pattern and so on.

```
(make-frame tyousetusuru2
        (is-token-of (value *change-position))
        (location (value *spatial-attribute)
                (importance 10))
        (lexeme (value "tyousetusuru"))
        (syntactic-info (cat V)
            (features (cat V) (subcat trans)
                    (vtype v-sahen)
                    (root tyousetusuru)))
        (subcategorization-info (req theme)
                            (opt agent goal source))))
```

Of course, many words have more than one lexical mapping. The various mappings of a particular form are indexed in the generation lexicon with numerals immediately following their frame names; thus we have tyousetusuru2, where the numeral identifies the form as having the second mapping in the set residing in the Japanese dictionary.

The name of the entry tyousetusuru2 and the is-token-of slot can be generated automatically from the entry's counterpart definition in the concept lexicon. Other lexical mappings for the Japanese word *tyousetusuru* appear in the dictionary and are indexed to frames other than `*change-position`.[1] The verb's mapping for `*change-position` is as follows:

```
(make-frame  *change-position
     (jhead
        ((tyousetusuru (cat V) (%location *spatial-attribute)))))
```

It is from this frame that we derive the concept name in the generation lexicon entry. That is, `(is-token-of (value *change-position))` is a lexical mapping rule based on the frame name `*change-position` in the concept lexicon.

An entry's meaning pattern can be viewed as one of the results of enhancing a concept lexicon concept or property for a lexical unit in a particular target language. This is the place to attempt to take care of the differences in the level of detail that different languages give to various concepts. Consider, for instance, the concept `*book`. Associated forms in English include *book, tome* and *volume*. Now, one can certainly enter several concepts (`*book`, `*tome`, `*volume`) in the domain model. But if this is considered unnecessary, then the generation lexicon for English can contain entries for the various words denoting types of books, each entry having a different meaning pattern. This would aid correct lexical selection.

Meaning patterns have slots for importance values; these are filled by integers from 1 to 10, inclusive, which serve to distinguish the saliency of various properties or relations in indentifying the lexical unit. This is illustrated in the earlier example of `tyousetusuru2`, where the importance value for the `location` slot is 10. This implies that the `(location (value *spatial-attribute))` slot-value pair is very important for generating the lexical unit *tyousetusuru*.[2]

Put differently, meaning patterns are knowledge sources for resolution of lexical synonymy during generation. A domain model may have only one concept, such as `*two-wheeled-vehicle`, to represent the meanings of any of the following English lexical units: *bicycle, motorcycle* or *tandem*. But if we need to generate those lexical units correctly from the same ILT representation, we require additional information about their differences. This information is stored in the entry's meaning pattern.

---

[1]The other concept frames in which *tyousetusuru* appears are `*display-event`, `*operate-display-device` and `*analog-rotate`. These concept frames would create entries with the names `tyousetusuru1`, `tyousetusuru3` and `tyousetusuru4`.

[2]The example at the end of this chapter provides an extended illustration of the role of the generation lexicon in generation mapping.

In the previous generation-lexicon entry, the `syntactic-info` slot values are required by the Japanese grammar for syntactic generation. When the entry `tyousetusuru2` is selected, the feature values

```
((cat V) (subcat trans)
 (vtype v-sahen)
 (root tyousetusuru)))
```

will constitute the initial f-structure.

The `subcategorization-info` slot specifies which semantic slots in the ILT are required or optional for a given entry. Before a generation lexicon entry can be chosen to lexicalize an ILT frame, the frame must be checked to see if it satisfies the entry's subcategorization requirements. The initial candidate set of lexical entries for realizing an ILT frame is filtered so that those entries whose subcategorization requirements are satisfied by the frame are further processed. This is crucial when more than one verb can be used to realize a single concept and where the verbs have different subcategorization requirements, not all of which may be appropriate. For example, the concept `*display-event` can be realized using entries from the English generation lexicon that correspond to the verbs *display*, *get* (as in *You will get an error message*) and *appear*. Yet *display* subcategorizes for an `agent`; *get* subcategorizes for a `beneficiary` and a `theme`; and *appear* subcategorizes for a `theme` and an optional `goal`. If an ILT contains an instance of `*display-event` that has only a `theme`, then only *appear* can be used to generate a grammatical output.

Generation lexicon entries are thus customarily used for open-class lexical selection. We noted at the outset that there are entries for nouns, verbs, adjectives and adverbs. It might be helpful at this point to provide a sample entry for each part of speech taken from the English generation lexicon.

The first example is the entry for the noun *shipping cardboard.* [3]

```
(make-frame shipping-cardboard
        (is-token-of (value *protection-material))
        (made-of (value *cardboard)
                (importance 10)))
```

---

[3]This lexical item appears in the corpus as part of the instructions for unpacking boxes containing computer components: *12. Remove the shipping cardboard.* Subsequent examples should be self-explanatory.

Notice that the syntactic value for `root` is `shipping_cardboard` (i.e., with an underscore) and the generation lexicon frame name is `shipping-cardboard` (with a hyphen). These conventions will be employed in all subsequent examples of multiple-word lexical entries.

```
(lexeme (value "shipping cardboard"))
(syntactic-info (cat N)
                (features (count yes)
                          (root shipping_cardboard)))
(subcategorization-info nil)
(morphological-info (infl (plural nil))))
```

The following example of a verb entry relates the root turn_on to *discrete-electronic-move-lever* (turning something on).

```
(make-frame turn-on
       (is-token-of (value *discrete-electronic-move-lever*))
       (cause-of (value *start-electricity*)
                 (importance 8))
       (discrete-position (value on-position)
                          (importance 10))
       (lexeme (value "turn"))
       (syntactic-info (cat V)
                       (features (particle on) (valency trans)
                                 (root turn_on)))
       (subcategorization-info (req agent theme discrete-position))
       (morphological-info (infl (regular))))
```

In the following entry for an adjective, note particularly the values of importance. The values for min and max indicate percentages for the range of *brightness*.

```
(make-frame dark
       (is-token-of (value *brightness*))
       (min (value 0)
            (importance 10))
       (max (value 33)
            (importance 10))
       (lexeme (value "dark"))
       (syntactic-info (cat adj)
                       (features (root dark)))
       (subcategorization-info nil)
       (morphological-info (infl (regular))))
```

Finally, here is an example of a generation lexicon entry for an adverb.

```
(make-frame ahead
       (is-token-of (value *direction*))
       (relation-range (value *forward*)
                       (importance 10))
       (lexeme (value "ahead"))
```

```
(syntactic-info (cat reg-adv)
                (features (root ahead)))
(subcategorization-info nil)
(morphological-info (infl (regular))))
```

Each generation lexicon entry has an `is-token-of` slot that links (or points) to the concept lexicon concept that can be lexicalized by other entries with this same pointer. In addition to lexemes that are morphologically unrelated (e.g., *finish*, *end* and *complete* as verbs), the entries associated with a particular concept (e.g., `*complete`) may also contain lexemes from different syntactic categories (e.g., *complete* as adjective, *complete* as verb, *completely* as adverb and *completion* the noun). Because some of the entries linked to a concept might not be of the appropriate category for the frame being lexicalized, we have a set of category heuristics to select the most appropriate part of speech. When an instance of a concept like `*complete` must be lexicalized, the generator chooses from only those entries that are syntactically appropriate.[4] Given the limitations on the domain, a simple set of heuristics is used to select likely lexicalization categories for an ILT frame; the set is based on the type of the frame and the context in which it appears.

- *Propositions*. Proposition heads are always realized as verbs.

- *Roles*. Role heads are realized as either nouns or adjectives.

- *Modifiers*. Modifiers are realized as adjectives when they appear inside role frames and as adverbs when they appear inside proposition frames.

These heuristics influence lexical selection by filtering the initial candidate set for only those generation lexicon entries that match the categories selected for the frame being realized.

To summarize so far, the generation lexicon entries are used in the open-class lexical realization of ILT frames. The best possible candidate can be selected from among these entries. This selection is performed based on several ensembles of information supplied by the generation lexicon: the meaning patterns, the subcategorization information and the syntactic part of speech.

As noted earlier, a particular generation module, the mapping rule interpreter, handles closed-class items and structural mappings. We now introduce the rules used by this module; they are discussed in greater detail in chapter 9.

---

[4]Category selection is only a subtask of the broader problem of text planning. Choosing appropriate syntactic structures is a well-known problem in natural language generation. The solution described here is not a general one.

6.3 Generation Mapping Rules

Generation mapping rules describe a mapping from semantic slot-value pairs to syntactic slot-value pairs. These rules consist of the following sets of subrules:

- Rules that map semantic case roles (agent, theme, goal, etc.) to syntactic functions or arguments (sub, obj, xcomp, ppadjunct, etc.)

- Rules to create specific features in the f-structure. These features include those whose values are determined by checking the existence of several slots and their values in the ILT. For example, a noun's number is determined by the presence or absence of *set as the head of the noun's role frame. If *set is absent, the value is singular: (number sg). If it is present, the value is plural: (number pl).[5] The possible values of mood (e.g., declarative, interrogative, imperative) and modality (e.g., necessity, ability and possibility) are determined by inspecting a combination of several slots in the ILT's speech-act frame: direct?, speech-act and time.

- Rules to create a new syntactic slot in the f-structure. The slot's value is in turn an f-structure that is not mapped directly from a semantic slot in the ILT. These rules are needed to create closed-class lexical items, such as adverbs (*yet, already*), prepositions, conjunctions and subordinate conjunctions.

- Rules that map the ILT frame clause into an embedded clause of the main f-structure. For instance, the rules are used for attaching relative clauses to objects and subordinate clauses to matrix clauses.

- Rules that create new f-structures by combining other f-structures, among them the creation of compound nouns in Japanese and coordinate structures in English and Japanese.

- Rules that delete and/or add information in an f-structure. In English, the passivization rule changes the feature that marks a verb's argument structure from trans to intrans.

Consider now the following rule format:

---

[5]Note that *set is also used in the ILT to indicate coordinate structures. A type slot indicates that the role is a coordinate structure (rather than a plural) and what type of coordinate structure it is.

```
(maprule <language> <mr-index> <mr-type> <predicate>
        <slot-mappings>)
```

This mapping rule shell consists of six basic parts:

1. `maprule` —This indicates that the list is a mapping rule.

2. `<language>` —Here, the target language is given; the values in KBMT-89 are e for English and j for Japanese.

3. `<mr-index>` —This index determines which ILT frame the rule should apply to, that is, whether it should apply to `proposition`, `clause` or `role`.

4. `<mr-type>` —There are two types of mapping rules, namely, `:any` and `:exclusive` (both of which are discussed in detail in chapter 9).

5. `<predicate>` —This is a LISP predicate. If it returns a non-nil value, then the rule can be fired; otherwise it cannot. Usually these LISP expressions are used as conditions for determining if the proper environment exists in which to apply a specific set of rules. For instance, if the current verb is transitive and the theme is focused, the rule for passivization is allowed to apply. Thus:

```
(maprule e :exclusive (and (lex-feature-p !lex 'valency 'trans)
                           (equal @frame.clause-id.focus 'theme))
    ((slot theme) => (slot subj))
    (feature! 'valency 'intrans))
```

6. `<slot-mappings>` —This is the mapping from semantic slot to syntactic slot. Hence, to map from a semantic case role to a syntactic function, an active verb that takes an `agent` and a `theme` will have the following slot mappings:

```
((slot agent) => (slot subj))
((slot theme) => (slot obj))
```

Now recall that generation mapping rules handle closed-class lexical mappings. The English generation mapping rule in the following example can be used to create an f-structure for the closed-class aspectual adverbs *yet* or *already*, depending on the input ILT.

```
(maprule e *proposition :any (if (equal @frame.completion 'yes)
                                 t
                                 nil)
        ((expr (if (equal @frame.p-quantifier 'negation)
                  'yet
                  'already))
        =>
        (slot advadjunct)
        (list !fsslot (cons '(position end) !slotfs)))))
```

The rule's contents are interpreted as follows:

1. This is an English mapping rule (maprule e).

2. It is applied to the *proposition frame of the ILT.

3. The rule can be used in conjunction with any (:any) mapping rule that applies to that frame.

4. If the value of the completion slot in this frame of the ILT is yes, then perform the mapping that follows; otherwise do not.

5. Create the slot advadjunct in the f-structure being built.

6. If the value of the p-quantifier (proposition quantifier) slot of the frame is negation, assign the advadjunct slot the value ((root yet)); otherwise, assign the value ((root already)). It is at this step that lexical selection of this closed-class item actually occurs.

7. Last, add (position end) to the list that is the value of advadjunct.

The resulting (truncated) f-structure is then either of the two below.

```
(...
 (advadjunct ((position end) (root already)))
 ...)


(...
 (advadjunct ((position end) (root yet)))
 ...)
```

An example of a mapping that is specific to Japanese is the negation raising rule that raises the negation in a role frame to the level of proposition frame. The negative marker *no* modifying nouns in English cannot be represented similarly in Japanese. Intuitively, the sentence *The computer has no programs* must be rendered as *The computer does NOT have any programs* in Japanese. This kind of movement of "negative" information is achieved through a generation mapping rule (see the following) that replaces the combination of the negative determiner *no* and a noun with just that noun and attaches the negative feature *not* to the head concept. The rule follows.

```
(maprule j *proposition :any
    (or (and (atom @frame.agent)
             (eq @frame.agent.r-quantifier 'negation))
        (and (atom @frame.theme)
             (eq @frame.theme.r-quantifier 'negation))
        (and (atom @frame.domain)
             (eq @frame.domain.r-quantifier 'negation))
        (and (atom @frame.experiencer)
             (eq @frame.experiencer.r-quantifier 'negation))
        (and (atom @frame.range)
             (eq @frame.range.r-quantifier 'negation)))
(slot negation hitei))
```

This rule cannot handle more complicated negative sentences, such as those employing double negatives or negation with *always* or *both*.

Generation mapping rules are also applied to structural mappings. A structural mapping rule assigns ILT slots to appropriate syntactic slots to create an f-structure. This f-structure is the input to the syntactic generation module that will produce a grammatical string. For example, the KBMT-89 corpus contains the following:

(6.1)   66. Did the printer test run error free and the printer test pattern print correctly?
          YES—Go to Step 67.
          NO—Record any error message. Go to "Printer Problem Determination Procedures."

Note the opening numeral and the responses "YES" and "NO." Now consider the following rule for English:

```
(maprule e *proposition :any t
    ((slot clause-response) => (slot response))
    ((slot number-bullet) => (slot number-bullet)))
```

This rule can apply to every *proposition frame. The mappings in the second and third lines may be read as follows: If the *proposition frame contains a clause-response slot, map the f-structure associated with that slot to the syntactic slot response—that is, put yes or no in the response slot;

and if the `*proposition` frame contains a `number-bullet` slot, map the f-structure associated with that slot to the syntactic slot `number-bullet`—that is, put `1.`, `2.` or `3. ...` in the `number-bullet` slot.

6.4 Annotated Example

The remainder of this chapter presents the ILT for the Japanese sentence in (6.2) and a trace showing the f-structure output of some of the mapping rules applied in the generation of the sentence.

(6.2)   Sindan tesuto sekusyon o mite kudasai.
         "Please see the diagnostic testing section."

First, the ILT:

```
(dolist (frame '(clause1 proposition1
                 role1 role2 role3 role99
                 speech-act1 aspect1 time1))
        (erase-frame frame))

(make-frame clause1
   (ilt-type (value clause))
   (clauseid (value clause1))
   (propositionid (value proposition1))
   (speechactid (value speech-act1)))

(make-frame proposition1
   (ilt-type (value proposition))
   (propositionid (value proposition1))
   (clauseid (value clause1))
   (is-token-of (value *proceed-through-text))
   (aspect (value aspect1))
   (time (value (after time1)))
   (agent (value role1))
   (goal (value role2)))

(make-frame role1
   (ilt-type (value role))
   (roleid (value role1))
   (clauseid (value clause1))
   (is-token-of (value *reader))
   (reference (value definite)))

(make-frame role2
   (ilt-type (value role))
   (roleid (value role2))
   (clauseid (value clause1))
   (is-token-of (value *section))
```

```
        (string-is (value Diagnostic_Testing))
        (convey (value role3))
        (reference (value definite)))

(make-frame role3
    (ilt-type (value role))
    (roleid (value role3))
    (clauseid (value clause1))
    (is-token-of (value *test))
    (end (value no))
    (purpose (value role99))
    (reference (value indefinite)))

(make-frame role99
    (ilt-type (value role))
    (roleid (value role99))
    (clauseid (value clause1))
    (is-token-of (value *diagnose)))

(make-frame speech-act1
    (speech-act (value request-info))
    (direct? (value yes))
    (speaker (value author))
    (hearer (value role1))
    (time (value time1)))

(make-frame aspect1
    (phase (value begin))
    (iteration (value 1)))

(make-frame time1
        (is-token-of (value *time)))
```

The following trace illustrates a series of five successful rule applications. Some rules have been deleted for cogency. Each instance of "Firing Rule" designates an attempt to apply a rule.

```
--------------------------------------------------
                    Firing Rule
--------------------------------------------------
Frame: role3
Lex: testing
FS: ((root tesutosuru) (cat N))
```

Here, a `role3` frame has been found and realized as the generation lexicon entry `testing` whose syntactic feature values are `((root tesutosuru) (cat N))`.

The following mapping rule determines if there is a modifier in the `role3` frame. If there is, the syntactic structure of the role frame is marked as a compound noun and the f-structure of the modifier (filler of `attached-to`, `convey`, `for-purpose`, etc.) is mapped to an `xadjunct` slot in the f-structure of the role frame.

```
(defrule j *role
   :any
   (or (frame-accessor frame 'attached-to)
       (frame-accessor frame 'convey)
       (frame-accessor frame 'for-purpose)
       (frame-accessor frame 'label)
       (frame-accessor frame 'material)
       (frame-accessor frame 'property)
       (frame-accessor frame 'purpose))
   ((slot attached-to) => (slot xadjunct))
   ((slot convey) => (slot xadjunct))
   ((slot for-purpose) => (slot xadjunct))
   ((slot label) => (slot xadjunct))
   ((slot material) => (slot xadjunct))
   ((slot property) => (slot xadjunct))
   ((slot purpose) => (slot xadjunct))
   (feature compnoun CN)

Predicate returns role99.
Slot xadjunct added.
Feature (compnoun CN) added.
```

Here, the generator reports that it has found `role99` to be a modifier of the `role3` frame. It then returns the following new f-structure for `role3`:

```
((compnoun CN) (xadjunct ((root sindansuru) (cat N)))
 (root tesutosuru) (cat N))
```

Similarly, the `role2` frame is realized as the generation lexicon entry `section`.

```
-------------------------------------------------
                Firing Rule
-------------------------------------------------
Frame: role2
Lex: section
FS: ((root sekusyon) (cat N))
```

Then, this same rule is applied to the `role2` frame.

```
(defrule j *role
   :any
   (or (frame-accessor frame 'attached-to)
       (frame-accessor frame 'convey)
```

```
        (frame-accessor frame 'for-purpose)
        (frame-accessor frame 'label)
        (frame-accessor frame 'material)
        (frame-accessor frame 'property)
        (frame-accessor frame 'purpose))
     ((slot attached-to) => (slot xadjunct))
     ((slot convey) => (slot xadjunct))
     ((slot for-purpose) => (slot xadjunct))
     ((slot label) => (slot xadjunct))
     ((slot material) => (slot xadjunct))
     ((slot property) => (slot xadjunct))
     ((slot purpose) => (slot xadjunct))
     (feature compnoun cn)

Predicate returns role3.
Slot xadjunct added.
Feature (compnoun CN) added.
```

The modifier of `role2` turned out to be the `role3` frame. We now have the following f-structure for `role2`:

```
((compnoun CN)
 (xadjunct
  ((compnoun CN) (xadjunct ((root sindansuru) (cat N)))
   (root tesutosuru) (cat N)))
 (root sekusyon) (cat N))
```

Here, the `proposition1` frame is realized as the generation lexicon entry `see`.

```
--------------------------------------------------
                   Firing Rule
--------------------------------------------------

Frame: proposition1
Lex: see
FS: ((vtype v-1dan) (subcat trans) (root miru)
     (subj-case ga) (obj-case o) (cat V))
```

The following rule maps the semantic case fillers of `source` and `goal` into the syntactic slots `ppadjunct` and `obj`, respectively.

```
(defrule j *proposition
   :any
   (equal (frame-accessor frame 'is-token-of)
          '*proceed-through-text)
   ((slot source) => (slot ppadjunct))
```

```
                        (list !fsslot
                              (cons '(part kara) !slotfs)))
    ((slot goal) => (slot OBJ))
```

```
Predicate returns T.
Slot OBJ added.
```

Because `role3` fills the `goal` slot of `proposition1`, the f-structure of `role3` is mapped to the `obj` slot in the f-structure of `proposition1`.

```
((obj
   ((compnoun CN)
    (xadjunct
     ((compnoun CN) (xadjunct ((root sindansuru) (cat N)))
      (root tesutosuru) (cat N)))
    (root sekusyon) (cat N)))
  (vtype v-1dan) (subcat trans) (root miru) (subj-case ga)
  (obj-case o) (cat V))
```

```
-------------------------------------------------
                    Firing Rule
-------------------------------------------------
```

```
Frame: proposition1
Lex: see
FS: ((obj
       ((compnoun CN)
        (xadjunct
         ((compnoun CN) (xadjunct ((root sindansuru) (cat N)))
          (root tesutosuru)
          (cat N)))
        (root sekusyon) (cat N)))
      (vtype v-1dan) (subcat trans) (root miru) (subj-case ga)
      (obj-case o)
      (cat V))
```

The following rule can map a `response` (*yes* or *no*) or a number tag (*1., 2.,* ...) associated with the sentence; it also attaches the (`formal +`) feature to each proposition frame.

```
(defrule j *proposition
  :any
  t
  ((slot clause-response) => (slot sent-tag))
  ((slot number-bullet) => (slot sent-num))
  (feature formal +)
```

```
Predicate returns T.
Feature (formal +) added.
```

Since the `proposition1` frame has no `clause-response` or `number-bullet`, the mapping rule attaches only the (`formal +`) feature.

```
((formal +)
 (obj
  ((compnoun CN)
   (xadjunct
    ((compnoun CN) (xadjunct ((root sindansuru) (cat N)))
     (root tesutosuru)
     (cat N)))
   (root sekusyon) (cat N)))
 (vtype v-1dan) (subcat trans) (root miru) (subj-case ga)
 (obj-case o) (cat V))


-------------------------------------------------
                 Firing Rule
-------------------------------------------------
Frame: proposition1
Lex: see
FS: ((formal +)
     (obj
      ((compnoun CN)
       (xadjunct
        ((compnoun CN) (xadjunct ((root sindansuru) (cat N)))
         (root tesutosuru)
         (cat N)))
       (root sekusyon) (cat N)))
     (vtype v-1dan) (subcat trans) (root miru) (subj-case ga)
     (obj-case o)
     (cat V))
```

This last rule determines the f-structure's `mood` slot value.

```
(defrule j *proposition
   :any
   t
   ((expr
     (cond ((and
              (equal (frame-accessor frame 'clauseid
                      'speechactid 'speech-act)
                      'command)
              (equal (frame-accessor frame 'clauseid
                      'speechactid 'direct?)
                      'yes))
             'imp)
           ((equal (frame-accessor frame 'clauseid
                    'speechactid 'speech-act)
                    'request-info)
            'ques)
           (t 'dec)))
   => (slot mood))
```

Because proposition1 has a speech-act frame whose semantic slots include (speech-act (value command)) and (direct? (value yes)), the mapping rule adds (mood ((root imp))) to the f-structure:

```
Predicate returns T.
Slot (mood ((root imp))) added.
```

The final f-structure, which can be input to the syntactic generator, is as follows:

```
((mood ((root imp))) (formal +)
 (obj
  ((compnoun CN)
   (xadjunct
    ((compnoun CN) (xadjunct ((root sindansuru) (cat N)))
     (root tesutosuru)
     (cat N)))
   (root sekusyon) (cat N)))
 (vtype v-1dan) (subcat trans) (root miru) (subj-case ga)
 (obj-case o) (cat V))
```

Chapter 7

Source Text Analysis

■ MARION KEE, LORI S. LEVIN AND STEPHEN MORRISSON

7.1   Introduction and Overview

The Revised Extended Standard Theory of syntax and the continuing development of the Chomskian "principles and parameters" approach to syntax presuppose the existence of a set of "theta roles" that are carried by lexical items, most notably verbs.[1] Most syntacticians now accept the existence of such roles, or at least of a fundamental predicate-argument relation, though exactly how many kinds of roles there and what they should be called remain topics of debate. However, a number of basic roles are usually agreed upon; these include, but are not limited to, agent, source, goal and theme. While even these are open to dispute, it is possible in a limited domain or application to define and apply them in a useful way.

   The job of the KBMT-89 analyzer is to extract predicate-argument relations from natural language sentences. These relations are, as was explained in chapter 3, syntactically encoded by case markers, word order, agreement markers and so forth. To extract the predicate-argument relations, it becomes necessary to "decode" the

---

[1]These have historically been referred to as "case roles." The *locus classicus* is, of course, Fillmore 1968.

syntactic representation of the relations. Therefore, a case-frame analysis must be combined with syntactic parsing. This chapter describes the procedure for this undertaking.[2]

The KBMT-89 analyzer, illustrated in figure 7.1, uses Tomita's universal parser,[3] guided by analysis knowledge (data files), to turn an input sentence in the source language into a semantic frame representation of the meaning of the sentence. The knowledge structures brought to bear are the analysis grammars, the mapping rules and the concept and analysis lexicons.[4]

The process of creating a case-frame is driven by syntactic analysis of the input sentence. If the parser operated with only an analysis grammar, the output would be a syntactic f-structure. The mapping rules mediate between the syntactic analysis grammars and the concept lexicon. (An explanation of how the parser interprets the mapping rules and makes use of semantic knowledge from the concept lexicon will be given later, in the account of the mapping rule interpreter.) The parser uses semantic restrictions embodied in the concept lexicon to guide treatment of syntactic ambiguities encountered in its analysis of the input. Further, it uses the concept lexicon's concepts as templates for the mapping rules to instantiate as case-frames. The result of the parser's interaction with the concept lexicon, via the mapping rules, is a partly disambiguated case-frame.

In the process of interleaving syntactic parsing with the mapping rules, semantic information is added to the syntactic f-structure. Syntactic f-structures containing

---

[2]The KBMT-89 approach to semantic representation was conditioned in part by previous work on the Xcalibur natural language database interface project; see Carbonell et al. 1983, 1985. The project relied on case-frame parsing. A major technique developed in Xcalibur and, later, in the Natural Language OPS (NLOPS) projects was the use of a two-stage frame transformation process in the parsing component. NLOPS, 1985-1987, was designed to make it easier for nonspecialists to use OPS-5, a rule-based package for building expert systems. NLOPS parsed natural language descriptions of rules and automatically generated actual OPS rules from these descriptions. It also had a generation component that turned OPS rules into natural language output. In NLOPS as well as Xcalibur the natural language input was processed with a case-frame parser; the parser output was transformed, using a separate module, into the desired frame-based semantic representation of the input. The parser had no general inferencing mechanism built into it; inferencing was done in the transformation module and was made as general as possible. This not only increased efficiency for both the parsing and inferencing components of the system but also made it far easier to debug the parsing grammars and inference rules. This approach generally parallels the parser/augmentor structure used to derive ILTs in KBMT-89.

[3]Discussed in the following section and the references therein.

[4]A discussion of the rationale for this configuration of the analysis knowledge bases can be found in Tomita, Kee, Mitamura, and Carbonell 1987.

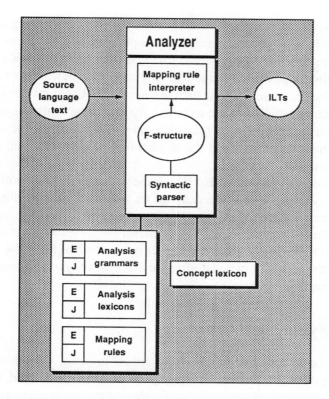

Figure 7.1: **The KBMT-89 analyzer. 'E' and 'J' designate English and Japanese.**

all applicable semantic information constitute the output of the analysis phase. The semantics associated with a particular portion of the syntactic parse is located in a special feature (designated sem; see section 7.3) in the f-structure representation of that syntactic segment.[5] In what follows, the phrase "the semantics of an f-structure" or just "the semantics" will be used to designate the result of applying mapping rules to the f-structure.

The semantic frame representation is an intermediate form; it is not yet an interlingua text. Its structure is largely determined by the structure of the source

---

[5]For use in debugging, such structures can be further processed by the parser to produce a semantically organized frame representation of the input. This representation instantiates the relevant concepts from the concept lexicon that were encountered during the parse and omits purely syntactic information about the input.

language sentence. This follows from a decision not to have the parser perform structural transformations on the semantic output frames it produces. Rather, we have placed this function in the augmentor. The augmentor also adds information that is not explicitly present in the source language text but which may reasonably be inferred from the parser output; such inferences are based on knowledge about the source language and from the context. By assigning to the augmentor those tasks associated with higher-level manipulation of instantiated concepts, we render both the instantiation process and the augmenting process substantially easier to debug and maintain.

This separation of functions also allows the parser to do what it does best, that is, build up structures, without the need for an additional functionality to perform transformations on those structures. The construction of the analysis knowledge sources will determine just how closely the parser output conforms to the structures needed in the ILT. But the ILT inherently raises issues, such as temporal relationships between clauses, not encountered during the linear activity of parsing (these issues are discussed in chapter 2).

7.2   The Syntactic Parser

The parser used in KBMT-89 has been described in detail in numerous places.[6] Consequently, there is little need to repeat such description. Instead, we will offer general remarks on the motivation for the *kind* of parser required by the project and account for modifications made to the Tomita parser.

One of the advantages of interlingua translation systems over direct and transfer systems is that the ILT is language-independent; that is, the source and target languages are never in direct contact. This theoretically allows the construction of a machine translation system in which any potential source and target languages could be selected, requiring minimal modifications to the computational structure. Clearly, then, any such system will eventually need to be able to parse numerous source languages, and a universal parser simplifies the task of system maintenance. It will take a language grammar as input, rather than build the grammar into the interpreter proper.

Viewing multiple languages from this perspective, the linguistic structure is no

---

[6] Among these are Tomita 1985; Tomita and Carbonell 1987; Tomita, Kee, Mitamura and Carbonell 1987; and the user's guide to the parser, Tomita, Mitamura, Musha and Kee 1988. In what follows, we rely extensively on these documents. Also, preambles to appendix A and appendix B provide details that are important for understanding examples and traces in this book.

longer a universal invariant that transfers across all applications (as it was for pure English language parsers), but rather it is another dimension of parameterization and extensibility. This is in a sense to say that the grammar and parser are distinct, and it is possible to change the one without changing the other. However, semantic information can remain invariant across languages (though, of course, not across domains). Therefore, it is crucial to keep semantic knowledge sources separate from syntactic ones, so that if new syntactic information is added it will apply across all semantic domains, and if new semantic information is added it will apply to all relevant languages. The universal parser attempts to accomplish this factoring without making major concessions to either run-time efficiency or semantic accuracy.

There are three kinds of knowledge sources (introduced in previous chapters). One contains syntactic grammars for different languages, another contains semantic knowledge bases for different domains and the third contains sets of rules that map syntactic forms (words and phrases) into the semantic knowledge structure. Each of the syntactic grammars is generally independent of any particular domain; likewise, each of the semantic knowledge bases is independent of any specific language.

The mapping rules are, however, both language- and domain-dependent, and a different set of mapping rules is created for each language/domain combination. Syntactic grammars, domain knowledge bases and mapping rules are written in a highly abstract, human-readable manner. This organization makes them easy to extend or modify but possibly machine-inefficient for a run-time parser.

The run-time grammar produced by the universal parser's multiphase compiler is an augmented context-free grammar, which is further compiled into a generalized LR (left-right) table to be used by a run-time parser based on Tomita's parsing algorithm.

The English grammar does not compile a syntactic component, semantic component and mapping rules (as it did in earlier versions of the system) but keeps these elements separate. It is the analysis lexicon that points to all three elements. The grammar contains rules that call the lexicons to obtain the entire definition of a word.

Unlike the English grammar, the Japanese grammar contains lexical information. But here, too, the grammar calls a lexical utility to obtain the semantics and mapping rule for a given word. The calls—but not the information itself—are compiled into the grammar.

An effect of this organization is that we can change the semantics, mapping rules and, in English, the syntactic features without recompiling the grammar. This has proved a valuable aid. For instance, it formerly took about 90 minutes to compile the various components into the grammars; this now takes 5 to 10 minutes.

7.3   The Mapping Rule Interpreter

The function of the mapping rule interpreter is to produce and manipulate the syntactic and semantic structures of a parse and, moreover, to produce these structures simultaneously.

Throughout, the key idea is *attachment*. That is, every NP or VP has a head to which other information is attached; and sentential structures also have heads to which accompanying information from phrases is attached. The characteristics of syntactic heads are defined in the syntactic grammar for each language; semantic heads are determined by the ways in which the concepts in the concept lexicon are related to each other. Overall, attachment is accomplished by the mapping rules. When syntactic attachments are made to f-structures, the mapping rules trigger the attachment of corresponding semantic information.

This is done in large part by mapping syntactic functions such as "subject" to semantic roles such as "agent."[7] The parse anchors a tokenized semantic representation to the syntactic head of a phrase.[8] In the KBMT-89 system, this semantic representation goes into the "semantics" (or sem) slot of the parser output.

There are several kinds of mapping rules to handle different kinds of semantic attachment: (i) headed and embedded lexical mapping rules and (ii) structural mapping rules. These mapping rules perform two key functions. First, they map lexical items onto concepts and, second, they fill slots in the concepts. Headed lexical mapping rules map lexical items onto concepts. They are used for syntactic heads of phrases and some modifiers. A typical example would be a noun phrase attached to a verb phrase. A headed lexical mapping rule maps the head of the NP onto a concept; this concept fills a slot in the concept that the VP maps to, via a relation identified by a slot name. This relation is specified by using an ordinary structural mapping rule and ordinary semantic restrictions. Structural mapping rules fill slots by associating a syntactic slot name with a semantic slot name. Heads of phrases are associated with structural mapping rules that place their arguments and certain kinds of modifers into slots. Embedded-head lexical

---

[7]The syntactic head/semantic head correspondence was developed in the Xcalibur system noted earlier.

[8]"Tokenized" indicates just that a token is created from the concept definition in the concept lexicon; nothing in the lexicon itself is altered by parsing.

mapping rules are used for some modifiers. A modifier with an embedded-head mapping rule maps to an attribute-value pair where the attribute corresponds to a semantic relation and the value maps to a (token of) a concept. To summarize, structural mapping rules specify a slot and where to find a filler in the syntactic structure; headed lexical mapping rules specify a concept that might later become a filler of a slot, but this slot is not specified. Embedded-head mapping rules specify a slot and a concept that fills it.

While the parser handles or accommodates arbitrary depth in the representations it creates, the ILT representation does not. The theory of generation adopted in KBMT-89 does not employ an arbitrarily deep recursive semantic definition of a phrase, and the ILTs that are fed into the generator have corresponding depth limitations. The augmentor takes deeply embedded portions of the parser output and expresses them in an acceptable syntax when creating the actual ILTs.

To recapitulate, the universal parser produces all the possible, that is, valid, f-structures that can be derived from the sentences parsed. Each of these syntactic f-structures has semantic features, and these features are created at the same time as the rest of the syntactic f-structure. The semantic component may thus be regarded as an additional feature of f-structures. To illustrate in processing terms, sem, a semantic feature, appears in the (abbreviated) f-structure for the sentence *Remove the tape.*[9]

```
((root remove)
 (tense present)
 (trans  +)
 (sem   (*sem* ((clausal-mark +)
                (mood imperative)
                (tense present)
                (theme
                 ((reference definite) (number singular)
                  ($map-data (*map* { map-str tape } ))
                  ($is-token-of sticky-tape) ($id (*id* 20))))) 
                (agent *reader*)
                ($map-data (*map* { map-str remove } ))
                ($is-token-of remove)
                ($id (*id* 19)))))) 
   .
   .
   . )
```

Thus, the semantic component is a visible part of the syntactic parse. This

---

[9]In the example, curly brackets are used to enclose the name of internal LISP structures, e.g., {map-str tape} .

approach, of simultaneously creating the syntactic and semantic structures, has produced a system able to eliminate useless partial parses before completing them. It does this by applying semantic constraints as soon as a phrase is analyzed.[10] This process is amplified below.

When parsing is completed, all possible semantic interpretations of the valid f-structures are passed to the augmentor. We can now say that the function of mapping rule interpretation is to provide the augmentor with all possible fillers of the f-structures' semantic slots. It is then up to the augmentor to determine what modifications must be made to produce a valid ILT.

Parser mapping rules can be divided into two classes: lexical and structural. Each class can be further subdivided.

7.3.1   Lexical Mapping Rules

There are two kinds of lexical mapping rules: *headed* and *embedded*.[11]

Generally, headed rules apply to nouns and verbs and embedded rules apply to determiners, adjectives and adverbs. Headed rules are used when the semantic role cannot be determined by the lexical entry alone. Embedded rules are used when the semantic role can be determined by the lexical entry alone. For example, the NP *personal computer* can fill the `theme` slot in *the personal computer broke* or the `source` slot in *remove the diskette from the personal computer* and so forth. However, we cannot determine merely from the NP *personal computer* which slots it fills.[12] We can do this, for instance, with *automatically*, which can fill only the slot `automated-p`.

In headed rules, the head noun or verb, in conjunction with the name of its part of speech, will point to a set of ontological concepts, that is, to entries in the concept lexicon. For instance, (`"disk"` (`cat N`)) will point to one or more entries in the concept lexicon. Only the root form of the word—and not a plural, for instance—will appear in a headed rule. Both the word and the concept specified in a headed rule are called "heads." The concept is a semantic head and the word is a syntactic head.

---

[10] A side effect of this approach is that the semantic head of the parse of a phrase must correspond to the syntactic head of the phrase. If the resulting semantic parse should in fact have a different semantic head, the augmentor will restructure it accordingly.

[11] See the discussion in chapter 5.

[12] The NP's relation to a verb will be determined by structural mapping rules, discussed later, and by the head noun's syntactic role in the verb phrase.

Following are abbreviated examples of headed mapping rules for *move* and *diskette*. Observe that in the first, the terminal natural language string does not match the name of the concept, where in the second it does. (Recall that each concept name is designated with an asterisk.) The point is that there is no theoretical significance in the choice of concept names.

```
("move" (cat V)
    (mapping
        (local
            (head (*change-location))))))
```

```
("diskette" (cat N)
    (mapping
        (local
            (head (*diskette))))))
```

Embedded mapping rules carry different information than do headed rules. While a headed rule points directly from a lexical root to a semantic head, an embedded rule points from a lexical root to a substructure that is either a filled relation or a filled property (see chapter 2). When we say that an embedded rule points to a filled relation, we mean that it points from a lexical root to a relation name and a semantic head; this head is the filler of the relation. An embedded rule that points to a filled property should be understood to point from a lexical root to a property name and a literal value; this literal value is the filler of the property.

To illustrate, the following embedded lexical mapping rule points from a lexical root to a relation and a semantic head. The lexical item *below* maps to the semantic head *text-group. In this case, *text-group attaches to a verb, filling that verb's goal slot, where goal is the relation that mediates between the verb and the embedded semantic head.

```
("below" (cat reg-adv)
    (mapping
        (local
            (embed (goal (*text-group (%textual-after $current-clause)))))))))
```

Embedded heads are themselves semantic heads of concepts, and they too can be modified. A modifier contains additional information either implied in the lexical item itself or carried in an adjective or adverb. In the preceding example, the embedded head `*text-group` is modified by information implied in the lexical item *below*, represented as (`%textual-after $current-clause`).

So, the parser output for the phrase *see below* will be (liberalizing notation for this example):

```
(*proceed-through-text
        (goal (*text-group
                (%textual-after $current-clause)))))
```

Here, `*proceed-through-text` is the *dominant* head, `*text-group` is the *embedded head* and *goal* is the relation between the dominant head and the embedded semantic head. (`%textual-after $current-clause`) is the modifier of the embedded semantic head. This conveys the meaning that the text referred to by the phrase *see below* appears after the text that the human reader is currently reading. The relation `goal` controls the selection of other concepts to which the embedded semantic head may be attached. That (`*text-group` (`%textual-after $current-clause`)) is associated with `goal` means it can only be attached to dominant heads that have `goal` slots, namely, those corresponding to certain verbs. Interpreting *below* as a `*text-group` is thus an inference drawn from its association (in the input sentence) with a particular kind of verb.

The following embedded lexical mapping rule points from a lexical root to a property and a literal value. The lexical item *automatically* maps to the combination of the property name *automated-p* and the literal value `yes`. This substructure can only attach to a dominant head that has the property slot `automated-p` included in its concept definition in the concept lexicon.

```
("automatically" (cat reg-adv)
    (mapping
        (local
            (embed (automated-p yes)))))
```

Using this mapping rule, the parser output for the phrase *a diskette is automatically loaded* should be as follows (again liberalizing notation):

```
(*load-software
        (focus theme)
        (theme (*diskette
                    (number singular)
                    (reference indefinite)))
        (automated-p yes))
```

A further account of attachment of properties and their values to dominant heads is given in section 7.3.3.

7.3.2 Structural Mapping Rules

The structural mapping rules are triggered by syntactic equations containing a syntactic slot name (again, see the discussion in chapter 5). Thus, the syntactic parsing process causes the structural mapping rules to fire. The KBMT-89 analysis grammar contains the following equation in the rule that expands a VP as V followed by NP.

```
((X0 obj) = X2)
```

Here, X0 is known as the dominant structure and X2 is the subordinate structure. During parsing, the syntactic slot is examined, and the corresponding slot mapping rule is found in the lexical entry for the head of the dominant structure. Then, if the syntactic restrictions are met and the semantic restrictions are valid, the semantics of the subordinate structure are attached to the semantics of the dominant structure using the semantic slot named by the structural mapping rule. Consider the following structural slot mapping rule associated with the word *remove*, which corresponds to the concept *remove.

```
(theme = obj)
```

The rule's output during parsing of the phrase *remove the diskette* is as follows:

```
[*remove
    (theme [*diskette])]
```

This structure contains two tokens, each indicated by square brackets. That is, the entire structure is a token that contains the embedded token *diskette. The token *remove is a value that exists when (X0 obj = X2) is encountered. Of course, this token can be modified, as noted earlier, without altering concept lexicon entries. As a token, the bracketed material in the example *cites* a named concept.

Semantic restrictions are applied when the token in the subordinate position is compared to the restrictions associated with the slot of the dominant token; these restrictions are set forth in the concept lexicon. So, for instance, the semantic restriction on the theme slot in the concept *remove is that it be *physical-object. Because *diskette is a *physical-object, it can be inserted into the theme slot of *remove.

There are also syntactic constraints on mapping rules. For example, the syntactic constraint (passive = -) might be associated with the structural mapping rule theme = obj. Before the mapping rule is applied, the syntactic constraint is unified with the dominant f-structure. The mapping rule will not apply if unification fails.

We have so far been discussing *semantic* or "standard" structural mapping rules. To recapitulate, a mapping rule is triggered when a syntactic equation causes a subordinate f-structure to be attached to a dominant f-structure. The mapping rule specifies a slot in the semantics of the dominant f-structure. This slot is filled with the semantics of the subordinate f-structure. The semantics of the subordinate f-structure must satisfy the semantic constraints on fillers of the slot.

Two other kinds of structural mapping rules were created because of the need to provide the ILT with information from the syntactic feature structure, where this information does not correspond to any ontological concept or relation. As was mentioned in chapter 1, the KBMT-89 corpora contain sentences that refer to the texts themselves in various ways (e.g., to sections in the texts), *and* they contain customary textual devices like enumerated lists. Further, some features of syntactic analysis, such as tense and mood, are required in the construction of ILTs (so to order time relations, for instance) but are not part of the domain and so are not represented in the concept lexicon.

One class of these special rules is the *unchecked semantic mapping rules*. When an unchecked rule is applied, the semantics of the subordinate f-structure are attached directly to the slot in the semantics of the dominant f-structure—but no semantic constraints are checked. This type of rule is required when the slot is not a relation in the ontology. (Such rules could, however, be used when the slot *is* a relation in the ontology and there is a desire to override the semantic constraints; but this was not done in KBMT-89.)

For instance, number-bullet is used to represent numbers and the punctuation marks that follow them in certain numbered sentences, and clausal-link is used in cases involving two clauses, as in a compound sentence. The number-bullet instance offers a more detailed example. Several sentences from the English corpus begin with a numeral from the computer manual, for instance:[13]

(7.1)   1. Remove the diskette from the diskette drive.

---

[13]This example is used later in an abbreviated trace and appears in the complete trace given in appendix A.

The English grammar is structured so that '1.' will be represented in the slot named `number-bullet` and '1' will map onto the concept (`*any-number (cardinality 1)`).[14] The syntactic slot `number-bullet` will map onto the slot `number-bullet` in the parser output, even though there is no conceptual entity that is a `*number bullet`. So, because `number-bullet` is not a relation in the ontology, there are no semantic restrictions to check.[15]

Now we can turn to syntactic promotion mapping rules. These are used when neither the slot nor the filler is represented in the concept lexicon, as is the case with mood and tense. Instead of attaching the semantics of the subordinate f-structure to the semantics of the dominant f-structure, the program simply copies the former into the semantics of the latter. That is, these rules merely take the syntactic value of the subordinate side and *promote* that value to the dominant side; no semantic restrictions are made.[16]

If the f-structure being mapped has been assigned semantics by previous mapping rules, the syntactic promotion rule ignores the semantic restrictions that would normally be applied to this structure. The structure is assumed to hold semantically correct values. These values will next be processed by the augmentor, not by the parser. This strategy was adopted primarily for efficiency in handling structures that are not lexically realized; tense and mood are again examples. Recall that the key reason for building the semantic and syntactic representations simultaneously was to reduce the number of valid parses. Because some syntactic components always map to valid semantic structures, there is no need at parse time to build these structures. The only requirement is that we preserve enough information to enable the augmentor to build these structures only in those parses that are successful.

Nothing is lost in forgoing semantic restraint checks for mood or tense—the restraints could not be violated by such in any case. Put differently, moods will just be stipulated as imperative, declarative and so on; thus there is no reason to make further checks at this phase of analysis.

---

[14]Of course, the question whether to represent numbers as concepts touches on fundamental issues in the philosophy of mathematics. In KBMT-89, numbers are stipulated to be special cases, and the problem is unresolved. The issue is touched on in chapter 5.

[15]Unchecked rules employ three equal signs, as in '`clausal-link === sadjunct`' or '`number-bullet === number-bullet`'.

[16]These rules are identified in the system by the appearance of double equal signs, e.g. '`mood == mood`.'

7.3.3 Semantic Restrictions

Semantic restrictions are performed to determine if a value that is a candidate to be instantiated as the filler of a frame's given slot is, in fact, a valid filler for that slot. Semantic restrictions are specified in the concept lexicon. In general, the possible valid fillers for a slot can be characterized as those that are instances of a particular frame or set of frames. For example, anything that fills an instance of the `theme` slot for the verb *remove* must be an instance of a concept that is a `physical-object`. The usual type of semantic restriction (that is, a list appearing in the definition of a given slot, which characterizes the possible valid fillers of that slot) is a *simple semantic restriction*.

Another source of semantic restrictions is the definition of a slot as a frame. When a frame definition for a slot is created, explicit specifications that characterize the function of that slot are required to be part of the definition. The range and domain specifications are examples. (Recall that the domain of a slot is the set of concepts that it can appear in; the range of a slot is the set of concepts that can appear as fillers of the slot.) Without frame definitions for slots, any particular slot might be more easily misused in the course of creating concept definitions. Thus, the interpreter checks to ensure that the slot has been defined as a frame.

Not every semantic restriction is a simple one; some consist of more complex sets of conditions. The following is a list of the kinds of semantic restrictions employed in KBMT-89. A candidate value *cannot* be a valid filler for a given slot if any of the following three conditions is true:

- There is no frame definition for the slot.

- There is a simple semantic restriction imposed by the concept in which the slot occurs (either direct or inherited) for that slot, and the filler is not valid for that simple semantic restriction. (This is just the normal function of a simple semantic restriction.)

- The frame in which the slot occurs does not specify a simple semantic restriction for that slot, and either or both of the following conditions hold:

  1. The frame definition for the slot specifies a simple semantic restriction for its range, and the filler is not valid under that restriction.

  2. The frame definition for the slot specifies a simple semantic restriction for its domain, and the frame in which the slot is contained is not valid under that restriction.

There are three kinds of lists that may be used in a concept lexicon frame definition to specify the simple semantic restriction on a given slot. They are as follows:

1. A list in which each element is a *literal value*. ("Literal value" is shorthand for "filler of a property" in the concept lexicon; note that concepts fill *relations*.) In this first case, a filler is valid if it is a member of this list.

2. A list in which each element is a concept name. In this case, a filler is valid if it matches any concept that meets the *is-a* test for one of the concepts named in this list.[17]

3. A list in which all values but one are concept names, and that one value is an *exception list*. An exception list is a list whose first element is *except* and whose remaining elements are concept names.[18] The test for filler validity in this third case includes the test described for the second case, but in addition the concept matched to the filler must not stand in the is-a relation to any of the concepts named in the exception list.

7.4 Sample Traces

The discussion of the mapping rule interpreter is illustrated here with an abbreviated trace of the processing of the English sentence that was given in (7.1), repeated here for convenience.

(7.1)   1. Remove the tape from the diskette drive

7.4.1 Disambiguation

To begin with, note that from the standpoint of lexical semantics, this sentence contains four points of disambiguation. First, the English verb *remove* is, in fact, vague. In some other languages a lexical distinction is made between removing an object from inside another object and removing it from another object's surface. For example, in Japanese, while *torinozoku* can be translated as "remove" in the

---

[17]The *is-a* inheritance relation links subclasses and superclasses of concepts. For example, *remove is-a *change-location. The relation is discussed in Nyberg 1988.

[18]Recall that if asterisks are pre- *and* postpended they designate semantic information in f-structures.

general case, the sense of "remove-from-on-surface-of" should be rendered as *toru*, while "remove-from-inside-of" should be rendered as *nukitoru*. In Russian, the equivalent of "remove-from-on-surface-of" is *snjat'*, while the equivalent of "remove-from-inside-of" is *vynut'*. This state of affairs requires that our domain model be developed so that this vagueness is resolved. One way of doing so is to give `*remove` the meaning of "remove-from-on-surface-of" and introduce a sister concept `*remove-from-inside-of`.

Consider, then, the concept lexicon frame for *remove*:

```
Frame Class:   ONTO   REMOVE
IS-A                  (change-location)
SUBCLASSES            (remove-sticky-tape remove-diskette)
DEFINITION            ("to take something from the surface of another
                         object and put it somewhere else")
THEME                 (physical-object)
SOURCE                (physical-object)
PRECONDITION          (ON remove.theme remove.source)
EHEAD                 ((remove (cat V)))
JHEAD                 ((torinozoku (cat V)))

SLOTS INHERITED FROM CHANGE-LOCATION:
PART-OF               (nil)
GOAL                  (physical-object)
THEME-PROPERTY        (location)
DISTANCE              (> 0)
      .
      .
      .
```

The frame for "remove-from-inside-of" might be crafted as follows (it was not used in KBMT-89):

```
Frame Class:   ONTO   REMOVE-FROM-INSIDE
IS-A                  (change-location)
SUBCLASSES            (remove-sticky-tape remove-diskette)
DEFINITION            ("to take something from inside another
                         object and put it somewhere else")
THEME                 (physical-object)
SOURCE                (physical-object)
PRECONDITION          (IN remove.theme remove.source)
EHEAD                 ((remove (cat V)))
JHEAD                 ((nukitoru (cat V)))

SLOTS INHERITED FROM CHANGE-LOCATION:
PART-OF               (nil)
GOAL                  (physical-object)
THEME-PROPERTY        (location)
DISTANCE              (> 0)
      .
      .
      .
```

Further problems of vagueness relating to *remove* can be uncovered. That is, one might remove a piece of tape adhering to the front of a diskette drive, and one might remove a reel or container of tape from atop a drive. While there was no need to address this ambiguity in KBMT-89, there are several ways one might begin to do so. The most obvious would be to add an additional condition to the concept lexicon frame above, perhaps (`remove.theme.atop-of remove.source`). Thereafter, decisions would need to be made in accordance with one's corpus and the languages involved. In other words, it is far from clear what sort of textual context would require removal of a roll of adhesive tape (or a diskette, for that matter) from *atop* a disk drive; certainly the presence of adhesive tape atop a drive would rarely occasion mention in a computer installation manual. Depending on the lexical semantics of the languages involved, one might even have to press the distinction between "affixed to" and "atop of" and broaden the definition of *remove* accordingly.

The second ambiguity pertains to the English lexeme *tape*. That is, there are tapes on which magnetic data are stored and tapes used to wrap parcels, fix torn pages and, in emergencies, to repair eyeglasses (of course, there are still other kinds of tape). In the example we are considering, the tape is adhesive tape, and it is used to cover the opening of a PC's disk drive as part of the process of packaging a PC for shipment. The sentence is among the instructions for unpacking a new computer.

In a sublanguage, this ambiguity is easily resolved. Because magnetic tapes will not appear in the domain of personal computers but adhesive tape will, given that it comes into play in their packaging, there is no ambiguity in this domain. That is to say, there is only one tape in the PC domain, and it is adhesive. This being the case, we need not account for magnetic tape in any of the applicable concept lexicon frames.[19]

This tacit constraint will continue to work in a larger domain. Consider that a corpus might require access to domains ranging across all computers. While some computers will clearly need magnetic tape, such computers do not have diskette drives. To be sure, however, some adhesive tape might be required in their packaging. In such a case, we would proceed much as above and note that adhesive tape is not a part-of these other computers either. In any event, such ambiguities did not arise in KBMT-89 and so are not addressed in the system's files or programs.

Third, the preposition *from* also is multiply ambiguous. However, in the KBMT-

---

[19]To be sure, we can imagine domains including personal computers *and* tape backups, but, as before, it should be a relatively simple matter to prevent lexical ambiguity.

89 environment, it is often possible to learn about the correct sense of a preposition with the help of the constraint on the `source` property of *remove. In other words, once the verb and the prepositional object are lexically disambiguated, the meaning of the preposition is, in a majority of cases, thereby determined.

Finally, the noun-noun compound *diskette drive* has to be processed. Noun-noun compounds are notoriously difficult to understand and translate, because even in simple compounds it is not easy to determine which property of the head noun (provided one can detect it first!) the modifier noun expresses. For instance, *IBM lecture* can mean (i) lecture at IBM (the property of location), (ii) lecture about IBM (the property of topic), (iii) lecture paid for by IBM (the property of sponsorship) and so forth. In KBMT-89, there is only a limited facility for resolving noun-noun compounds automatically. Therefore, we need either to make them a single lexical unit or to delegate the decision about their resolution to the augmentor. In the case of *diskette drive*, we decided on the former.

7.4.2 The Traces

Let us move on. Recall from chapter 5 the structure and notation for structural mapping rules. In the example at hand, the applicable rule is as follows:

```
("remove" (cat V)
                (features        (class default-verb-feat))
                (mapping
                 (local
                  (slot
                    (source = (ppadjunct (prep = from)))))
                 (class cb-th-verb-map)))
```

In the rule, `(class cb-th-verb-map)` will call the mapping rule class used for "caused-by-theme" verbs such as *control* and *disconnect* (verbs that take a `caused-by` slot and a `theme` slot).

```
(cb-th-verb-map
    (mapping
        (local
            (test (passive = -) (valency = trans))
            (slot (caused-by = subj)
                  (theme = obj)))
        (local
            (test (passive = +))
            (slot (caused-by = obl-agent)
                  (theme = subj))
            (sem-test (focus theme))))
```

```
(local
    (test (passive = +))
    (slot (theme = subj))
    (sem-test (focus theme)
              (caused-by unknown))))
    (class ag-th-verb-map)))
```

The second is required for the "agent-theme" verbs *contact, enter* and so forth.

```
(ag-th-verb-map
    (mapping
        (local
            (test (passive = -) (valency = trans))
            (slot (agent = subj)
                  (theme = obj)))
        (local
            (test (passive = -) (valency = trans))
            (slot (theme = obj))
            (sem-test (agent *reader)))
        (local
            (test (passive = +))
            (slot (agent = obl-agent)
                  (theme = subj))
            (sem-test (focus theme)))
        (local
            (test (passive = +))
            (slot (theme = subj))
            (sem-test (focus theme)
                      (agent unknown))))
        (class all-verb-map)))
```

Next, a rule to accommodate all verbs is summoned. Here, '`*predefined slot*`' is an indicator that calls for the use of an embedded mapping rule. The embedded-head mapping rules for `adv-comp` and `adv-conj` will name the slots they fill.

```
(all-verb-map
    (mapping (local
                (slot
                    (mood == mood)
                    (*predefined-slot* === adv-conj)
                    (*predefined-slot* === adv-comp)
                    (ability == ability)
                    (possibility == possibility)
                    (negation == negation)
                    (message-type == info-attn-getr)
                    (tense == tense)
                    (effect-of = (ppadjunct (prep = by)))
```

```
                              .
                              .
                              .
                          (location = (ppadjunct (prep = in)))
                          (location = (ppadjunct (prep = on)))
                          (location = (ppadjunct (prep = next to)))
                          (location = (ppadjunct (prep = out of)))
                          (frequency = (ppadjunct (prep = from)))
                          (perfective == perfective); have -ed
                          (progressive == progressive); be -ing
                          (*predefined-slot* = advadjunct)
                          (passive == passive)
                          (number-bullet === number-bullet)
                          (clause-response === response)
                          (clausal-link === sadjunct)
                          (necessity == necessity))
                     (sem-test (clausal-mark +)))))
```

A segment of the sentence's analysis is as follows. (The parse appears in full in appendix A, where it is annotated.) The segment illustrates the nested list representation of the semantics and syntax for the input sentence; this list constitutes input to the KBMT-89 augmentor. Recall that the semantic information appears in the sem sublists.

```
((sem
  (*sem*
   ((number-bullet
     (($is-token-of any-number) ($id (*id* 15))
      ($map-data (*map* { map-str (any-number-map) } ))
      (cardinality 1)))
    (clausal-mark +) (mood imperative) (tense present)
    (source
     ((reference definite) (number singular)
      ($map-data (*map* { map-str diskette drive } ))
      ($is-token-of diskette-drive) ($id (*id* 41))))
    (theme
     ((reference definite) (number singular)
      ($map-data (*map* { map-str tape } ))
      ($is-token-of sticky-tape) ($id (*id* 20))))
    (agent *reader) ($map-data (*map* { map-str remove } ))
    ($is-token-of remove) ($id (*id* 19)))))
  (number-bullet
   ((root 1) (value 1)
    (sem
     (*sem*
      (($is-token-of any-number) ($id (*id* 15))
       ($map-data (*map* { map-str (any-number-map) } ))
       (cardinality 1)))))))
```

```
(obj
  ((case acc)
   (sem
    (*sem*
      ((reference definite) (number singular)
       ($map-data (*map* { map-str tape } ))
       ($is-token-of sticky-tape) ($id (*id* 20)))))
   (ref definite) (det ((root the) (ref definite))) (root tape)
   (count no) (person 3) (number singular) (meas-unit no)
   (proper no)))
 (valency trans) (mood imperative) (tense present) (form inf)
 (ppadjunct
  ((prep from)
   (sem
    (*sem*
      ((reference definite) (number singular)
       ($map-data (*map* { map-str diskette drive } ))
       ($is-token-of diskette-drive) ($id (*id* 41)))))
   (ref definite) (det ((root the) (ref definite)))
   (root diskette_drive) (person 3) (number singular) (count yes)
   (proper no) (meas-unit no)))
 (root remove) (comp-type no) (passive -))


semantic candidate 1 of 1
[*remove
   (agent *reader)
   (theme [*sticky-tape
           (number singular)
           (reference definite)])
   (source [*diskette-drive
           (number singular)
           (reference definite)])
   (tense present)
   (mood imperative)
   (clausal-mark +)
   (number-bullet [*any-number (cardinality 1)])])]
```

Note that the string that precedes the final segment of the parse ('semantic ambiguity 1 of 1') should be understood to mean that there is only one reading—in other words, that there are no ambiguities.

Now we can display and comment on the example of a somewhat more complicated sentence: *1. Get the diagnostics diskette from the back of this manual.* The example is intended to illustrate how KBMT-89's semantic restrictions constrain the number of legitimate parses, yielding only the intended ones.

Observe in the following that the parser first tries to attach `diagnostics` to `get` as its `object`. The English verb *get* maps into two concepts: `*receive` and `*appear`. (The reason for this latter mapping is that for a sentence such as *You can get lower-case characters* ..., it was decided that *get* is best understood as meaning "cause to appear." This simplified the acquisition of the concept lexicon.) The noun *diagnostics* maps into one concept, namely, `*diagnose`. The structural mapping rule for *get* states that when the verb is in the active voice (which it is here), the syntactic object should occupy the `theme` slot of the concept into which the verb maps.

The first test shows the result of trying to attach `*diagnose` to `*receive` as its `object`. The test fails because the filler of the `theme` slot of the concept `*receive` must be an `*object`. However `*diagnose` is not an `*object` but, rather, an `*event`. The second test shows the result of trying to attach `*diagnose` to `appear`. It fails for the same reasons: `*diagnose` is not a `*display-object`. Note that even if the semantic restrictions were not violated, this part of the parse would have failed for syntactic reasons. As soon as the next word, *diskette*, is parsed, it develops that *diagnostics* is in fact not the object but only a part of it; the object is the noun phrase *diagnostics diskette*.

```
sem check new filler called with
RECEIVE THEME DIAGNOSE
semantic restriction should fail because of
  SIMPLE-SEMANTIC-RESTRICTION-FAILURE
semantic restriction:
  (OBJECT)
ok to attach [NO]

sem check new filler called with
APPEAR THEME DIAGNOSE
semantic restriction should fail because of
  SIMPLE-SEMANTIC-RESTRICTION-FAILURE
semantic restriction:
  (DISPLAY-OBJECT)
ok to attach [NO]
```

The third semantic test shows the result of trying to attach the concept `*diagnose` (into which the noun *diskette* maps) to the concept `*diskette`. The relevant structural mapping rule is (`*predefined-slot*` = `pre-nom-noun`). This is a general rule that applies to all (head) nouns. Each noun that occupies the syntactic pre-nominal-noun position has an embedded lexical rule that maps it into its appropriate concept. The embedded lexical rule contains a restriction that specifies which slot this concept has to fill in the concept into which the head noun maps. In this case the pre-nom-noun is *diagnostics*, and the head noun is *diskette*.

Now, the noun *diagnostics* has an embedded lexical mapping rule that maps it into the concept `*diagnose`, filling the `%purpose` slot: (`"diagnostics"` (cat N) (`%purpose *diagnose`)). This simply means that the concept *diagnose may be the filler of the purpose slot in any concept that has this slot. So in this case, because the concept *diskette has a purpose slot and *diagnose is a legitimate filler of the slot, the test succeeds.

```
sem check new filler called with
DISKETTE PURPOSE DIAGNOSE
ok to attach [YES]
```

The fourth test shows the result of trying to attach the concept *diskette to the concept *receive. This test succeeds since *diskette is an *object —the restriction on the filler of the theme slot in the concept *receive).

```
sem check new filler called with
RECEIVE THEME DISKETTE
ok to attach [YES]
```

The fifth test fails because the filler of the theme slot of the concept *appear must be a *display-object. But *diskette is not a *display-object.

```
sem check new filler called with
APPEAR THEME DISKETTE
semantic restriction should fail because of
  SIMPLE-SEMANTIC-RESTRICTION-FAILURE
semantic restriction:
   (DISPLAY-OBJECT)
ok to attach [NO]

sem check new filler called with
RECEIVE FREQUENCY BACK-OF-3D
semantic restriction should fail because of
  SIMPLE-SEMANTIC-RESTRICTION-FAILURE
semantic restriction:
   (LITERAL-ITERATION)
ok to attach [NO]

sem check new filler called with
BACK-OF-3D PART-OF MANUAL
ok to attach [YES]
```

Finally, the parser produces the correct output.

.
.
.

```
[*receive
  (agent *reader)
  (theme [*diskette
          (number singular)
          (purpose [*diagnose
                     (number singular)])
          (reference definite)])
  (source [*back-of-3d
            (number singular)
            (reference definite)
            (part-of [*manual
                       (number singular)
                       (reference definite)
                       (near +)])])])
  (tense present)
  (mood imperative)
  (clausal-mark +)
  (number-bullet [*any-number (cardinality 1)])])]
```

This output then constitutes part of the input to the augmentor. The structure and function of KBMT-89's augmentor are the subjects of the next chapter.

Chapter 8

Automatic and Interactive Augmentation

■ RALF D. BROWN

8.1 Motivation and Design

Computational efficiency drives and motivates the process of semantic interpretation in KBMT-89. If semantic constraints were absent or applied after syntactic processing, the system would have to cope with a great number of candidate syntactic parses for certain input sentences; indeed, syntactic ambiguities can number in the tens of thousands. It is therefore crucial to reduce the number of ambiguities early in the parsing process. This requirement motivated, at least in part, the design of the universal parser used in KBMT-89.

The approach further affects the generality of semantic interpretation. It is, for instance, necessary to retain in the analyzer's output the constituent structure that parallels the syntactic result. For the English sentence *Start the test*, the desired ILT output would reflect an instantiation of the event concept of *test* as the head of the proposition, with the implied concept of "reader" as its agent; the meaning of aspect.phase = begin would be attached to the proposition to represent the meaning of *start*. However, the semantic interpreter in KBMT-89 is constrained to produce the structure in which *start* is the head, because it corresponds to the head of the syntactic representation. So, if the desired output must conform to the

189

ILT format, an additional transformation must be performed on the analyzer output. This calls for a separate architectural component.

The analyzer architecture was designed so that no intersentential context is taken into account. This means that special techniques have to be developed to treat anaphora and other intersentential phenomena. A separate component of the system needed to be designed and implemented to support this functionality in order to avoid a reimplementation of the parsing module and a major complication of the testing and debugging process. For example, a phenomenon that occurs with regularity in translations from Japanese into English is ellipsis. In Japanese, subjects of sentences are often elided and require reconstruction. This process uses contextual (previous discourse) and world (domain model) knowledge to include the information missing from the source language text into the interlingua text and, through it, into the target language text.

There is no guarantee that the analyzer will produce a single structure as output. The original sentence might be genuinely ambiguous, in which case it is appropriate for the analyzer to produce representations of all the input's meanings. Another reason for producing more than a single output is that there might be errors or omissions in the knowledge base.

To solve these and related problems, KBMT-89 introduced the augmentor component. Its goal is to output a single ILT that represents the appropriate meaning of the source language text. The augmentor will therefore include preference rules for choosing among genuinely ambiguous candidate ILTs.[1]

The augmentor thus functions as a bridge between parsing and generation. As its name indicates, it augments the parser's output before passing the output on to the generator. Augmentation, as noted above, consists in adding any missing values that could not be determined from the input sentence and removing any ambiguities that the parser could not eliminate. While the augmentor is an integral part of the KBMT-89 system, it is nevertheless general enough to operate with any parser whose output can be transformed into compatible data structures and with any generation system that can accept interlingua texts in the format used by the KBMT-89 generators. This modular construction allows the system to be used as a natural language interface simply by replacing the target language generator with a module to translate an interlingua text into the language of the underlying system.

The augmentor has three main components: a format converter, an automatic augmentation module and an interactive augmentation module. A representation

---

[1]The system does not treat cases in which no candidate meanings are produced. It is assumed that this reflects incompleteness of ontological, grammatical or lexical knowledge.

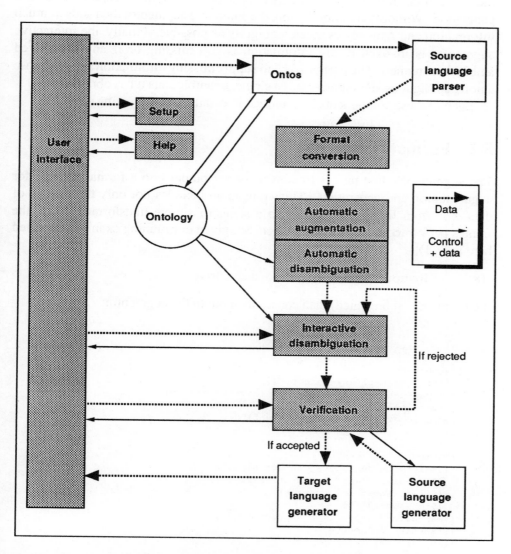

Figure 8.1: **Representation of the augmentor architecture. Augmentor components are shaded.**

of the augmentor architecture appears as figure 8.1. The format converter changes the data format from that produced by the parser to that used in augmentation and generation. Without user intervention, the automatic augmentor then adds as much information and removes as much ambiguity as possible. Finally, the interactive augmentor is invoked if any information is still missing or if any unresolved ambiguities remain. The user is asked to supply missing information and to choose among ambiguous alternatives until a single, unambiguous ILT is obtained.

Each of these components is examined in detail in the following sections.

8.2   Format Conversion

The augmentor's first task is to convert parser output into a format suitable for augmentation and generation. This conversion includes not only the change of data type from list to frame but also a series of simple transformations on the frames performed by a pattern matcher. So, given our running example, repeated here as (8.1),

(8.1)   Remove the tape from the diskette drive.

the following (abbreviated) data constitute input to the augmentor:

```
(((sem
   (*sem*
    ((number-bullet
      (($is-token-of any-number) ($id (*id* 1))
       ($map-data (*map* { map-str (any-number-map) } ))
       (cardinality 1)))
     (mood imperative) (tense present)
     ...

     (theme
      ((reference definite) (number singular)
       ($map-data (*map* { map-str tape } ))
       ($is-token-of sticky-tape)
       ($id (*id* 7))))
     ($map-data (*map* { map-str remove } ))
     ($is-token-of remove)
     ($id (*id* 5)))))
    ...

   (ppadjunct
    ((sem
      (*sem*
       ((reference definite) (number singular)
        ($map-data (*map* { map-str diskette drive } ))
        ($is-token-of diskette-drive) ($id (*id* 38)))))))
```

```
    (prep from) (dual nil) (near nil) (specific nil)
    (ref definite) (det ((root the) (ref definite)))
    (root diskette_drive) (person 3) (number singular)
    (count yes) (proper no) (meas-unit no)))
 (root remove) (comp-type no) (passive -)))
```

The generator expects an ILT in the form of a set of linked FRAMEKIT frames (Nyberg 1988) stored in a file as a list of make-frame commands. The set consists of one or more clauses, each with a proposition, a speech act and, possibly, other components. Propositions are further subdivided into roles and an aspect. First, the interlingua is given in Backus-Naur Form:

```
ILT    ::= (<target> <frame> <frame> ...)
target ::= E | J
frame  ::= (make-frame <name> (<slot1> <value>)
                               (<slot2> <value>)
                               ...)
value  ::= (value (common <filler>))
```

FRAMEKIT allows multiple views of the facets that are contained in a frame's slots. These views may be understood to constitute potentially conflicting world models. They are implemented as tagged lists within the facet. So,

```
(value (common 5)
       (alternate five))
```

is a value facet whose filler is 5 under the common view and five under the alternate view. Because only the common view is used in the augmentor, fillers will be placed directly within their facets in much of the following discussion. This approach should increase the clarity of the examples.

The augmentor output is given below in the format expected by the generator. The target language is English (E) and the ILT consists of a clause frame with three subframes, the last of which has three subframes representing the proposition's aspect and roles.

```
(e
(make-frame clause5393 (number-bullet (value (common role5391)))
            (ilt-type (value (common clause)))
            (speechactid (value (common speech-act5392)))
            (propositionid (value (common proposition5388)))
            (clauseid (value (common clause5393)))
            (frame-maker (value (common augmentor))))
```

```
(make-frame role5391 (reference (value (common definite)))
              (ilt-type (value (common role)))
              (roleid (value (common role5391)))
              (propositionid (value (common proposition5388)))
              (clauseid (value (common clause5393)))
              (cardinality (value (common 1)))
              (is-token-of (value (common *any-number)))
              (frame-maker (value (common augmentor))))
(make-frame speech-act5392 (time (value (common time5527)))
              (passive (value (common -))) (space)
              (direct? (value (common yes)))
              (speech-act (value (common request-action)))
              (ilt-type (value (common speech-act)))
              (speechactid (value (common speech-act5392)))
              (frame-maker (value (common augmentor))))
(make-frame proposition5388 (time (value (common (at time5527))))
              (agent (value (common agent5463)))
              (propositionid (value (common proposition5388)))
              (aspect (value (common aspect5394)))
              (ilt-type (value (common proposition)))
              (clauseid (value (common clause5393)))
              (source (value (common role5390)))
              (theme (value (common role5389)))
              (is-token-of (value (common *remove)))
              (frame-maker (value (common augmentor))))
(make-frame agent5463 (reference (value (common definite)))
              (ilt-type (value (common role)))
              (roleid (value (common agent5463)))
              (is-token-of (value (common *reader)))
              (clauseid (value (common clause5393)))
              (roleid (value (common role5459)))
              (propositionid (value (common proposition5388)))
              (frame-maker (value (common augmentor))))
(make-frame aspect5394
              (propositionid (value (common proposition5388)))
              (clauseid (value (common clause5393)))
              (ilt-type (value (common aspect)))
              (frame-maker (value (common augmentor))))
(make-frame role5390 (ilt-type (value (common role)))
              (roleid (value (common role5390)))
              (propositionid (value (common proposition5388)))
              (clauseid (value (common clause5393)))
              (dual (value (common nil)))
              (near (value (common nil)))
              (specific (value (common nil)))
              (reference (value (common definite)))
              (is-token-of (value (common *diskette-drive)))
              (frame-maker (value (common augmentor))))
(make-frame role5389 (ilt-type (value (common role)))
              (roleid (value (common role5389)))
              (propositionid (value (common proposition5388)))
              (clauseid (value (common clause5393)))
              (dual (value (common nil)))
              (near (value (common nil)))
```

```
(specific (value (common nil)))
(reference (value (common definite)))
(is-token-of (value (common *sticky-tape)))
(frame-maker (value (common augmentor))))))
```

8.2.1   Conversions

The first phase in converting parser output into interlingua text sees the extraction of the semantic parts of the output, along with several syntactic features. Next, the frames corresponding to each of the components of the resulting nested list structure are created, producing the "bare" ILTs containing only that information appearing directly in the parser output. Once the frame hierarchy has been constructed, a variety of simple transformations are performed. These transformations include moving slots from one frame to another, mapping combinations of slot values into other slots or values, mapping plurals into sets of objects, and promoting some subframes into separate clauses. After these transformations are complete, the result is passed to the automatic augmentation unit. The bare ILT is as follows (using an abbreviated notation for clarity):[2]

```
[clause1377
    (speechactid
        [speech-act1375
            (time time1376)
            (space)
            (direct?)
            (speech-act)])
    (propositionid
        [*remove
            (number-bullet
                [*any-number
                    (cardinality 1)])
            (mood imperative)
            (tense present)
            (source
                [*diskette-drive
                    (reference definite)
                    (number singular)])
            (theme
                [*sticky-tape
                    (reference definite)
                    (number singular)])
            (agent *reader)])]
```

---

[2]The numerals appended to frame names are generated sequentially to ensure that the names are unique.

Observe that a "place-holding" speech-act frame, empty except for the time stamp, has been added at the beginning of the bare ILT. The frame contains a "time stamp" for the time of the utterance. The time of the proposition will be set relative to this time stamp.

Some information is not where the generator expects it to be after the straightforward conversion from f-structure to linked frames has been performed. The first transformation thus adds values to the proper frames and removes them from the frames in which the parser placed them. The second transformation maps combinations of slot values into other slots or values. Both of these transformations are performed by a pattern matcher, which compares the values of specified slots and adds new slots and values when a match is found. The matched slots are optionally deleted before the new values are added. So, for instance, the second transformation replaces the `tense` slot with a `time` slot and gives a time relative to that in the speech-act frame's `time` slot.

The parser does not represent all plurals in the same way, so it is necessary to transform some into the set notation expected by the generator. The transformation consists of removing the `number` slot and creating a set whose member type is the object with the plural number and whose cardinality is greater than 1. This transformation is also accomplished with the pattern matcher. It uses the option to recursively apply the pattern starting at each frame in the ILT, rather than starting only at the topmost clause frame.

Certain slots indicate links between the constituent clauses of a sentence. Because the parser outputs a single embedded structure, the values of those slots will appear as subframes in the hierarchy generated by the initial conversion to linked frames. Thus, the final, simple transformation promotes the subframes to clauses, with their own speech acts and aspects. This transformation is accomplished first by scanning each frame of the ILT. Next, each subframe pointed to by a special slot is promoted to a proposition frame with a newly created clause frame, speech-act frame and aspect frame. The link is then changed from the subframe (which is now a proposition) to the newly created clause frame. A discourse cohesion marker is then added to the main and the new clause frames. The process of flattening subframes into separate clauses is shown in the following example (abbreviated for clarity). The subframes

```
(make-frame role1
            (clauseid (value (common clause1)))
            (ilt-type (value (common role)))
            (roleid (value (common role1)))
            (clausal-link (value (common role2)))
              ;; other slots
```

```
)
(make-frame role2
            (clauseid (value (common clause1)))
            (ilt-type (value (common role)))
            (roleid (value (common role2)))
                ;; other slots
)
```

are transformed into the following by creating a new clause frame and an associated speech-act frame.

```
(make-frame role1
            (clauseid (value (common clause1)))
            (ilt-type (value (common role)))
            (roleid (value (common role1)))
            (clausal-link (value (common clause2)))
                ;; other slots
)
(make-frame clause2
            (clauseid (value (common clause2)))
            (ilt-type (value (common clause)))
            (propositionid (value (common role2)))
            (speechactid (value (common speech-act2)))
                ;; other slots
)
(make-frame role2
            (clauseid (value (common clause2)))
            (ilt-type (value (common proposition)))
                ;; other slots
)
(make-frame speech-act2
            (clauseid (value (common clause2)))
            (ilt-type (value (common speech-act)))
                ;; other slots
)
```

The link from role1 to role2 has been redirected to the new clause frame clause2, which has role2 as its proposition and the new speech-act frame, speech-act2, in its speechactid slot. After all of the above transformations, our previous bare ILT now looks like this:

```
[clause1377
    ($sentence$ sentence 11:  1. Remove the tape from the diskette drive.)
    (main-clause yes)
    (number-bullet
        [*any-number
            (reference definite)
            (cardinality 1)])
```

```
(speechactid
    [speech-act1375
        (time time1376)
        (space)
        (direct? yes)
        (speech-act request-action)])
(propositionid
    [*remove
        (time (at time1376))
        (agent
            [*reader
                (reference definite)])
        (source
            [*diskette-drive
                (reference definite)])
        (theme
            [*sticky-tape
                (reference definite)])])])]
```

8.2.2   Implementing the Conversions

The parse is received in a nested list format. The semantic information that is extracted is also a list of nested lists that must be converted to a set of linked FRAMEKIT frames. This is called *list-to-frame conversion*. The component lists represent either slots or frames, depending on the nesting level. If the component represents a frame, then all of its elements must be lists representing the frame's slots, one of which is of the form ($is-token-of parent) and specifies the inheritance link to be used. However, if the list also contains a sublist of the form ($is-not-a-frame t), then the entire list represents a value rather than a frame.

If the component represents a slot, then the first element is the slot's name and the remaining elements are either fillers (if not lists) or subframes (if lists). The one exception to this rule is the *multiple* filler, which is in the form of a list. Each of the elements in the remainder of the *multiple* list is treated as if it had appeared directly in the component, rather than nested one level deeper.

The conversion proceeds recursively. Given the semantic section of the parse, a frame is created that inherits (through the is-token-of link) from the frame named by the $is-token-of element of the list. For each remaining element, if it is a list, the slot named by the first element of the sublist is created and filled with the remaining values of the sublist. If any of the elements of the sublist is itself a list, the conversion is called recursively, and the filler placed in the slot is the name of the frame created by the recursive call.

Let us examine the following fragment of the semantic information from the

F-structure at the beginning of this section.

```
(($id (*id* 5))
 ($is-token-of remove)
 ($map-data (*map* { map-str remove }))
 (number-bullet (($is-token-of any-number)
                 ($id (*id* 1))
                 ($map-data (*map* { map-str (any-number-map)}))
                 (cardinality 1))))
```

The first step in converting the preceding into a set of FRAMEKIT frames is to apply a minor simplification, which allows the second step to be considerably simpler. To do this, the item contained in a list of the form (`$is-token-of x`) is made to be the first element of the list containing such a list, and values in sublists inside (`$id x`) and (`$map-data x`) lists are promoted to be elements of the latter lists. Applying this simplification, we get

```
(remove ($id 5)
        ($map-data remove)
        (number-bullet (any-number
                        ($id 1)
                        ($map-data (any-number-map))
                        (cardinality 1))))
```

Next, we create a proposition frame that contains an `is-token-of` link to the concept specified by the first element of the list, `remove`:

```
(make-frame proposition1
        (frame-maker (value augmentor))
        (is-token-of (value remove)))
```

For each remaining element of the list, we create a slot and fill it with the given values, unless they are lists. Thus, after processing the next two elements, we have

```
(make-frame proposition1
        (frame-maker (value augmentor))
        (is-token-of (value remove))
        ($id (value 5))
        ($map-data (value remove)))
```

For the final element of the list, the filler is itself a list, so we recursively build another frame, this time a role frame.

```
(make-frame role2
       (frame-maker (value augmentor))
       ($id (value 1))
       ($map-data (value any-number-map)))
       (cardinality (value 1)))
```

role2 now becomes the filler of the number-bullet slot for proposition1, resulting in the following set of frames.

```
(make-frame proposition1
       (frame-maker (value augmentor))
       (is-token-of (value remove))
       ($id (value 5))
       ($map-data (value remove))
       (number-bullet (value role2)))
(make-frame role2
       (frame-maker (value augmentor))
       ($id (value 1))
       ($map-data (value any-number-map)))
       (cardinality (value 1)))
```

To make an ILT, we now add a clause frame and speech-act frame and identify each frame with an ilt-type slot and appropriate clauseid, roleid and propositionid slots.

```
(make-frame clause4
       (frame-maker (value augmentor))
       (clauseid (value clause4))
       (speechactid (value speech-act3)))
       (propositionid (value proposition1))
       (ilt-type (value clause)))
(make-frame speech-act3
       (frame-maker (value augmentor))
       (clauseid (value clause4))
       (ilt-type (value speechact))
           ;; The rest of this frame will be created by the
           ;;  pattern matcher and in subsequent processing.
)
(make-frame proposition1
       (frame-maker (value augmentor))
       (is-token-of (value remove))
       ($id (value 5))
       ($map-data (value remove))
       (number-bullet (value role2))
       (clauseid (value clause4))
       (propositionid (value proposition1))
       (ilt-type (value proposition)))
```

```
(make-frame role2
        (frame-maker (value augmentor))
        ($id (value 1))
        ($map-data (value any-number-map)))
        (cardinality (value 1))
        (clauseid (value clause4))
        (propositionid (value proposition1))
        (roleid (value role2))
        (ilt-type (value role)))
```

This ILT is then submitted for automatic and interactive augmentation and, if necessary, disambiguation.

Now the *pattern matcher* operates on an interlingua text by applying a list of transformations to the ILT frames. Each transformation consists of a (possibly empty) pattern that is to be matched and a (possibly empty) replacement specification. The pattern and replacement are separated by a token that indicates whether to remove the matched slots of the pattern after the replacement specification has been executed.

The pattern to match consists of an optional '*', indicating a global matching, followed by zero or more slot matches. If a global matching is used, the following slot matches and replacement are applied to each frame in the interlingua text, not just to the topmost clause frame. A slot match may have one of five forms:

- `(path-spec slot-value)`

- `(= path-spec slot-value)`

- `(!= path-spec slot-value)`

- `(! path-spec)`

- `(gensym root-symbol)`

Here, `path-spec` specifies the frame and slot to test; `slot-value` is the value the slot must have; an equal sign indicates that the value must be present directly in the specified frame and not inherited; a '!=' indicates that the value of the slot must differ from the given value; and an exclamation point means that the slot must be missing from the ILT frame being tested. The fifth form creates a new symbol using `root-symbol` as the root of the symbol's name and binds it to the match variable `root-symbol`.

Match variables are created whenever the `slot-value` is of the form `(var <variable>)` or the form `gensym`. The first appearance of a variable causes it to be bound to the value of the slot; on subsequent appearances, the value of the slot must be the same as the value to which the variable has been bound. The match variable ilt is predefined and indicates the frame on which the match is being performed.

The path-spec lists the path through which the desired frame and slot may be reached. It is a list in which each element but the last specifies a link to traverse to reach the next frame. The last element is the desired slot within the final frame. For example, the path specification (propositionid aspect phase) means "get the value of the propositionid slot in the current frame and make that the new frame. From this new frame, get the value of the aspect slot, and make that the frame being considered." The desired value is then the value of the phase slot in that frame. The slot match ((propositionid aspect phase) end) means that the value of the phase slot must be end.

The replacement specification consists of zero or more replacements, which may take any of three forms:

- (path-spec new-value)

- (remove path-spec path-spec ...)

- (eval lisp-code)

The first form adds one or more new values to the specified frame and slot, creating any intermediate frames that do not exist. Before adding the new values, any components of the form (var <variable>) are replaced by the value to which the variable is bound or by nil if there is no binding for the variable. Unlike the variable binding and substitution for slot matches, the variables may be nested inside other lists. Thus, if the variable foo is bound to 3, the replacement

```
((contents) (boxes (number (var foo))))
```

will add (boxes (number 3)) to the contents slot of the current frame.

The second form stipulates that the slots specified by path-specs be erased. A frame is never implicitly erased, even if its last slot has been erased. The slotname '*' may be used to request explicitly that a frame and all its slots be erased, rather than just a specific slot.

The final of the three forms allows arbitrary LISP code to be executed. As in the first form, variable substitutions are performed on the code before executing it.

Once conversions are fully debugged, they may be recoded as handwritten LISP code to reduce execution time. Unlike handwritten code, the pattern matcher must always support the most general possibilities. It also performs duplicate work in many cases. For instance, it will repeatedly follow the same path if multiple patterns in the conversion begin with the same path prefix.

8.2.2.1 Sample Conversion

It is worth illustrating format conversion with an extended example. Four conversion patterns are illustrated. In the first, the `number-bullet` slot is moved from the proposition frame to the clause frame:

```
(((propositionid number-bullet) (var num))
 ==>
 ((number-bullet) (var num)))
```

Second, a time value is created for the speech act frame:

```
((gensym time)
 -->
 ((speechactid time) (var time)))
```

Next, all past tenses are turned into a time relation specifying that the action took place before the speech act:

```
(*
 ((tense) past)
 ((clauseid speechactid time) (var time))
 -->
 (remove (tense))
 ((time) (before (var time))))
```

Finally, some unconditional additions are required to fill in values not handled elsewhere:

```
(
 -->
 ((speechactid speaker) author)
 ((speechactid hearer) reader))
```

We now apply each conversion in turn to the following ILT (abbreviated by removing housekeeping slots not needed in this example):

```
(make-frame clause5
        (clauseid (value clause5))
        (speechactid (value speech-act4))
        (propositionid (value proposition1)))
(make-frame speech-act4
        (clauseid (value clause5)))
(make-frame proposition1
        (is-token-of (value remove))
        (number-bullet (value role2))
        (clauseid (value clause5))
        (propositionid (value proposition1))
        (tense (value past))
        (agent (value role3)))
(make-frame role2
        (cardinality (value 1))
        (clauseid (value clause5))
        (propositionid (value proposition1))
        (roleid (value role2)))
(make-frame role3
        (is-token-of (value *reader))
        (clauseid (value clause5))
        (propositionid (value proposition1))
        (roleid (value role3)))
```

Applying the first conversion, we find that there is indeed a number-bullet slot in the frame pointed to by the propositionid slot of clause5. We therefore bind the value role2 to the match variable num. Since all slot matches were successful, we now remove the matched slot (because the conversion uses '==>' instead of '-->') and then add the value of the variable num, which is role2, to the frame clause5. The clause and proposition frames are now as follows:

```
(make-frame clause5
        (clauseid (value clause5))
        (speechactid (value speech-act4))
        (propositionid (value proposition1))
        (number-bullet (value role2)))
(make-frame proposition1
        (is-token-of (value remove))
        (clauseid (value clause5))
        (propositionid (value proposition1))
        (tense (value past))
        (agent (value role3)))
```

Applying the second conversion, we generate a new symbol, time6, and bind it to the match variable time. Since all slot matches were successful, we now add the value to the time slot of the frame speech-act4, which becomes

```
(make-frame speech-act4
        (clauseid (value (clause5))
        (time (value (time6)))
```

For the third conversion, the slot matches will be applied to each frame in the ILT. The first match fails for all but the `proposition1` frame, so we will discuss only that frame. Having succeeded with the first match, the pattern matcher applies the second match to the `proposition1` frame, which also succeeds, binding the value `time6` to the match variable `time`.

Now that all the slot matches have succeeded, the pattern matcher performs the right-hand side of the conversion. Since '`-->`' was used, neither of the matched slots is removed. However, the `tense` slot is removed by the (`remove` (`tense`)) form. Then a `time` slot is added with filler (`before time6`); this is the result of substituting the value of the match variable `time`. The proposition frame emerges as:

```
(make-frame proposition1
        (is-token-of (value remove))
        (clauseid (value clause5))
        (propositionid (value proposition1))
        (agent (value  role3))
        (time (value (before time6))))
```

The fourth and final conversion has no slot matches, so it automatically succeeds. The `speaker` and `hearer` slots are added to the `speech-act4` frame, resulting in the final ILT:

```
(make-frame clause5
        (clauseid (value clause5))
        (speechactid (value speech-act4))
        (propositionid (value proposition1))
        (number-bullet (value role2)))
(make-frame speech-act4
        (clauseid (value clause5))
        (speaker (value author))
        (hearer (value reader))
        (time (value time6)))
(make-frame proposition1
        (is-token-of (value remove))
        (clauseid (value clause5))
        (propositionid (value proposition1))
        (agent (value role3)
        (time (value (before time6))))
```

```
(make-frame role2
        (cardinality (value 1))
        (clauseid (value clause5))
        (propositionid (value proposition1))
        (roleid (value role2)))
(make-frame role3
        (is-token-of (value *reader))
        (clauseid (value clause5))
        (propositionid (value proposition1))
        (roleid (value role3))))
```

8.3   Automatic Augmentation

The augmentor's automatic component has the tasks of filling in all information missing from the interlingua text and of removing any ambiguities the parser has left in that text. The automatic component has a single module, MARS (Multiple Anaphor Resolution Strategies). MARS's function is limited to determining the referents of pronouns and definite noun phrases; remaining augmentation resides in the augmentor's interactive component. Our specifications called for single sentences to be parsed without regard to context; MARS is therefore normally disabled because it requires information about context.

Anaphora is, of course, a common phenomenon in natural language communication, whether it be complex multiparty human discourse, more constrained bilateral human-computer dialogue, or even narrative or expository text. Anaphors typically refer back to other constituents in the same sentence or to constituents in earlier utterances in the discourse. MARS currently deals only with the latter (intersentential anaphora).

8.3.1   Multiple Anaphor Resolution Strategies

MARS performs its resolution based on the integration of multiple knowledge sources: sentential syntax, case-frame semantics, dialogue structure and general world knowledge. The underlying theoretical tenet is this:

T1 *Anaphor resolution is not an autonomous process; it requires access to and integration of all the knowledge sources used for dialogue and text interpretation. These linguistic knowledge sources are brought to bear in the form of constraints or preferences encoded as multiple resolution strategies.*

The knowledge sources MARS uses to resolve intersentential anaphora follow, along with statements of the anaphoric resolution strategies.[3]

Certain anaphors carry constraints (on number, gender, case, etc.) that must be satisfied by the candidate referents. The strategy here is trivial:

T2 *Eliminate from consideration all candidate referents that violate the local constraints of the anaphor in question.*

For example, in (8.2) we may eliminate *John* as the referent of *she* because the name violates the local constraint that the referent be female.

(8.2)   John and Mary went to the movies.
          She paid for the tickets.
          [she = Mary]

Further, case-role semantics imposes constraints on what can fill the case roles. If they are filled by an anaphor (which specifies few if any semantic features), the case-role constraints must also be satisfied by the anaphor's referent. This move eliminates from consideration all candidate referents that violate constraints on the case role occupied by the anaphor. The strategy here is also fairly simple:

T3 *Eliminate from consideration all candidate referents that violate any case constraint imposed on the anaphor in question. In the absence of hard constraints, prefer those candidates that accord with typical case fillers.*

This strategy is illustrated by (8.3).

(8.3)   John took the cake from the table.
          He ate *it*.
          [it = cake]

Here, the referent of *it* must be edible; tables are not, and this eliminates *table* from consideration.

Using knowledge about the world, it is possible to say that a candidate antecedent cannot be the referent of an anaphor because some action occurring between the referent and the anaphor invalidates the inference that they denote one and the same object or event. The strategy is simple, but it requires a fairly large amount of knowledge to be useful for a broad range of cases:

---

[3]A more detailed discussion of these knowledge sources is given in Carbonell and Brown 1988, from which some of the following examples are adapted.

T4 *Eliminate from consideration all candidate referents associated with actions whose postconditions violate the preconditions of the action containing the anaphor.*

Now consider the following example.

(8.4)   John gave Tom an apple.
           He ate the apple.
           [he = Tom]

The assumption that *John* is the referent of *he* violates the precondition on *eat*, namely, that the actor possess the item being eaten, because the postcondition of *give* is that the actor no longer possess the object that was given.

A pervasive form of "linguistic inertia" manifests itself as a preference to assign the referent of an anaphor to the entity in the discourse context that filled the corresponding semantic case role in an earlier utterance. This is a generalized form of case-role parallelism, which has proven crucial in ellipsis resolution (Carbonell 1983b; Carbonell et al. 1985; Carbonell and Hayes 1987), although in anaphora resolution it is demoted from the status of a categorical constraint to that of a preference.[4] The semantic preference strategy can be stated as follows:

T5 *Search first for acceptable referents in the antecedent phrase (or phrases) that occur in the same semantic case role as the anaphor. If a match satisfying all constraints is found, look no further; otherwise, search the other case roles.*

In (8.5), for example, the preferred referent for *it* would be the recipient in a previous utterance, that is, the dog rather than the robot.

---

[4]The preference strategies described here should not be confused with Preference Semantics (Wilks 1975; Fass 1988), as they are distinct and quite different. Some of the major differences are:

1. MARS includes syntactic preference strategies as well as semantic preferences. In addition, preferences such as intersentential recency may be considered to operate at the text level, rather than being syntactic or semantic.

2. Lexical disambiguation is not a goal in itself but a (highly useful) by-product of attempts to match pronominal anaphors and definite noun phrases against candidate antecedents. The analyzer is expected to perform the bulk of the lexical disambiguation.

3. Separate preference strategies are used for various feature sets rather than a monolithic "semantic formula." This allows independent weighting of the various preferences.

(8.5)   a. The robot gave the dog a bone.
            John also gave *it* some water.
            [it = dog]

       b. The robot gave the dog a bone.
            It also gave John some water.
            [it = robot]

To consider more evidence in support of semantic case role persistence, note the following example, with three possible referents to the anaphor *him*. It is clear that *Peter* is the preferred referent, once again because of the persistence of the underlying semantic recipient case.

(8.6)   John carried the box of papers from Bill to Peter.
            He also sent *him* Mary's books.
            [he = John; him = Peter]

Topicalized structures should be searched first for possible anaphoric referents. The topicalization strategy may be stated as follows:

T6 *First search a syntactically topicalized part of the candidate antecedent clause (or clauses) for the referent of the anaphor. If an acceptable referent is found, search no further; otherwise search the rest of the clause(s).*

Consider the cleft constructions in (8.7).

(8.7)   a. It was Mary who told Jane to go to New York.
            Why did *she* do *it*?
            [she = Mary]

       b. It was Jane who went to New York at Mary's bidding.
            Why did *she* do *it*?
            [she = Jane]

Here, the topicalized person becomes the referent of the anaphor *she*, even though the underlying action is essentially the same in both cases. Observe that this is merely a preference: If 'Jane' were replaced by 'Peter' in (8.7), both instances of 'she' would follow gender constraints and refer to Mary.

When the previous context contains many sentences, one must consider the fact that anaphoric references become less common as distance from the referent increases. Hence, one should select the most recent of otherwise equivalent candidates as the referent of the anaphor. The most straightforward method for preferring more recent candidates is to give this preference a full weight for those candidate referents closest to the anaphor and ever-decreasing partial (even negative) weights for increasingly distant candidates.

8.3.2   Integrating the Strategies

To apply a set of diverse strategies, such as those presented above, one needs to make a distinction between constraints (which cannot be violated) and preferences (which discriminate among candidates satisfying all constraints). The resolution method employed by MARS works by applying the constraints first, thus reducing the number of candidate referents for the anaphor in question.[5] The preferences are then applied to each of the remaining candidates. If more than one preference applies, and each suggests different candidate referents for the anaphor in question, all of which have passed the constraint tests, then the anaphor is considered to have a truly ambiguous referent. Thus, when faced with conflicting knowledge sources of nearly equal strength, MARS simply reduces the space of possible anaphoric referents to those that are accepted by constraints and indicated as most desired by one or more preferences.

Because the strategies are independent of each other, they may be applied in any order. Thus, a fully parallel application of the strategies is possible. Depending on the number of processors available, one can either apply all strategies to a candidate in parallel, one strategy to all candidates at once, or all strategies to all candidates in parallel.

A slight modification of the above method enables the resolution of partially specified, definite noun phrases with an antecedent noun phrase. To do this, the head nouns and the remaining slots in the noun phrase are evaluated, in conjunction with other local constraints, for agreement with the candidate referent. The head noun of the candidate must be the same as, or an instance of, the head noun of the reference. For the remaining slots, it suffices if corresponding slots are unifiable with each other or are missing from either the definite noun phrase or the candidate referent. It is not considered an error if there are no candidates that pass all constraints; therefore, it is distinguished from the case that obtains with anaphors, which must have a suitable referent.

---

[5]In a parallel implementation, candidates violating constraints would merely be flagged as invalid and left for removal at the end of the resolution process.

8.3.3 Implementing the Resolution Strategy

MARS, the anaphor resolver, uses the techniques outlined above: local constraints, case-role semantic constraints, pre- and postcondition constraints, case-role persistence, intersentential recency preference and syntactic topicalization preference. The anaphor resolver operates on the set of instantiated semantic case frames provided by the format converter; it attempts to resolve pronouns and definite noun phrases in the parse of the newest sentence using earlier parses as contextual grounds to mine for candidate referents.

Candidate referents are derived by extracting noun phrases from the most recent previous sentences. The number of sentences examined may be changed, allowing the future addition of discourse phenomena to restrict further the sentences that are examined for candidate referents.

The preferences use a voting method to determine which candidate referent is most preferred. Each preference strategy is given an individual weight and may vote with less than its full weight for less-preferred candidates, such as case-role persistence in a referent several sentences removed from the anaphor.

In addition to ruling out candidates, the case-role and local anaphor constraints may also cast votes for those allowable candidates most closely matched to the anaphor or corresponding to typical fillers. In effect, these strategies indicate a preference in the absence of hard constraints. For example, the gender constraint would prefer a candidate reference of female gender over one of indeterminate gender when resolving an anaphor of female gender, while at the same time eliminating all candidates of male gender.

After applying the preferences, the most desired candidate referent is unified with the reference to restrict the range of possible values as much as possible. For instance, if *she* is determined to refer to *doctor*, all future anaphoric references to the doctor will be required to have female or unknown gender. If, however, multiple candidates have received nearly the same number of votes, the anaphor is considered to be ambiguous.

8.4 Interactive Disambiguation

In its final phase, the augmentor provides for interactive disambiguation of the set of ILTs produced by format conversion and automatic disambiguation. The objective here is to reduce the set of ILTs to a single, unambiguous interlingua text representing the original sentence.

The disambiguation system requires an interactive component, because it will

not always be possible for the automatic part to reduce a sentence to a single parse.[6]
The augmentor must therefore ask the user to make a choice among the alternatives
that it is unable to choose among. Users should be questioned as nontechnically
as possible; then they need not be linguists to use the system. We have designed a
series of menus asking the user to select among alternatives, using (by default, but
user-configurable) the source language to display those alternatives.[7]

8.4.1   Starting Up

When the augmentor is first loaded , the user is asked a series of questions about
configuration. First, the other components of the KBMT-89 system may be started
up from the workstation running the augmentor by specifying the component name
and the name of the machine on which it is to be executed.

Next, the location of the ontology to be used by the augmentor is specified.
Normally, a preconfigured default ontology is used, but this may be overridden (to
use an experimental version, for example).

The remaining questions affect the actual operation of the augmentor. They
include

- Which language will be used by the user interface;

- What the source and target languages will be;

- Whether to use the parser or read previously produced parse files;

- Whether to use the target-language generator or produce ILT files;

- What the name of the corpus is containing the sentences used for previously
  produced parse files;

- Whether to generate paraphrases;

- Whether to use MARS; and

- How detailed to make the execution trace in the trace window.

---

[6]There are two reasons for this: incompleteness in the grammars, the lexicons or the domain
model; and genuine ambiguity that can remain when no intersentential context is available.

[7]Providing support for additional languages is merely a matter of adding the appropriate messages
to a table, because a table lookup is applied to all messages before they are displayed.

8.4.2 The User Interface

The augmentor's screen has two principal sections—the input/output panel and the augmentor query area. (A sample screen is given as figure 8.4 in the sequence of screen displays below.) The input/output panel consists of three fields in the bottom half of the screen. In the topmost field, the user enters a sentence. A reverse-video line between the top and center fields serves as a status line, indicating the system's progress through a translation or giving reminders of the action the user is expected to take. The center field is used to ask the user (possibly after a session of interactive disambiguation) to verify that a source-language paraphrase of the original sentence conveys the intended meaning. The bottom field will then display the translation of the original sentence.

To the right of the input/output panel, the main menu allows the user to perform a variety of operations:

- Invoke help;

- Set the system's operating parameters;

- Choose whether or not a confirming paraphrase is generated;

- Reset the anaphor resolver so that prior context is discarded;

- Read source text from a file;

- Process all parses stored in a directory;

- View a graphical representation of the ILT;

- Consult the ontology via the Ontos knowledge acquisition tool;

- Evaluate an arbitrary LISP expression; or

- Exit the KBMT-89 system.

Unlike the input/output panel, the contents of the augmentor query area change depending on how the user and augmentor are interacting. As many as four windows may appear in the query area at any one time. The window types mediate word selection, role selection and reference selection.[8] Additionally, Ontos windows may be popped up over the augmentor.

---

[8]It is expected that future implementations will include attachment selection.

8.4.3 Using the Augmentor

When the augmentor is loaded and ready, the cursor will be placed in the top field of the input/output panel. If the parses are being read from a file, the user enters the number of the sentence to use, and the system then proceeds to read the parse from the file corresponding to that sentence. If the parses are being taken directly from the parser, the user enters the actual sentence to be parsed.

During the course of an interactive session, as previously noted, as many as four windows may be visible in the query area at one time. Whenever more than one window is displayed, the user may choose to answer the questions in any convenient order. In most cases, making a selection in one window will change the contents of other windows, as the augmentor eliminates alternatives.

The word-selection menu is used when the parser and automatic disambiguator are unable to determine which of various senses of a word is correct. The menu presents a list of descriptions of those senses, and the user chooses from the list.

The role-selection menu is used when the parser and automatic disambiguator are unable to determine which of various roles a phrase may fill, such as `destination` or `goal`. In such cases, the menu presents a list of the roles for the user to choose from.

The reference-selection menu comes into play when the automatic disambiguator is unable to determine a unique referent for a pronoun or noun. The menu presents a list of the referents that the augmentor was unable to choose from. It presents this list along with the sentences in which the referents appear, thus providing context.

When only a single parse remains, whether through automatic disambiguation or user interaction, a paraphrase of the original sentence is generated in the source language and placed in the verification field of the screen's input/output panel. The user is then asked if this paraphrase accurately reflects the content of the original sentence. Because such paraphrasing can be time consuming, the main menu contains an option to allow the paraphrasing to be turned on or off at will. When paraphrasing is turned off, the resulting unambiguous parse is sent to the generator or a file without verification.

When a verified ILT is produced, the result may either be stored in a file or be sent to the generator for immediate translation. If the sentence was read from the keyboard and is being stored in a file, the user would be asked to enter the name under which the sentence is to be stored. If the augmentor read a parse from a file, it will save the resulting ILT in a previously specified directory using the same base name and extension.

8.4.4 Example

In this section, we present an account of an actual run of the KBMT-89 augmentor. For this example, a subset of the full system was run on a single IBM-RT workstation. Key screen configurations are illustrated throughout.

First, we enter the sentence to be translated, in this case, *7. Set the Power switch on the system unit to On.* The augmentor then passes that sentence to the parser and awaits the result.[9] The augmentor displays the message 'Parsing ...' on the status line (figure 8.2). Once it has read in the candidate parses, the augmentor converts them from the list-of-lists format produced by the parser to an isomorphic set of FRAMEKIT frames. It then augments these by making explicit various implicit data and performing structural rearrangements. This is indicated on the status line along with the number of candidate parses being processed (figure 8.3).

After augmentation and disambiguation, any remaining ambiguity in the candidate parses prompts an interactive disambiguation session. In this case, four menus appear, indicating that there are at least four points at which the candidate parses differ (figure 8.4). We will work with the bottom-left menu first, as it has the most entries and so, we hope, will reduce the ambiguity most quickly. Before deciding on discrete-electronic-move-lever as the appropriate meaning of *set*, however, we decide to look at the synonyms that are stored in the lexicon for each of the possible meanings (figure 8.5).

After we make this selection and click DONE, the augmentor discards those candidate parses that do not contain any of the selected values of the local ambiguity for which the menu was generated. In this case, the number of candidate parses drops from fourteen to six, as indicated on the status line, and another menu replaces the one just completed (figure 8.6). We may select multiple items on a menu if we are unsure of the correct one.

We now select on-position from the upper left-hand menu; this reduces the number of candidates to two and removes three of the menus, as two of the other menus were not independent of the upper left-hand menu. A new menu appears, and we are left with just two menus (figure 8.7). After selecting YES on the upper left-hand menu, only a single candidate parse remains. This is passed to the English generator for paraphrasing (figure 8.8). The English parser was, unfortunately, not able to generate from the ILT, and the augmentor must thus display the raw ILT in the center window (figure 8.9). We will respond affirmatively to the verification

---

[9]For convenience in this particular test, parse results were read from a file produced earlier. For expository purposes, we will continue the account as if it included augmentor-parser communication.

question in the input window; this allows the augmentor to proceed with the translation, which then appears in the bottom window (figure 8.10).[10] If the paraphrase were incorrect, we would be asked to fill out the menus again, this time restoring any parses removed by the automatic disambiguation. This permits us to make a different choice on one or more menus, or correct a mistake made by the automatic disambiguator.

8.5   Implementation Details

8.5.1   LISP Dependencies

The augmentor makes use of a variety of features of Carnegie Mellon University's COMMONLISP system. These include an integrated programmable editor and interprocess communication functions.

The Hemlock editor integrated into the COMMONLISP system provides the primitives to display windows and menus and to accept user input from them. Because the user might not always be able to select a specific alternative from a menu, or the menu might reflect true ambiguity, it is helpful to allow the user to select multiple items from the menu and retain all alternative parses containing any of those items. The editor is programmed to display multiple-selection menus for the interactive disambiguation and call an action function with the selected items when the user selects the DONE item on the menu.

The translation system is designed as a distributed system, with the parser, augmentor and generators each running in separate LISP systems (which are normally running on different machines). Thus, it becomes necessary to communicate between parts of the translation system, that is, to achieve interprocess communication. During testing, files may be used to store the results of one stage in the translation for later use by the next phase. However, during an actual user session, it is also necessary to communicate control between the LISP systems. The augmentor controls the parser and generator using a LISP package that interfaces with the interprocess communication features of the operating system. This package allows the augmentor to send a LISP function call to the remote LISP and optionally to await the return of a result.

---

[10]Had the translation been similarly unsuccessful, the augmentor would have displayed the raw ILT in the translation window.

Figure 8.2: **Parsing the input sentence.**

Figure 8.3: **Processing the candidate parses: automatic augmentation.**

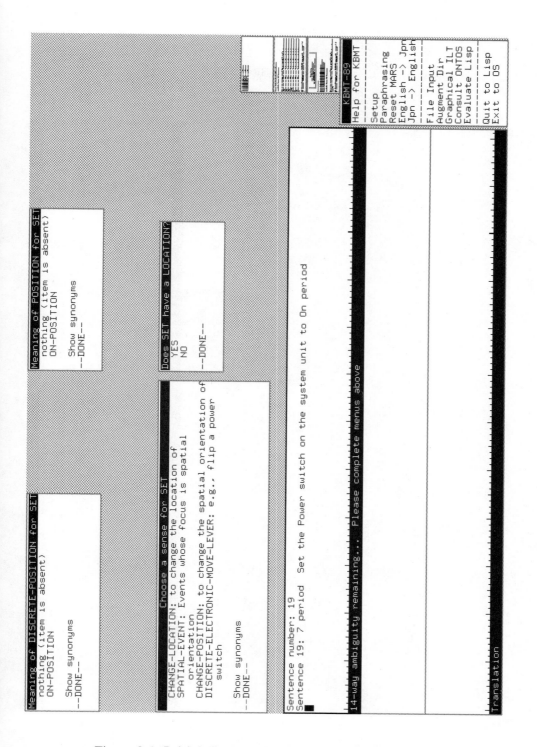

Figure 8.4: **Initial display of four menus, the maximum.**

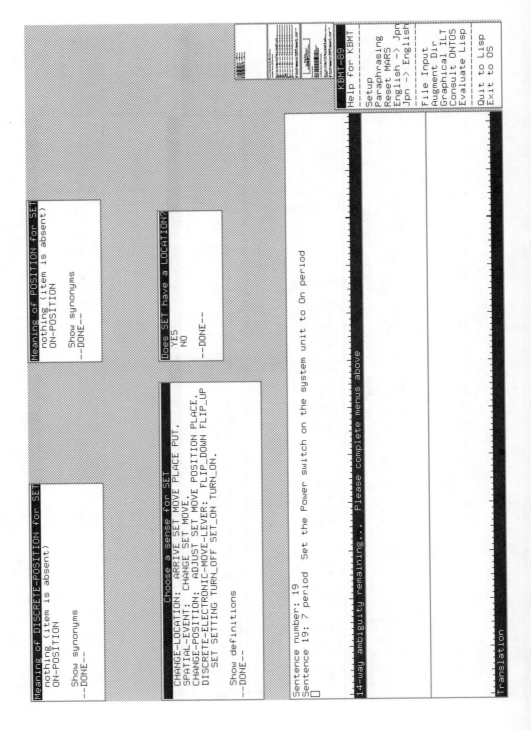

Figure 8.5: **Checking the lexicon for various senses of the verb** *set*.

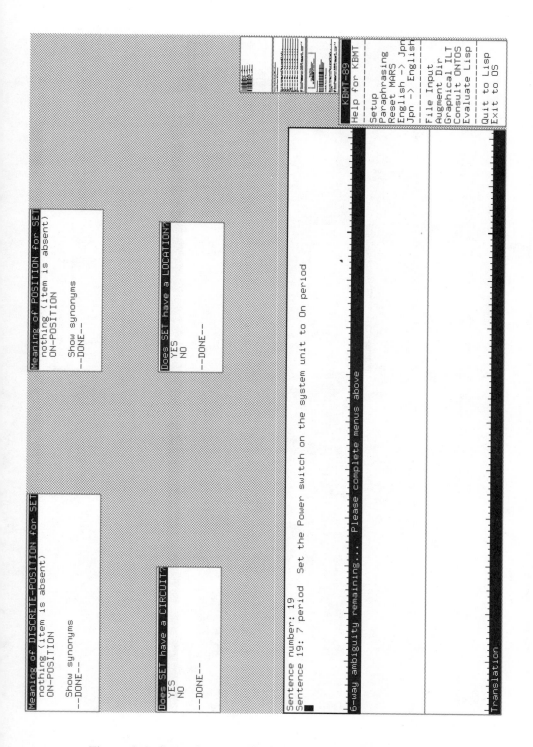

Figure 8.6: **Second set of menus, after disambiguating** *set*.

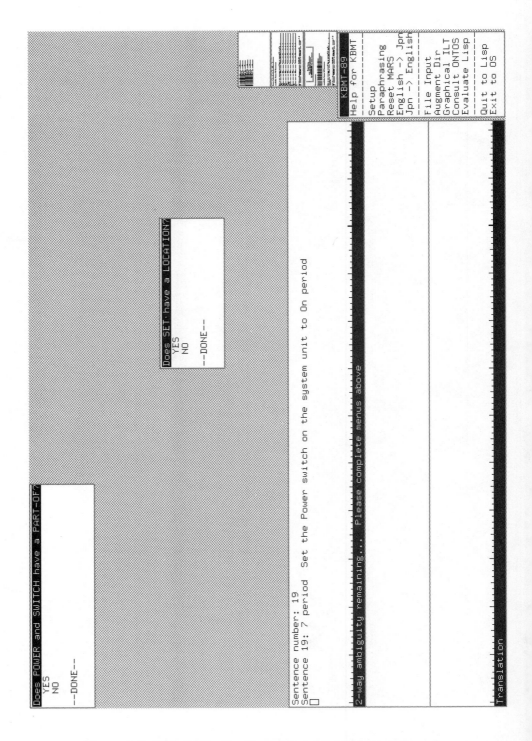

Figure 8.7: **Third set of menus, after selecting meaning of** *on*.

Figure 8.8: **Generating a paraphrase for verification after disambiguation.**

Figure 8.9: **Verifying the paraphrase produced from the disambiguated parse.**

Figure 8.10: **Display of the final translation of the input sentence.**

8.5.2   Composite ILTs

To reduce the number of queries needed to disambiguate a parse, a composite
ILT containing all values from all ambiguous parses is created. The augmentor
can then ask a single question for each slot filler in the composite ILT that has
multiple values, rather than ask the user to choose among a potentially huge
number of parses. Additionally, the composite ILT allows easy comparisons among
the original parses, permitting straightforward elimination of incomplete parses
which are occasionally produced along with complete parses.

A detailed example should help illuminate the process. Consider the following
three highly abbreviated ILTs (which do not represent a real sentence):

```
1. (make-frame proposition1
          (is-token-of (value (common *event)))
          (agent (value (common role4))))
   (make-frame role4
          (is-token-of *reader)
          (number singular))

2. (make-frame proposition2
          (is-token-of (value (common *change-position)))
          (agent (value (common role5)))
          (goal (value (common role7))))
   (make-frame role5
          (is-token-of *reader)
          (number singular))
   (make-frame role7
          (is-token-of (value (common *3d-orientation)))
          (position (value (common level))))

3. (make-frame proposition3
          (is-token-of (value (common *change-location)))
          (agent (value (common role6)))
          (destination (value (common role8))))
   (make-frame role6
          (is-token-of *reader)
          (number singular))
   (make-frame role8
          (is-token-of (value (common *desktop))))
```

Each of the three ILTs is processed in sequence, adding slots and frames to the
composite ILT as needed to contain all the values from the original ILT. If the slot
contains a value, it is placed in the `values` facet of the composite slot. If the
slot contains the name of another frame in the candidate ILT, the name is placed in
the `subframe` facet of the composite slot, and a new frame of the composite is
created if it is the first filler. If a new frame is created, the name is also placed in
the `value` facet of the current composite frame. Each time a candidate ILT frame

is processed, its name is placed in the $frames slot of the composite frame. When all candidates have been processed, the $frames slot is used to determine whether any candidates are missing slots from the corresponding frame.

Since the composite ILT is initially empty, a new frame is created in the composite for each frame in the first candidate. Each slot in the composite is filled with a list consisting of the value in the original frame and the name of that frame.

After processing the first candidate ILT, the composite is as follows:

```
(make-frame composite9
        ($frames (value proposition1))
        (is-token-of (values ((*event) proposition1)))
        (agent (subframe (composite10 proposition1))
               (value composite10)))
(make-frame composite10
        ($frames (value role4))
        (is-token-of (values ((*reader) role4)))
        (number (values ((singular) role4))))
```

Next, the second candidate is processed. As before, new frames and slots are added when necessary. If a slot already exists in the composite, the value in the original slot is compared to the values listed in the composite slot. If the value is not already present, then a new filler is added in the form of a two-element list containing the value and the frame name; otherwise, the name of the frame is added to the list of frames associated with the value. After adding the second candidate ILT, the composite appears thus:

```
(make-frame composite9
        ($frames (value proposition1 proposition2))
        (is-token-of (values ((*event) proposition1)
                             ((*change-position) proposition2)))
        (agent (subframe (composite10 proposition1 proposition2))
               (value composite10))
        (goal (subframe (composite11 proposition2))
              (value composite11)))
(make-frame composite10
        ($frames (value role4 role5))
        (is-token-of (values ((*reader) role4 role5)))
        (number (values ((singular) role4 role5))))
(make-frame composite11
        ($frames (value role7))
        (is-token-of (values ((*3d-orientation) role7)))
        (position (values ((level) role7))))
```

We proceed similarly for the third candidate ILT, which results in

```
(make-frame composite9
        ($frames (value proposition1 proposition2 proposition3))
        (is-token-of (values ((*event) proposition1)
                             ((*change-position) proposition2)
                             ((*change-location) proposition3)))
        (agent (subframe
                  (composite10 proposition1 proposition2
                               proposition3))
               (value composite10))
        (goal (subframe (composite11 proposition2))
              (value composite11))
        (destination (subframe (composite12 proposition3))
                     (value composite12)))
(make-frame composite10
        ($frames (value role4 role5 role6))
        (is-token-of (values ((*reader) role4 role5 role6)))
        (number (values ((singular) role4 role5 role6))))
(make-frame composite11
        ($frames (value role7))
        (is-token-of (values ((*3d-orientation) role7)))
        (position (values ((level) role7))))
(make-frame composite12
        ($frames (value role8))
        (is-token-of (values ((*desktop) role8))))
```

We now examine the $frames slot of each composite ILT frame. A value of nil is placed in each slot of the composite for those frames that did not have the corresponding slots. In other words, each frame listed in the $frames slot—but not listed among a particular slot's fillers—will be placed in the list of frames associated with the nil filler.[11] After adding the missing frames (in this case, only for the goal and destination slots of composite9), the $frames slot is erased because it is no longer necessary. The final composite ILT appears as follows:

```
(make-frame composite9
        (is-token-of (values ((*event) proposition1)
                             ((*change-position) proposition2)
                             ((*change-location) proposition3)))
        (agent (subframe
                  (composite10 proposition1 proposition2
                               proposition3))
               (value composite10)
        (goal (subframe (composite11 proposition2))
              (value composite11)
```

---

[11]FRAMEKIT considers a missing slot to be equivalent to a slot whose filler for the desired facet and view is nil.

```
                        (values (nil proposition1 proposition3)))
            (destination (subframe (composite12 proposition3))
                          (value composite12)
                          (values (nil proposition1 proposition2)))))
(make-frame composite10
        (is-token-of (values ((*reader) role4 role5 role6)))
        (number (values ((singular) role4 role5 role6))))
(make-frame composite11
        (is-token-of (values ((*3d-orientation) role7)))
        (position (values ((level) role7))))
(make-frame composite12
        (is-token-of (values ((*desktop) role8))))
```

It is now simple to determine that the `agent` subframes of all three candidates were indistinguishable (there is only one filler for the `values` facets of each slot in the composite frame), while all three candidate ILTs differed in the `is-token-of` slot (each filler lists only a single frame containing that value).

8.5.3   Removing Discarded ILTs

After the composite ILT has been created, a series of menus is built to acquire information from the user about which parses should be retained and which should be discarded. For each slot in the composite ILT that has multiple values, a multiple-selection menu is created; this allows the user to select possible fillers for the slot. Similarly, for each group of mutually exclusive slots in a composite frame (i.e., each original frame contains at most one of the slots), a case-role selection menu is displayed, asking the user to choose which of the cases may be filled.

Once the user has made these selections, we accomplish disambiguation by removing those ILTs that do not contain any of the selected values in the appropriate frame. This removal is accomplished by first extracting from the composite ILT the lists of frames for each of the selected values. For each of those frames, the topmost clause frame in its ILT is recovered using a link stored in the frame, creating a list of the candidate parses that are to be retained. The composite ILT is then recursively traversed to adjust the frames of the candidate parses listed within each composite ILT frame. For each slot-filler combination, the list of frames associated with that combination is examined; those frames that are not contained in one of the parses to be retained are removed from the list. When no frames remain for a particular value, that value is removed from the slot in the composite ILT.

Chapter 9

Target Text Generation

■ Eric Nyberg III, Rita McCardell, Donna Gates AND Sergei Nirenburg

This chapter describes the design and implementation of the KBMT-89 generation module. Section 1 discusses the overall design of the generator. Section 2 describes the lexical selection knowledge structures and algorithms. Section 3 describes the meaning-to-syntax mapping phase. Section 4 describes the generation of output strings using a target language grammar. Section 5 presents the control structure of the entire generation module.

9.1   Design of the Generation Component

The generation module of the KBMT-89 system produces target language sentences from the ILT output by the analysis and augmentor modules. There are three main phases in the generation task:

1. *Lexical selection.* For each frame in the ILT, the most appropriate lexical item(s) must be selected.

2. *F-structure creation.* The ILT and the set of appropriate candidate lexemes are analyzed to determine an acceptable grammatical structure for the target utterance. A syntactic functional structure (or *f-structure*) is produced by

231

mapping semantic fields in the ILT (e.g., `agent`) to corresponding fields in the f-structure (e.g., `subj`), as determined by the properties of the chosen lexemes.

3. *Syntactic generation.* The syntactic generation phase produces an output sentence, using the target language generation grammar to properly inflect and order lexical items in the target utterance.

The lexical selection module of the system is a modified version of the lexical selection algorithm used in DIOGENES-88 (Nirenburg et al. 1988). The structural mapping module (which creates an f-structure from the ILT) was designed specially for the KBMT-89 system. A set of mapping rules is interpreted by a program called the *mapper* when ILT frames are mapped onto syntactic f-structures. The GENKIT grammar compiler is used to produce a run-time syntactic generator that produces surface strings from syntactic f-structures.[1]

The control structure of the generator is general and extensible, and it will support both further research and more sophisticated use of knowledge in generation. However, the restricted focus of the present domain makes unnecessary the consideration of text ordering and other trans-sentential phenomena. Furthermore, the relatively detailed granularity of the concept lexicon made the use of collocational restrictions unnecessary during generation.[2]

The architecture of the generation module is shown in figure 9.1. ILT frames are first input to the lexical selection module, which stores the appropriate lexical choices in the frames themselves. The ILT frames are then input to the mapper, which fires any appropriate mapping rules for the target language and creates an f-structure from the ILT frames. This f-structure is then passed through to the precompiled generation grammar, which produces an output sentence in the target language.

9.2   The Lexical Selection Module

While the main task in natural language understanding is robust lexical *disambiguation*, the major lexicon-related task of a natural language generator is to perform

---

[1]GENKIT compiles a functional unification grammar and produces LISP code that may be called directly for run-time syntactic generation (Tomita and Nyberg 1988).

[2]A description of the use of collocational restrictions in generation can be found in Nirenburg et al. 1988.

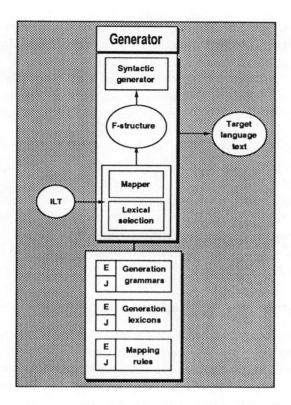

Figure 9.1: **Architecture of the generation module.**

principled *selection* of target language lexical items, based on lexical, semantic, pragmatic and discourse knowledge available in the input.

In this section, we discuss the types of input meanings that must be realized and the structure of the generation lexicon. We also discuss the use of subcategorization knowledge and a meaning matching metric for lexical selection. Then we present a formal description of the algorithms used for lexical selection.

9.2.1 Types of Meanings and Types of Realizations

Recall that the ILT contains information about the meanings of propositions, as well as nonpropositional information about modality, speech acts, focus, discourse relations and so forth. Propositional meanings are typically realized by open-class items (nouns, verbs, adjectives, adverbs) and sometimes by closed-class items (determiners, prepositions, conjunctions, etc.). Nonpropositional meaning can be realized with the help of lexical items, word order or particular syntactic structures.

In what follows, we concentrate on the selection of open-class lexical items. The KBMT-89 generator does a substantial amount of processing of nonpropositional meaning as well, in the spirit of Pustejovsky and Nirenburg (1987). However, we cannot claim a sufficient degree of coverage of that set of phenomena to describe it in detail here. This will be one of the major directions for future research.

The lexical selection module of a natural language generation system should make use of both context-dependent and context-independent information. Thematic role subcategorization is an example of the use of context-dependent information in generation. Lexical selection based on the "distance" between a given input meaning and a generation lexicon entry is an example of a context-independent process, since it does not take into account any constraints on other ILT meanings in selecting the realization for a given ILT component.

The next two subsections illustrate how these types of information influence the process of lexical selection.

9.2.2   Context-Dependent Selection: Subcategorization

Thematic-role subcategorization in lexical selection is essentially the problem of comparing the thematic roles of various lexical candidates with the roles of a given input role or proposition in the ILT to be realized. Each noun and verb in the generation lexicon is subcategorized for the thematic roles that are either required, optional or forbidden if that lexeme is chosen as a realization.

For example, verbs like *move* expect an agent and a theme and, optionally, a source and a goal. Verbs like *appear*, on the other hand, occur only with a theme (never an agent), and verbs like *be* can require a domain and a relation-range, as in *The keyboard is the primary input to the system.* There are, of course, many other subcategories of English verbs and nouns.

When a lexical item is selected for a particular ILT frame, the contents of that frame must be checked against subcategorization requirements of the lexical item. For example, if a candidate verb subcategorizes for an agent and a theme, the ILT frame must contain both an agent slot and a theme slot for the verb to be selected.

Two knowledge sources for subcategorization must be defined for each language to be generated:

- A list of all possible thematic roles used to subcategorize each category (or part of speech) in the language. This information is defined with a subcat macro and usually placed at the beginning of the generation lexicon. For

example, the thematic roles used for English verb subcategorization in the
KBMT-89 domain are defined as follows:

```
(subcat english verb (agent theme
                      experiencer
                      source goal beneficiary
                      domain relation-range
                      theme-reference
                      theme-property instrument))
(subcat english noun (convey string-is
                      number-representation
                      agent theme goal instrument
                      relation-range domain))
```

- A specific subcategorization pattern for each generation lexicon entry, where appropriate. The subcategorization pattern lists the required and optional slots in the ILT frame. If a thematic role is not mentioned, then it must not appear. For instance, consider the generation lexicon entry for the verb *add*:

```
(make-frame add
   (is-token-of (value  *appear))
   (lexeme (value "add"))
   (syntactic-info (cat V)
                   (features (valency trans) (root add)))
   (subcategorization-info (req agent theme) (opt goal))
   (morphological-info (infl regular)))
```

The verb *add* requires that an agent and a theme be present, and that a
goal is optional. It also specifies that no roles other than agent, theme
and goal be present.

Nouns in the generation lexicon likewise contain required and optional thematic
roles. The lexical units *note* and *message* illustrate how thematic-role subcategorization works for nouns:

```
(make-frame note
   (is-token-of (value  *text-group))
   (convey (value  *communicative-content) (importance 10))
   (lexeme (value "note"))
   (syntactic-info (cat N)
                   (features (count yes) (root note)))
   (subcategorization-info (req convey))
   (morphological-info (infl regular)))
(make-frame message
   (is-token-of (value  *text-group))
   (lexeme (value "message"))
   (syntactic-info (cat N)
                   (features (count yes) (root message)))
   (subcategorization-info (opt convey string-is))
   (morphological-info (infl regular)))
```

Message can optionally take `convey` and `string-is` slots. However, *note* must have a `convey` slot filled with an instance of the concept `*communicative -content`. When no `convey` slot is mentioned in the ILT, then the lexeme *message* is chosen because its thematic-role slots are optional. When both `convey` and `string-is` are present, only *message* can be chosen. (*Note* is not subcategorized to take a `string-is` slot.) For example, notice the difference between the '*IBM personal computer basic*' *message* and *the note*.

When only the `convey` slot is present within the ILT, either word can be selected. The generation lexicon entry for *note*, however, constrains the `convey` slot to be filled with the concept `*communicative-content`. If this is not the case, then *message* will be selected by virtue of the meaning matching metric. However, if the slot is filled with a role whose concept is `*communicative-content`, then *note* will be selected.

9.2.3 Context-Independent Selection: The Matcher

Context-independent lexical selection is the task of comparing the meaning of each lexical realization candidate with the input meaning to determine the best lexical choice. KBMT-89 matches an ILT frame's slots against the *meaning pattern* slots of candidate generation lexicon entries. In the absence of a perfect match, the matcher must determine exactly how far the input ILT frame is from such a match with the generation lexicon pattern. Mismatches are assigned penalties proportional to how much the two frames differ in meaning.

Both ILT frames and the meaning patterns of generation lexicon entries are collections of slots, whose fillers are members of *domains* that are predefined for each slot. Slot fillers can be symbols (e.g., `(temperature (value tepid))`) or numerals (e.g, `(weight (value 141.5))`).

The domains (or value sets) from which slot filler values are taken can be unordered, ordered discretely (hereafter, *ordered*) or ordered continuously (hereafter, *continuous*). An example of an unordered set would be `occupations`; an ordered set `months-of-the-year`; and a continuous set `height`. Note that the slot fillers of a continuous set can contain only numeric values.

The cardinality of slot fillers in meaning patterns can be *single* as in `(sex (value female))`, *enumerated* as in `(subjects (value physics math history))` or *range* as in `(age (value (0 100)))`.

The matching metric is based on the following heuristics:

- If there is a difference in the types of slot fillers or the domains of the filler values in the ILT and generation lexicon meaning pattern, then the match is declared inadequate and a maximum distance is assigned.

- The quality of the match is proportional to the size of the intersection of the actual slot fillers in the ILT and generation lexicon frames, which is then modified by the size of the domain itself.

- Each slot in a generation lexicon meaning pattern is rated with respect to its importance for the meaning expressed by the frame. A mismatch on a less important slot will have a smaller influence on the overall score of the match.

- The quality of a match between two frames is a weighted sum of the quality of the matches of the individual frame slots.

For the matching program, it is assumed that the ILT frame contains all the slots found in the generation lexicon meaning pattern. Conversely, the ILT frame can (and regularly will) contain more slots than the generation lexicon frame. This is because an ILT frame corresponds not to a *single* lexical unit but rather to an *entire* phrase (such as a noun phrase, complete with various modifiers). Lexical selection proceeds in two phases: first, the heads of phrases (typically, nouns and verbs) are generated, and then the modifiers (typically, adjectives and adverbs, but frequently such recursive elements as prepositional phrases and relative clauses) are selected.

In what follows, we describe the empirically derived scoring functions used in DIOGENES, along with the algorithm that uses the scoring function to calculate an aggregate penalty for the slots in an ILT input frame and a generation lexicon entry.

Fillers are compared for each slot that is present in both the ILT and the lexicon entry. If the fillers are equal, then the slots match perfectly and no penalty is assigned. If the fillers do not match perfectly, a penalty is computed for that slot. The function used to calculate the penalty depends on the type of slot filler (e.g., `single`, `enumerated` or `range`). Once the penalty is computed, it is weighted according to the importance of that slot to a successful match (i.e., the importance value within the lexicon entry) and added to the total penalty for the match. The penalty functions for the three types of slot fillers are described below.

9.2.3.1 Single Element Fillers

An *ordered domain* with single element fillers can be exemplified by a set of single `temperature` values:[3]

---

[3]`temperature` is one of the physical object attributes within the ontological *is-a* hierarchy from which ILTs are produced (Nirenburg et al. 1987b).

```
(make-frame temperature
  (instance-of (value slot))
  (element-type (value symbol))
  (domain-type (value ordered))
  (cardinality (value single))
  (elements (value (cold cool tepid lukewarm warm hot  scalding))))
```

Suppose we are trying to match `temperature` slots in an ILT frame and a generation lexicon (GL) entry:

ILT: `(temperature (value cool))`
GL: `(temperature (value lukewarm))`

The penalty assigned to a mismatch depends on two variables:

- D: the distance between the fillers in the *ordered* set of values
- C: the size of the domain of values.

The quality of the match depends, of course, on the distance between the two fillers. However, it is important to consider the size of the filler domain as well. The larger a domain, the higher the chance that the two fillers will diverge. Consequently, the penalty is lessened for larger domains, the distance between the fillers being equal. (If there are only two elements in the domain, for example, there is a 50% chance of the correct filler appearing in the input, so a larger penalty is assigned if it does not.)

A simple equation relates these two variables:

$$P = \frac{W \times D}{\mathcal{F}(C)} \qquad (9.1)$$

where W is a numerical weight on the distance between the fillers and $\mathcal{F}$ is a damping function on the size of the domain. These parameters are added to the equation for calibration purposes (calibration is discussed briefly in section 9.2.3.5).

The matching of single element fillers from *unordered domains* is quite similar to matching single fillers in ordered domains. The difference lies in the fact that the distance between the fillers is no longer meaningful, since they are not ordered with respect to one another. The penalty assigned to the match becomes a function merely of the size of the domain (and hence the probability of the correct filler appearing):

$$P = \frac{W}{\mathcal{F}(C)} \qquad (9.2)$$

A *continuous domain* is basically an ordered domain with numeric fillers that are equally spaced. The elements of the domain are defined by giving its endpoints (or closed interval) and the unit size of representation to be used in computing the distance between fillers. As an example, consider the following alternate definition of the attribute `temperature`. Equation (9.1) can also be used to compute the penalty for continuous domain sets.

```
(make-frame temperature
  (instance-of (value slot))
  (element-type (value number))
  (domain-type (value continuous))
  (cardinality (value single))
  (unit-size (value 0.1))
  (elements (value (0 100)))))
```

As before, suppose we are trying to match `temperature` slots between an ILT and a generation lexicon frame:

ILT: `(temperature (value 93.7))`
GL: `(temperature (value 98.6))`

Before evaluating equation (9.1), both the distance between the two fillers and the distance between the endpoints of the closed domain interval are computed using the defined `unit-size` value. Then the evaluation of the equation proceeds as before.

9.2.3.2 Enumerated Fillers

An enumerated filler can be treated essentially as a set of single fillers. Basically, an enumerated slot's penalty depends on the number of single fillers that appear in one set (i.e., either of the lexicon entry or the ILT frame) but not the other. More specifically, the penalty for the slot will depend on (i) the individual penalty for each single filler in the entry's enumerated set when compared with the ILT slot's fillers and (ii) penalties for any single fillers in the ILT slot's enumerated set that are not accounted for by the entry. After these penalties have been determined, they can be combined to obtain the total slot penalty.

The following rules are used to determine a penalty for each single filler in the enumerated set of a generation lexicon entry:

- If the single filler is a member of the ILT slot's enumerated filler set, the penalty is 0.

- Otherwise, we calculate a single-filler penalty for this filler compared with *each* of the single fillers in the ILT slot using the earlier equations. The penalty for this single filler will be the *minimum* of these penalties.[4]

Besides penalizing each filler in the entry that does not appear in the ILT's set of fillers, we also penalize for each filler in the ILT's set that does not appear in the entry. Each such filler is assigned a penalty using equation (9.2).

Once we have calculated penalties for individual fillers, we can combine them to obtain a penalty for the entire slot. This can be done in two distinct ways, which are now described.

Consider first the following slot within an ILT frame:

```
(wheels (value 3 4))
```

This slot expresses the idea of "3 *or* 4 wheels." `wheels` is an enumerated slot that uses a *disjunctive* penalty-combining operator because a vehicle cannot have *both* 3 *and* 4 wheels.

Total slot penalty for a disjunctive enumerated slot, therefore, is calculated by taking the *minimum* of the individual penalties described above. So, for example, if the lexicon entry being compared to the ILT frame with the above slot contained the slot

```
(wheels (value 2 4 18))
```

the total slot penalty would be 0; the slots are considered to match because the entry is able to represent a 4-wheeled vehicle.

In other cases, enumerating more than one single filler within a slot does not indicate that any one of the values is sufficient (as with disjunctive slots), but that the fillers are meant to be combined to give the full meaning. For example, consider the slot

```
(color (value green blue))
```

This can be taken to mean that the color is "green *and* blue," that is, aqua.

For this type of slot, all the individual penalties found earlier must be combined to determine the entire slot penalty. The total penalty is thus the *average* of the individual penalties. The only way to get a penalty of 0 in this case is to match the entire slot *exactly*. So, for example, comparing the preceding

---

[4]Note that if the domain is *unordered*, all single-filler comparisons yield the exact same penalty; so the *minimum* of single-filler penalties equals whatever value the first comparison yields.

slot to (color (value blue green)) will give a penalty of 0, comparing to (color (value green)) or (color (value blue)) will give a penalty P greater than 0 and comparing to (color (value red)) will give a penalty larger than *P*.

9.2.3.3 Range Fillers

The elements of range fillers may be either numbers or symbols. For instance, the range of temperature might be expressed as freezing to scalding, or as 32.0 to 101.7. The function used to calculate the penalty for mismatched range fillers is identical in both cases.

If two range fillers do not match exactly, several factors are taken into account when calculating the size of the penalty: the size of each filler, the size of the intersection between the fillers and the size of the domain. In determining the size of any of these sets, we want a count of the number of domain elements between the determined endpoints (inclusive). For numeric ranges, the size of a set *S* is equal to the difference between the endpoints divided by the unit-size of the domain. For symbolic ranges, the size of *S* is simply equal to the number of symbolic elements between the endpoints (inclusive).

The sizes of each filler and domain are therefore simple to calculate, since the ranges are given. The intersection between the two fillers may fall into any of the following categories:

1. The ILT filler and the generation lexicon filler overlap, and the resulting intersection is smaller than either filler.

2. The fillers overlap, and the ILT filler is contained within the lexicon filler.

3. The fillers overlap, and the lexicon filler is contained within the ILT filler.

4. The fillers do not overlap.

The first three cases above are easy to calculate, and the result is simply the endpoints of the intersection set. In the fourth case, when the fillers do not overlap, the intersection is indicated by a negative number that represents the distance between the nearest endpoints of the two fillers.

The function used to calculate penalties for range fillers employs the following variables:

- S_i: the size of the ILT filler

- S_g: the size of the generation lexicon filler

- I: the size of the intersection between the two fillers, where negative values indicate the distance between disjoint fillers

- C: the size of the domain

- W_i: a weighting function dependent upon the ILT filler size

- W_g: a weighting function dependent upon the lexicon filler size

- W_{int}: a weighting function dependent upon the size of the intersection

- $\mathcal{F}(C)$: a damping function dependent upon the domain size

The overall mismatch penalty (at the slot level) is computed by the following function:

$$P = \frac{W_i(S_i - I) + W_g(S_g - I) - W_{int}(I)}{\mathcal{F}(C)} \tag{9.3}$$

The first two terms in the numerator are designed to account for the two types of intersection in the second and third categories above. If some of the ILT filler falls outside the intersection, then $S_i - I > 0$, and the first term will increase the penalty. If some of the filler lies outside the intersection, the second term will increase the penalty. The determination of how much is added in each case is dependent upon the weighting functions W_i and W_g. The penalty is decreased by the size of the third term, which is the weighted size of the intersection. (This counteracts the additive factor of I in the first two terms when $I < 0$.) Finally, the entire penalty is divided by the weighted size of the domain, which accounts for the varying probability of matching in larger domains.

9.2.3.4   The Frame Level

Once all of the slots have been compared using the appropriate equation, the *overall* score for the match between the ILT frame and the lexicon entry is produced according to the following formula:

$$S = \frac{\sum_{i=1}^{n} I_i \times P_i}{\sum_{i=1}^{n} I_i} \tag{9.4}$$

where the P_is are mismatch penalties between each slot of the ILT frame, and the entry and the I_is are *importance values* for the corresponding slots of the entry's meaning pattern. (The slots in an ILT frame do not contain importance values.)

9.2.3.5 Calibration

The functions in equation (9.3) can be calibrated to yield results with an intuitive interpretation. For example, for most applications, the W_g function should be quite low because a subrange of a given range should reveal a valid instance of the concept. Conversely, the function W_i should be quite high, signifying an entry that does not fit into the specified range.

9.2.4   The Lexical Selection Algorithm

The following is a simplified version of the top-level lexical selection algorithm.

```
candidate-set := GL-search (current-frame, GL)
if cardinality(candidate-set) = 0
   then candidate-set := interactively-augment-GL (current-frame)
subcat-set := subcat-match-p (current-frame, candidate-set,
                              target-language)
current-candidate := select-best (subcat-set, current-frame)
```

The function `generation-lexicon-search` searches the generation lexicon and produces an initial set of candidate lexical realizations by obtaining all entries that are instances of the same concept as the ILT role or proposition (i.e., that have the same `is-token-of` value).[5]

Subcategorization information is processed by the function `subcat-match-p` to filter the initial set of generation lexicon entries returned by the function `generation-lexicon-search`. The process retains only those entries whose subcategorization patterns are satisfied by the ILT frame to be generated.

After `subcat-match` processes any relevant subcategorization information, the function `select-best` is called to perform context-independent lexical selection based on the quality of the match between the meaning pattern of the ILT role or proposition frame and the weighted meaning patterns of the generation lexicon entries in the candidate set. A penalty is computed for each potential candidate, and the candidate with the lowest final penalty is then returned.

Once the head of the lexical item has been realized, modifiers may be selected. The function `unrealized-slots` checks to see if there exist properties (or slots) in the ILT role or proposition that are not accounted for by the lexical selection for the head. If all properties have been accounted for, then

---

[5]Full formal descriptions of the lexical selection algorithms are given in Nirenburg and Goodman 1989.

lexical processing terminates for that ILT frame. Otherwise, each remaining property will be realized as one lexical unit, that is, as a single word. The KBMT-89 generator will realize two different types of modifiers—*attribute* and *relational*. Attribute modifiers are derived from properties such as "color" and "size," while relational modifiers are those derived from features such as `part-of` and `made-of`. The modifier type (either attribute or relation) of each unrealized slot is determined, and the appropriate lexical selection function is triggered. The functions `attribute-lexical-selection` and `relational-lexical selection` use essentially the same set of algorithms (*generation lexicon-search* and *select-best*) for choosing phrase modifiers such as were employed for selecting phrase heads, with some slight modifications.

9.3   F-Structure Creation

This section describes the rules that are used to map ILT frames into syntactic f-structures in the first phase of target language generation.

In the following subsections, the BNF-like specification for the mapping rules is presented, some example rules are given, the algorithm for the mapper itself is described and a sample mapping rule file is presented.

9.3.1   Mapping Rules

Here we describe the BNF for mapping rules and provide examples to illustrate how the various fields within a rule should be used (square brackets indicate optionality).

- `<mrule> := (maprule <target><index><mr-type> <predicate> <mslot>*)`. Each mapping rule has a target, index, type and predicate field, and one or more slot fields. These fields are described below.

- `<target> := E | J`. This field is used to indicate the target language of the given rule. The symbol 'E' is used to identify rules for English and 'J' is used to identify rules for Japanese.

- `<index> := <ilt-type> | <lex-class>`. This field is used to associate a rule with the entity that it maps. There are two methods of indexing: by ILT type and by lexical class. In the first case, the type of the ILT frame being mapped is used to access rules for mapping; in the second case, the lexical item selected for the head of the phrase for the frame is used.

- `<mr-type> := :exclusive | :any`. This field is used to control the behavior of rules when they are fired:

  - `:exclusive`: Only one `:exclusive` rule may be fired on a single ILT frame during mapping. This allows the mapping-rule writer to create a set of mutually exclusive structural mappings for a single type of frame. All mappings in an `:exclusive` rule must succeed or the rule will not fire.

  - `:any`: There is no limit to the number of `:any` rules that may fire on a single frame. Each mapping in an `:any` rule that succeeds is used, even if not all of the mappings are successful. For this reason, it is possible to place all of the `:any` mappings for an ILT frame into a single rule. However, clarity dictates that only conceptually related `:any` mappings should be grouped into the same rule (e.g., mappings that generate `ppadjuncts`).

- `<ilt-type> := *clause | *proposition | *role ...` The `<ilt-type>` field is a symbol denoting an ILT frame type (e.g., `*role`, `*proposition`, etc.).

- `<lex-class> := (any lexical root)`. This field is a symbol denoting either a lexical root (e.g., `throw`) or a lexical class (e.g., `change-of-location`) that the rule should fire on.

- `<predicate> := (LISP expression)`. The `<predicate>` field is an evaluable COMMONLISP expression. When evaluated, the `<predicate>` must return a non-`nil` value for the rule to fire. The context present when the rule is fired can be accessed in one of two ways:

  - *Path abbreviation.* The `<predicate>` can contain a symbol of the form `@<start>[.<field>]*`. The @-sign indicates that the rest of the symbol should be treated as a path abbreviation. `<start>` can be either `frame` or `lex`, depending on whether the user intends to access the ILT frame or the lexicon frame that has been selected. Each `<field>` should be either a slot name or a facet name. For example, the path `@frame` returns the frame being mapped; the path `@frame.agent` returns the frame filling the `agent` slot of the frame being mapped; the path `@lex.syntactic-info.verb-class` will access the verb class facet of the syntactic information slot of the lexicon frame.

- *Context variables.* The variables `!frame` and `!lex` are bound to the frame being mapped and its lexicon entry, respectively, and can be accessed freely inside the `<predicate>`. Although the system user can employ `@frame` and `!frame` interchangeably, the use of `@frame` symbols creates an extra function call where the use of `!frame` does not. As a result, `!frame` and `!lex` should be used for efficiency when no path is required.

- `<mslot> := <feature> | <slot> | <mapping>`. This field can take six basic forms:

  1. *Slot addition:* A slot is added directly to the f-structure.
  2. *Feature addition:* A feature is added directly to the f-structure.
  3. *Slot-to-slot mapping:* A slot in the ILT frame is mapped to a slot in the f-structure.
  4. *Slot-to-feature mapping:* A slot in the ILT frame is mapped to a feature in the f-structure.
  5. *Expr-to-slot mapping:* An evaluated expression provides the value for a slot in the f-structure.
  6. *Expr-to-feature mapping:* An evaluated expression provides the value for a feature in the f-structure.

  Rather than describing each type of `<mslot>` separately, we will later present and discuss some sample rules that contain examples of each type.

- `<feature> := (feature <feature-name> [<value>])`. This field specifies a particular feature in an f-structure.

- `<slot> := (slot <slot-name> [<value>])`. This field specifies a particular slot, either in the ILT or in an f-structure.

- `<mapping> := (<lhs> => <rhs> [<post-process>])`. Each mapping contained in the rule will have a left-hand side denoting the portion of the ILT to be mapped, a right-hand side denoting the target structure in the f-structure and an optional post-process field that indicates some action to be applied to the result of mapping; see the discussion following.

- `<lhs> := <slot> | <expr>`. The left-hand side of a mapping may contain either a slot specification or an expression.

- `<rhs> := <slot> | <feature>`. The right-hand side of a mapping may contain either a slot specification or a feature.

- `<expr> := (expr <expr-form>)`. An expression is a LISP form, explicitly labeled with the tag `expr`.

- `<expr-form> := (LISP expression)`. Like `<predicate>`, this may include a path abbreviation.

- `<value> := (LISP expression)`. This is an unevaluated LISP expression.

- `<feature-name> := (LFG feature)`. This field is a symbol denoting an LFG feature.

- `<slot-name> := (ILT, f-structure)`. This field is either an ILT or an f-structure slot.

- `<post-process> := (LISP expression, evaluated)`. This field may access `!frame`, `!iltslot`, `!fsslot` or `!slotfs`.

- `<mclass> := (mapclass <target> <lex-class> (<lex-class>*))`. This field provides the mapper with inheritance information for lexical classes; see the discussion following.

9.3.1.1 Some Sample Mapping Rules

This subsection describes several mapping rules to illustrate the concepts previously introduced. Since the distinction between `:any` and `:exclusive` rules is only important when several rules are fired together, we defer discussion of this until section 9.3.3.

- **Slot Addition**

```
(maprule e *role :any t
  (slot cat NP))
```

Here the target language is e, (English), the rule is for ILT frames that are members of the `*role` class and the `<predicate>` field is t, so there are no restrictions on the rule. The rule contains a single `<mslot>`, namely, `(slot cat NP)`, which is an example of *slot addition*. If this rule is present, the slot `(cat ((root NP)))` will be added to each f-structure constructed from a `*ROLE` frame.

- **Feature Addition**

```
(maprule e *role :any t
  (feature cat NP))
```

The target language is e, the rule is for ILT frames that are members of the
*role class and the <predicate> field is t, so there are no restrictions
on the rule. The rule contains a single <mslot> — (feature cat NP)
— which is an example of *feature addition*. If this rule is present, the feature
(cat NP) will be added to each f-structure constructed from a *role
frame.

- **Slot-to-Slot Mapping**

```
(maprule e *proposition :exclusive @frame.object
  ((slot agent)   => (slot subj))
  ((slot object)  => (slot obj)))
```

Here the <predicate> is @frame.object. The rule will not be fired
unless there is an object present in the ILT frame. In this case, the agent
and object slots will be filled with role frames, each of which will have
been mapped already. Each role frame will contain a current-fs slot,
which is accessed by the mapper and is the value returned by the left-hand slot
in the mapping. This f-structure will be placed inside the slot designated by
the left-hand slot in the mapping; this is an instance of *slot-to-slot mapping*.
For example, if ((root boy)) was returned from the left-hand slot in the
first mapping, then the slot (subj ((root boy))) will be placed into
the f-structure.

```
(maprule e *role :any t
  ((slot reference) => (slot ref)))
```

This slot-to-slot mapping is similar to the previous one except that the left-
hand slot does not resolve to an f-structure. Here, the reference slot is
filled with a nonframe symbolic value (e.g., definite). This value will be
placed inside the slot indicated by the right-hand slot in the mapping. The
mapper will place the value inside the form ((root <value>)), so a
slot value of definite in the ILT frame will add the slot (ref ((root
definite))) to the f-structure as a result of this mapping.[6]

---

[6]If the value returned by a left-hand slot is a symbol, it is wrapped inside ((root <symbol>));
otherwise, it is assumed to be a list containing a root, and nothing special takes place.

- **Slot-to-Feature Mapping**

```
(maprule e *role :any t
  ((slot reference) => (feature ref)))
```

By changing the right-hand side of the mapping to a feature specification, we have an example of *slot-to-feature mapping*. No extra structure is added by the mapper, as in the case of slot-to-slot mapping of a symbolic value. This mapping will add the feature (ref definite) to the f-structure, assuming that the value of the reference slot is definite.

- **Expr-to-Slot Mapping**

```
(maprule e *proposition :any t
  ((expr (case @frame.clauseid.speechactid.speech-act
          (assertion      'declarative)
          (request-info    'interrogative)
          (request-action 'imperative)))
   => (slot mood)))
```

This rule is an example of *expr-to-slot mapping*. The left-hand expression is evaluated and may contain path abbreviations and/or access the global variables mentioned before. The value returned by evaluating the expression is the value of the left-hand side. Assuming that the speech-act slot of the frame attached to the proposition by the clauseid and speechactid links is filled with assertion, this value will be declarative. Since the right-hand side is a slot and this value is symbolic, the slot (mood ((root declarative))) will be added to the f-structure. (If the value returned were a list expression rather than a symbol, it would have been placed directly into the slot without adding a root).

- **Expr-to-Feature Mapping**

```
(maprule e *proposition :any t
  ((expr (case @frame.clauseid.speechactid.speech-act
          (assertion      'declarative)
          (request-info    'interrogative)
          (request-action 'imperative)))
   => (feature mood)))
```

This rule is an example of *expr-to-feature mapping*. The left-hand expression is evaluated as in the previous example. Since the right-hand side is a feature specification, the feature (mood declarative) will be added to the f-structure.

- **The Optional** `<value>` **Field**

  When a slot or feature specification appears on the right-hand side of an `<mslot>`, it may contain an explicit value, for example:

  ```
  (feature mood imperative)
  ```

  If an explicit value is present in the right-hand side, it is used instead of the value returned by the left-hand side of the mapping.

- **Expansion of Slot Names**

  It is often useful to create a rule that maps a whole class of slots (for instance, all modifier slots for `*roles`). However, the basic notation requires that a rule explicitly state the slot to be mapped. The mapper also supports the expansion of keyword slot names. If the symbol denoting the slot name in the left-hand side of a slot mapping is a keyword (e.g., `:modifier`), then the mapper will access the `map-expansion` slot in the frame for a list of slot names to map. For example:

  ```
  (maprule e *role :any t ((slot :mod) => (slot apadjuncts)))
  ```

  This rule will try to map role modifiers into the `apadjuncts` slot. The frame `*role` (which any ILT role will inherit from) should contain a `map-expansion` slot with the appropriate facet:

  ```
  (add-filler 'role 'map-expansion ':mod
    '(quote (color size age made-of ... )))
  ```

  When the rule in the example is fired, the particular role being mapped will inherit the `map-expansion` slot from `*role`. The mapper will look for the `:mod` facet in the `map-expansion` slot, which is filled with a list of slots. In general, the facet filler accessed in the `map-expansion` slot for the expansion keyword should be an evaluable LISP form: either a quoted list of slots to map or an arbitrary expression that can calculate the slots to map. The variable `!frame` is bound to the frame being mapped and can be accessed by the slot expansion expression.

- **Post Processing**

  Each <mslot> can contain an optional third field (<post-process>). This can be used further to modify the result of the original mapping. The <post-process> field should be filled with an evaluable LISP expression. This expression is evaluated with the following context variables set: !frame, !iltslot, !fsslot and !slotfs. So, !frame is the ILT frame being mapped; !iltslot is the name of the slot in the frame that is being mapped (if the left-hand side is an "Expr," !iltslot will be bound to expr); !fsslot is the name of the slot (or feature) being created in the f-structure; and !slotfs is bound to the contents of that slot as produced by processing the left-hand side. If a <post-process> form is used, it should produce a valid structure for a full f-structure slot when evaluated, that is, it should be a list containing a slot name and an f-structure for the slot contents. For example, if !fsslot is subj and !slotfs is ((root boy)), then the mapping

  ```
  ((slot agent) => (slot subj) (list !fsslot !slotfs))
  ```

  will produce the slot (subj ((root boy))). To map a slot to another slot and add a feature, for example, a mapping like this can be used:

  ```
  ((slot agent) => (slot subj) (list !fsslot (cons '(case nom) !slotfs)))
  ```

  Here the ILT agent is mapped to the subj slot, and the feature (case nom) is added to the slot's f-structure.

9.3.2 Mapping Rule Files

Now we can describe the format of mapping rule files and the process by which they should be loaded.

In addition to specifying mapping rules, the system user can employ the <mclass> form to provide the mapper with inheritance information for lexical classes. For example,

```
(mapclass e throw (change-of-location))
```

indicates that `throw` should inherit any mapping rules associated with `change-of-location`. The first item in the `mapclass` form is the inheritor, and the list of items that follows defines the classes that the inheritor inherits from.[7]

A mapping rule file should contain valid `maprule` forms, as described earlier. If the file contains @ path abbreviations, it should be loaded with `load-gen-mrule-file`.

This function activates a special readtable that expands the @ path abbreviations into the appropriate access function calls. If a file containing abbreviations is loaded with `load`, an error will be generated when the rules containing abbreviations are fired. If there are no abbreviations in the file, `load` may be used safely.

9.3.3   The Mapper and Its Algorithm

Here we describe the top-level function in the mapper, the algorithm that it implements, and how to trace the mapper's execution during debugging.

The top-level function that should be called to map a single frame is called `mapgen`:

function **MAPGEN** (frame target)
>   The frame argument should be a valid FRAMEKIT frame; otherwise an error is generated. The target language should have some mapping rules associated with it, or an error will be signaled. The mapping rules for the indicated target language are fired on the frame, and the resulting f-structure is the value returned by `mapgen`.

The mapping rules associated with the frame are fired in the following way:

1. The `current-candidate` slot in the frame is filled with a symbol denoting the generation lexicon entry that was selected for the frame (e.g., `throw`).

2. Any rules for the target language that are indexed on the selected root are retrieved.

---

[7]In the current implementation, inheritance is supported for lexical classes only. It is intended that lexical indices and inheritance be used to support structural mapping and that ILT-indexed rules be used to support the selection and mapping of closed-class slots and features (e.g., `mood`). For this reason, inheritance is currently not supported for ILT types.

3. Any rules for any lexical class that the selected root inherits from are retrieved.

4. Any rules for the target language that are indexed on the type of the ILT frame (e.g., `*role`) are retrieved.

5. The rules retrieved are fired in the order given above, one at a time, and the resulting f-structure is returned.

Two distinctions are made between `:exclusive` and `:any` rules.

First, when `mapgen` is originally called on the frame, it erases the value of the `exclusive-map?` slot in the frame. When an `:exclusive` rule fires sucessfully, this slot is filled and no other `:exclusive` rule will be fired.[8] In contrast, an `:any` rule can always fire, no matter which rules have fired previously on the same frame.[9]

Second, when an `:exclusive` rule is fired, all of the `<mslot>` mappings in the rule must succeed, or the rule will fail and none of its mappings will be invoked. When an `:any` rule is fired, any of the `<mslot>` mappings can be successful and will be processed, even if not all of the mappings in the rule are successful.

Mapping rules associated with a single index (lexical class or ILT type) will be fired in the order they were loaded. Hence, the order of mapping rules in the mapping rule file is significant. For `:any` rules, there should be no real effect of ordering, but for `:exclusive` rules (where the first successful rule "locks out" the others), ordering should be performed with care.

As described earlier, mapping rules can access the context variables `!frame` and `!lex`. The former is bound to the ILT frame being mapped; the latter is bound to the selected root.

The following variable may be set to enable mapper trace output:

variable ***MTRACE*** (default: nil)

>If the variable `*mtrace*` is non-`nil`, the mapper will output trace statements that indicate how each mapping rule is processed. This is useful for debugging or demonstrating the mapper's algorithm.

---

[8]This slot is erased when the mapper exits, so it will have no effect on other processes accessing the ILT frame.

[9]The `:exclusive` mechanism is provided so that the grammar writer can define mutually exclusive structural mappings.

For example, the following is a sample transcript for a call to `mapgen`. For each rule that is fired, the mapper traces the current frame, lexical root and the f-structure's intermediate state. The rule definition is printed, followed by statements that indicate what occurred when each `<mslot>` was processed. Then the resulting f-structure is printed. (Note: Since `mapgen` also returns the final f-structure as its value, the final f-structure appears twice in this example.)

```
* (mapgen 'prop1 'e)


--------------------------------------------------
                 Firing Rule
--------------------------------------------------
Frame: prop1
Lex: throw
FS: ((root throw))

(defrule e change-of-location
   :exclusive
   T
   ((slot agent) => (slot subj))
   ((slot patient) => (slot obj)))

Predicate returns T.
Slot subj added.
Slot obj added.


((obj ((cat NP) (root mary))) (subj ((cat NP) (root joe))) (root throw))
--------------------------------------------------
                 Firing Rule
--------------------------------------------------
Frame: prop1
Lex: throw
FS: ((obj ((cat NP) (root mary))) (subj ((cat NP) (root joe))) (root throw))

(defrule e *proposition
   :any
   T
   ((slot foo) => (feature mood)))

Predicate returns T.
Feature (mood imperative) added.

((mood imperative) (obj ((cat NP) (root mary))) (subj ((cat NP) (root joe)))
 (root throw))
((mood imperative) (obj ((cat NP) (root mary))) (subj ((cat NP) (root joe)))
 (root throw))
```

The following is a sample mapping rule file. The rules are trivial and not intended to demonstrate how to write rules. Rather, it is the intention here to show what should be done in a mapping rule file in addition to defining mapping rules.

```
(erase-mrule-inheritance 'e)   ; remove any existing inheritance info

(erase-mrules 'e)              ; remove any existing mapping rules
;; Define some sample rules:
(maprule e change-of-location :exclusive t
  ((slot agent) => (slot subj))
  ((slot patient) => (slot obj)))
(maprule e action :exclusive t
  ((slot agent) => (slot dummy))
  ((slot patient) => (slot dummy)))
(maprule e *proposition :any t
  ((slot foo) => (feature mood)))

;; Define inheritance classes:
(mapclass e throw (change-of-location))

(mapclass e change-of-location (action))
```

9.4 Syntactic Generation: GENKIT

KBMT-89 makes use of a tool called GENKIT (Tomita and Nyberg 1988) to generate target language strings from the f-structures output by the mapping process; that process is discussed in the previous section. GENKIT is a grammar compiler that compiles source grammars in a unification-based formalism into a set of COMMONLISP functions that can be called directly during generation, without reference to the grammar itself.

As described in chapter 4, there are two generation grammars, one each for English and Japanese. These are precompiled into files containing COMMONLISP functions, which are in turn are compiled and loaded into the run-time translation system.

The syntactic structures produced by the parser and the syntactic structures accepted as input by the generator are indistinguishable. The latter, as f-structures, capture the constituent structure of the utterance, the lexical entries (roots) of the constituents and the tense and agreement features of the constituents, where appropriate.

The process of generating a string of words from a syntactic f-structure is basically the reverse of parsing. In the (simplified) grammar rule

```
(<DEC> <==> (<NP> <VP>)
```

a constraint equation places the information from the <NP> inside the subject of the <DEC> during parsing; in generation, the f-structure for a <DEC> will be broken up into its constituent parts, each of which will be generated by further recursive applications of grammar rules. In this case, the embedded f-structure that fills the subject slot of the declarative f-structure will be used as input to all of the rules that can possibly generate an <NP>. The generator follows a top-down, depth-first strategy for applying rules during generation. If the current search path fails, the generator backs up to the next applicable rule. This process continues until a successful generation is found, or until all of the rules are exhausted.

The generator compiler creates a set of COMMONLISP functions that represents the target language grammar. Each function, GG-X (where X is any syntactic category), implements all rewrite rules from the grammar whose left-hand symbol is <X>. When GG-X is called with the f-structure representation of a source language string, and if that string can be generated by expansion of the non-terminal <X>, then GG-X returns the representative target language string.

The process of constructing GG- functions consists in reading rewrite rules from the file containing the target language grammar and adjusting the appropriate GG- function after each rule is read. The first time a rewrite rule for <X> is read, the basic shell of the GG-X function is created, and the COMMONLISP code implementing that rule is added as a clause of or:

```
(defun  GG-X   (x0)
  (or  **lisp code for first rewrite rule** ))
```

The argument passed to GG-X, namely, X0, will be an f-structure.

This new function is stored in a list with the other GG- functions. Each time a rewrite rule for <X> is read from the grammar file, function GG-X is retrieved from this list, and the code for the new rule is added as the last argument to the or predicate.

To summarize: For every nonterminal category in the generation grammar, GENKIT creates a corresponding COMMONLISP function to generate structures of that category. For each rule that expands a particular category, a piece of code is generated that implements the constraints and assignments of the rule.

Let us consider an example in greater detail. In the case of verbs, GENKIT creates a function GG-V by building code for all the rules of type

```
(<V> --> ...)
```

GG-V will contain a block of code corresponding to each grammar rule.

Consider the following rules for the verb *pull*.

```
(<V> --> (p u l l)
        (((x0 root) =c pull)
```

```
            (*or* (((x0 form) =c finite)
                   ((x0 tense) =c present)
                   (*or* (((x0 number) =c plural)
                          ((x0 person) =c (*or* 3 2 1)))
                         (((x0 number) =c singular)
                          ((x0 person) =c (*or* 2 1)))))
                  (((x0 form) =c inf)))
            ((x0 valency) =c trans)))

(<V> --> (p u l l s)
         (((x0 root) =c pull)
          ((x0 form) =c finite)
          ((x0 tense) =c present)
          ((x0 number) = singular)
          ((x0 person) = 3)
          ((x0 valency) =c trans)))

(<V> --> (p u l l e d)
         (((x0 root) =c pull)
          (*or* (((x0 form) =c pastpart)
                 ((x0 passive) =c +)
                 ((x0 valency) =c intrans))
                ((*or* (((x0 form) =c finite)
                        ((x0 tense) =c past))
                       (((x0 form) =c pastpart)
                        ((x0 passive) =c -)))
                 ((x0 valency) =c trans)))))

(<V> --> (p u l l i n g)
         (((x0 root) =c pull)
          ((x0 form) =c prespart)
          ((x0 valency) =c trans)))
```

These rules are then compiled into the COMMONLISP function by GENKIT.

```
(defun GG-V (x0)
  (if (equal *trace-rules* 'all) (gentrace "~a called with ~a" 'GG-V X0)
      (gentrace "~a called" 'GG-V))
  (let (result)
    (setq *trace-rule-indent* (+ *trace-rule-indent* *trace-rule-indent-factor*))
    (setq result
          (or
           <code for first rule>
           <code for second rule>
           <code for third rule>
           <code for fourth rule>))
    (setq *trace-rule-indent* (- *trace-rule-indent* *trace-rule-indent-factor*))
    (gentrace "~a returns ~a" 'GG-V result)
    result))
```

Finally, the code for the rule for *pull* is given.

```
(let ((X (list (list (list 'X0 X0))))))
   (and (P=CA (X0 root) pull)
      (setq x
            (append
             (let ((X X))
                (and (P=CA (X0 form) finite) (P=CA (X0 tense) present)
                     (setq X
                           (append
                            (let ((X X))
                               (and (P=CA (X0 number) plural)
                                    (P=CA (X0 person) (*OR* 3 2 1))))
                            (let ((X X))
                               (and (P=CA (X0 number) singular)
                                    (P=CA (X0 person) (*or* 2 1))))))))
             (let ((X X))
                (and (P=CA (X0 form) inf)))))
      (P=CA (X0 valency) trans)
      (or-dolist (FS X)
                 (let ((result-string ""))
                    (and
                     (setq result-string
                           (concatenate 'string result-string ""
                              (symbol-name 'P)))
                     (setq result-string
                           (concatenate 'string result-string ""
                              (symbol-name 'U)))
                     (setq result-string
                           (concatenate 'string result-string ""
                              (symbol-name 'L)))
                     (setq result-string
                           (concatenate 'string result-string ""
                              (symbol-name 'L))))
                    (if (equal result-string "") nil result-string)))))
```

9.5   Control

9.5.1   Top-Level Generation Algorithm

The top-level function in the generation module is called `realize-node-top-down`. It accepts two arguments: an ILT frame to be realized in the target language and the expected syntactic category of the target phrase.[10]   Lexical selection proceeds, assigning the best possible lexical choice of the appropriate category to the frame. Then any modifiers of the frame (including both embedded roles

---

[10]The expected syntactic category is determined by the following heuristics. If the frame is a role, then it will be realized as a noun or an adjective, in that order. If the frame is a proposition, it will be realized as a verb. If the frame is a modifier, it will be realized as an adverb if it is embedded in a proposition; otherwise it will be realized as an adjective.

and attributes) are realized recursively. Subsequently, an f-structure is constructed by applying the generation mapping rules for the given ILT type. This f-structure is returned as the result of `realize-node-top-down`. This f-structure is then passed to the `generator` function, created during compilation of the target GENKIT grammar, which produces a target language string from the f-structure. The algorithm for `realize-node-top-down` is shown here:

```
Realize-Node-Top-Down (Frame, Cat):
    Bind (CandidateSet, OrderedCandidateSet, CurrentCandidate, FStructure)
    CandidateSet = GL-Search (Frame)
    CandidateSet = FilterCat (CandidateSet, Cat)
    CandidateSet = FilterSubcat (Frame, CandidateSet)
    OrderedCandidateSet = SelectBestWord (Frame, CandidateSet)
    CandidateSet = SkimBestPenalties (OrderedCandidateSet)
    CurrentCandidate = FindBestEntry (CandidateSet)
    InvokeDemon (*realize-modifiers*, Frame)
    FStructure = InvokeDemon (*build-f-structure*, Frame)
    Return (FStructure)
```

The following submodules are called during the generation process:

1. *GL-Search.* This function finds any generation lexicon entries that might be used to realize the input frame.

2. *FilterCat.* This function removes any entries from the candidate set that do not match the *Cat* argument.

3. *FilterSubcat.* This function removes any entries from the candidate set whose subcategorization pattern does not match that of the ILT frame to be realized.

4. *SelectBestWord.* This function assigns a penalty to each candidate depending on how well it matches the meaning of the ILT frame to be realized, and orders the candidate set to correspond to the penalties assigned, that is, in increasing order.

5. *SkimBestPenalties.* This function finds all entries that share the lowest penalty.

6. *FindBestEntry.* This function decides which of the remaining entries to choose, in the event that *Cat* contains more than one possible category for realization. It makes use of heuristic rules such as *When a role may be realized as either a noun or an adjective, always try to use a noun first.*

7. *InvokeDemon.* This function searches for generation demons stored in the generation control knowledge base and fires them to process modifiers and build f-structures for frames once a lexical entry has been selected.

9.5.2   Control Knowledge

The process of realizing nodes in the ILT proceeds as described in the preceding for every type of ILT frame (`clause`, `proposition`, `role`, etc.). A separate knowledge base is used to support specific types of processing for specific types of ILT frames; it describes the steps that should be taken to realize each type. Hence, the top-level algorithm mentions general steps to be taken, and the knowledge base describes the specific tasks that embody each general step with respect to a particular ILT type. For example, to complete the general task of realizing any embedded modifiers for a `role` frame, the generator must realize any embedded role frames and any attributional modifiers. As a result, the generation knowledge frame for `role` contains two `realize-modifiers` generation demons: `realize-roles` and `realize-mods`. The implementation of generation demons is illustrated here.

```
(defun define-generation-frames ()

  (make-frame role
    (is-a (value (common ilt-type)))
    (map-expansion (:mod (common (get-values !frame 'modifier-slots))))
    (generation-demons
      (realize-modifiers (common (realize-roles !frame)
                                 (realize-mods !frame)))
      (build-f-structure (common (build-fs !frame '*ROLE)))))
  (make-frame modifier
    (is-a (value (common ilt-type)))
    (generation-demons
      (realize-modifiers (common))
      (build-f-structure (common (build-fs !frame '*MOD)))))
  (make-frame proposition
    (is-a (value (common ilt-type)))
    (map-expansion (:mod (common (get-values !frame 'modifier-slots))))
    (generation-demons
      (realize-modifiers (common (realize-roles !frame)
                                 (realize-mods !frame)))
      (build-f-structure (common (build-fs !frame '*PROPOSITION)))))
  (make-frame clause
    (is-a (value (common ilt-type)))
    (generation-demons
      (realize-modifiers (common (realize-clause-prop !frame)))
      (build-f-structure (common (build-fs !frame '*CLAUSE))))))
```

Two demons must be defined for each ILT type: `realize-modifiers` and `build-f-structure`. These must be defined so that the top-level algorithm can fire the appropriate demons when `invoke-demon` is called. The description of the demons is simple and straightforward. There are three COMMON-LISP functions that serve as demons: `realize-roles`, `realize-mods` and `build-fs`. `realize-roles` and `realize-mods` are general, in that they can process any kind of ILT frame; `build-fs` must be called with the particular type of mapping rule to fire when mapping the frame. (Section 9.3.1.1 describes the mapping phase and the significance of the `map-expansion` slot).

The ILT frames to be processed are linked to the generation knowledge frames via the `ilt-type` slot, which should be present in each ILT frame and have a value from the set (`clause, proposition, role, clause`). When an ILT frame is processed, the particular demons to be fired are inherited through the value of `ilt-type`.

Appendix A

Annotated English-Japanese Trace

A.1 Preamble

This appendix contains a trace of the KBMT-89 system's analysis, augmentation and generation components. Except as noted, the following introductory remarks, as well as the preamble, apply to this appendix and to appendix B, which also has its own preamble. The reader is urged to consult earlier chapters, especially 7, 8 and 9, for a fuller description of the processes displayed in the appendices.

For this trace, the source language is English and the target language is Japanese. Annotations are provided throughout to comment on or explain various phenomena. The source text input is *1. Remove the tape from the diskette drive.* Note that the sentence begins with an integer and a period, as in an enumerated list, and it ends with a period. This punctuation mark is represented as `period`.

This and the subsequent appendix (a Japanese-to-English example) were produced using a utility that can generate dribble traces with various levels of detail. Some settings produce too much unilluminating detail, some too little. It was necessary to edit the two traces in several ways.

First, relics of implementation (that is, strings of no computational significance) and various housekeeping slots were excised. System messages were standardized.

Second, extra blank lines were added at various places. The spaces were inserted by hand to improve display of the traces and the marginal annotations. Relatedly,

263

in the English-Japanese example, the f-structures produced at various points during generation appear in their raw form; but the f-structures in the Japanese-English example were "pretty-printed" by hand to improve readability

Next, to constrain otherwise very long examples, lines displaying the flagging of inapplicable rules were omitted.

Also, some few ILT frames were elided when they presented extra, unilluminating and unnecessarily complicating levels of nesting. These deletions are flagged in the annotations.

Finally, in the "Analysis" sections of both traces, lines that appear repetitious were deleted. The apparent redundancy embodied in the lines is a function of KBMT-89's run-time, left-right parser. This is explained as follows. The parser uses a *shift-reduce* mechanism. The Lexical Functional Grammar is compiled into a large table of states. The state table encodes the relationship between a parser state and the set of valid actions (shift and reduce) available at that state, the actions being indexed by an input token corresponding to the next word (or character) in the input string. A *shift* action is one that accepts a word from the input string and changes to a new state in the LR table. A *reduce* action is one that unifies the results of earlier actions and shifts to a new state in the table. The combined actions of shifting and reducing allow the parser to build a complete f-structure for a sentence as determined by the grammar.[1]

Now, an active state is created using (i) the state table, (ii) the current state and (iii) the next (unshifted) word in the input string. Active states are collapsed when they have the same original state, but not when they have the same action (destination state). While multiple activations of the same rule might appear to be spurious, this is normal behavior for a shift-reduce parser. When more than one shift action is available during the shift phase, copies of the word in question are shifted into each of the currently active shift states. Often the active states generated from the shifts will contain identical reduce actions. These reduce actions appear as rules in the trace output. For example, one version of the English-Japanese trace contained the following lines when the first appearance of the English word *the* was parsed:

```
rule # 362 E-KBMT89F-362     <DET>(31) --> <$WORD$>(30)
rule # 362 E-KBMT89F-362     <DET>(32) --> <$WORD$>(30)
```

The apparent repitition of the same action means that there is more than one distinct parse path that is being followed at that point in the parse. But in that

---

[1]Some aspects of parsing in KBMT-89 were discussed in chapter 7; building f-structures during parsing was covered in chapter 3. For more details concerning shift-reduce parsing, see Tomita 1986.

only one path is used by the end of the parse to build a complete structure, the rules indexed (by node identifiers) to inapplicable paths were removed from the English-Japanese and Japanese-English traces.[2]

KBMT-89's bottom-up LR parser can be used in word-based mode for English or character-based mode for Japanese. For English, the parser treats one word at a time. For each word, it builds all possible legal structures until there are no more applicable rules. It then goes to the next word and tries to combine the structure built for the previous word or words. That is, at each stage the parser attempts to build a complete structure, or one that takes into account all the words so far parsed. This of course is the very point of bottom-up, LR parsing.

In the following trace, each word (or string treated like a word—e.g., '1') is highlighted at the beginning of the set of rules that were applied. PERIOD, REMOVE and so forth likewise appear at the point at which they are being parsed. They serve as indices or placemarkers and are produced automatically during the trace.

The rules that follow each word are those that actually applied or successfully fired, thus contributing to the building of a candidate structure at that point. However, most of the structures will not be used in the final parse tree or structure. For instance, the following rule

```
rule # 247 E-KBMT89F-247    <CARD-NUM>(2) --> <$WORD$>(1)
```

is used in the final parse tree (given at the end of the next section). But the one immediately following it—

```
rule # 116 E-KBMT89F-116    <Q>(3) --> <CARD-NUM>(2)
```

—is not. This rule would have been used if the integer 1 were a quantifier in the sentence; it is not. Neither does the integer represent a quantity <QUANT> (e.g., *a 6-foot cable*). Rather, it is eventually understood to be a cardinal numeral (<CARD-NUM>). Here is the rule that is ultimately successful and therefore appears in the final tree:

```
rule # 247 E-KBMT89F-247    <CARD-NUM>(2) --> <$WORD$>(1)
```

---

[2]We are exploring ways of collapsing these branches; currently, the computational cost of recognizing the redundancy outweighs the cost of allowing different parse paths to perform redundant actions.

Each rule display has the same general structure: a number, a name and the corresponding phrase structure rule. These parts are identified and described in figure A.1.

The rightmost part of each line in the "Analysis" sections contains the phrase structure rule that applied at that point. The numbers in parentheses identify the preceding category's node in the phrase structure.

Most of the abbreviations are general and should be transparent (e.g., NP, DET, V and so forth). Several symbols require an introduction, however.

<START> rules are needed to identify the topmost node in any complete phrase structure tree in word-based parses. In the English-Japanese trace below, the rule appears only after either 1. or the entire sentence, 1. Remove the tape from the diskette drive. In the former case, the string is initially read as an NP followed by a period. However, the parser soon learns that there is more of the sentence to be analyzed, and the first <START> rule therefore cannot apply. Each sentence must use at least one successful <START> rule.

<$WORD$> is a special phrase-structure category used to identify the terminal node associated with each word. It triggers lexical lookup in analysis, for example, <$WORD$>(19) --> REMOVE. For our sentence-opening string, <$WORD$> fires the part-of-speech rule CARD-NUM ("cardinal number").

Others symbols include <MEASURE-NP>, which stands for "measurement NP" and is used in case a quantity is a measurement; <S/PRE-SENT>, which is used for presentential sentences such *Yes*, *No* and, for our purposes, *1.*; <CN>, which is a "compound noun"; and <*N1> and <*N2>, which are inserted into the grammar by the parser to handle ordering for compound nouns at the the lexical item level (they are unrelated to <N1> and <N2>).

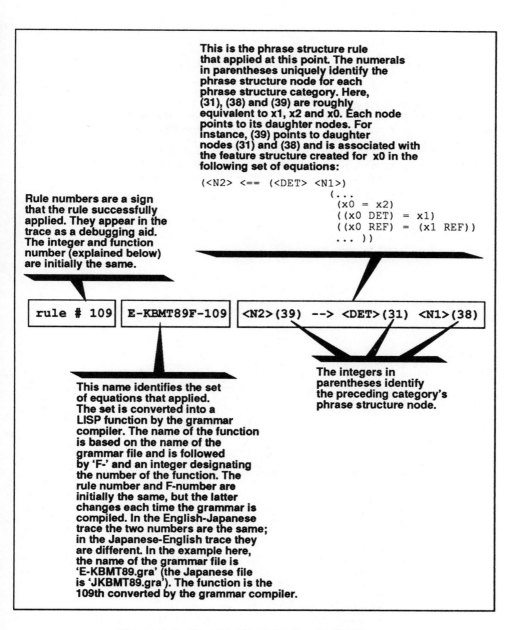

This is the phrase structure rule that applied at this point. The numerals in parentheses uniquely identify the phrase structure node for each phrase structure category. Here, (31), (38) and (39) are roughly equivalent to x1, x2 and x0. Each node points to its daughter nodes. For instance, (39) points to daughter nodes (31) and (38) and is associated with the feature structure created for x0 in the following set of equations:

```
(<N2> <== (<DET> <N1>)
              (...
               (x0 = x2)
               ((x0 DET) = x1)
               ((x0 REF) = (x1 REF))
               ... ))
```

Rule numbers are a sign that the rule successfully applied. They appear in the trace as a debugging aid. The integer and function number (explained below) are initially the same.

```
rule # 109    E-KBMT89F-109    <N2>(39) --> <DET>(31) <N1>(38)
```

This name identifies the set of equations that applied. The set is converted into a LISP function by the grammar compiler. The name of the function is based on the name of the grammar file and is followed by 'F-' and an integer designating the number of the function. The rule number and F-number are initially the same, but the latter changes each time the grammar is compiled. In the English-Japanese trace the two numbers are the same; in the Japanese-English trace they are different. In the example here, the name of the grammar file is 'E-KBMT89.gra' (the Japanese file is 'JKBMT89.gra'). The function is the 109th converted by the grammar compiler.

The integers in parentheses identify the preceding category's phrase structure node.

Figure A.1: **Description of rules in the trace.**

A.2   Analysis

```
parsing sentence:
1 period  Remove the tape from the diskette drive period
```

```
1
```

<$WORD$>
*causes a lexical rule
to fire.   The next
four rules build on the*
<CARD-NUM> (2)
structure.

```
    rule #  386 E-KBMT89F-386    <$WORD$>(1) --> 1
    rule #  247 E-KBMT89F-247    <CARD-NUM>(2) --> <$WORD$>(1)
    rule #  116 E-KBMT89F-116    <Q>(3) --> <CARD-NUM>(2)
    rule #  143 E-KBMT89F-143    <QUANT>(4) --> <CARD-NUM>(2)
    rule #  193 E-KBMT89F-193    <N>(5) --> <CARD-NUM>(2)
    rule #  194 E-KBMT89F-194    <NP>(6) --> <CARD-NUM>(2)
    rule #  198 E-KBMT89F-198    <CARD-NUM-COORD>(7) --> <CARD-NUM>(2)
    rule #  142 E-KBMT89F-142    <MEASURE-NP>(8) --> <QUANT>(4)
    rule #  131 E-KBMT89F-131    <CN>(9) --> <N>(5)
    rule #  219 E-KBMT89F-219    <N-COORD>(10) --> <N>(5)
    rule #  207 E-KBMT89F-207    <NP-COORD>(11) --> <NP>(6)
    rule #  152 E-KBMT89F-152    <MOD>(12) --> <MEASURE-NP>(8)
```

<CN>
*at phrase level allows
the input word to be
the first item in a com-
pound noun.*

```
PERIOD
    rule #  386 E-KBMT89F-386    <$WORD$>(14) --> PERIOD
    rule #  380 E-KBMT89F-380    <@PERIOD>(16) --> <$WORD$>(14)
    rule #    1 E-KBMT89F-1      <START>(17) --> <NP>(6) <@PERIOD>(16)
```

<START>
is triggered by <NP>
and <@PERIOD>.

```
REMOVE
    rule #  386 E-KBMT89F-386    <$WORD$>(19) --> REMOVE
    rule #  262 E-KBMT89F-262    <V>(20) --> <$WORD$>(19)
    rule #  225 E-KBMT89F-225    <V-A>(21) --> <V>(20)
    rule #   57 E-KBMT89F-57     <V2>(22) --> <V-A>(21)
    rule #   91 E-KBMT89F-91     <V-COORD>(23) --><V-A>(21)
    rule #   54 E-KBMT89F-54     <VP>(24) --> <V2>(22)
    rule #   53 E-KBMT89F-53     <VP2>(25) --> <VP>(24)
    rule #   34 E-KBMT89F-34     <VP-ADV-S>(26) --> <VP2>(25)
    rule #   63 E-KBMT89F-63     <IMP>(27) --> <VP2>(25)
    rule #   99 E-KBMT89F-99     <VP2-COORD>(28) --> <VP2>(25)
```

<V-COORD>
*identifies the coordi-
nate structure built
by the grammar rule.*
<V-A> *is name of the
f-structure(s) used to
build the f-structure
for the left-hand side of
the rule.*

```
THE
    rule #  386 E-KBMT89F-386    <$WORD$>(30) --> THE
    rule #  362 E-KBMT89F-362    <DET>(31) --> <$WORD$>(30)
```

```
TAPE
    rule #  386 E-KBMT89F-386    <$WORD$>(34) --> TAPE
    rule #  349 E-KBMT89F-349    <N>(35) --> <$WORD$>(34)
    rule #  131 E-KBMT89F-131    <CN>(36) --> <N>(35)
    rule #  219 E-KBMT89F-219    <N-COORD>(37) --> <N>(35)
    rule #  112 E-KBMT89F-112    <N1>(38) --> <CN>(36)
    rule #  109 E-KBMT89F-109    <N2>(39) --> <DET>(31) <N1>(38)
    rule #  215 E-KBMT89F-215    <N1-COORD>(41) --> <N1>(38)
    rule #  104 E-KBMT89F-104    <N3>(42) --> <N2>(39)
    rule #  211 E-KBMT89F-211    <N2-COORD>(43) --> <N2>(39)
    rule #  104 E-KBMT89F-104    <N3>(44) --> <N2>(40)
```

```
rule # 211  E-KBMT89F-211    <N2-COORD>(45) --> <N2>(40)
rule # 100  E-KBMT89F-100    <NP>(46) --> <N3>(42)
rule # 207  E-KBMT89F-207    <NP-COORD>(48) --> <NP>(46)
rule #  55  E-KBMT89F-55     <VP>(49) --> <V2>(22) <NP>(46)
rule # 207  E-KBMT89F-207    <NP-COORD>(50) --> <NP>(46)
rule #  53  E-KBMT89F-53     <VP2>(52) --> <VP>(49)
rule #  34  E-KBMT89F-34     <VP-ADV-S>(53) --> <VP2>(52)
rule #  63  E-KBMT89F-63     <IMP>(54) --> <VP2>(52)
rule #  99  E-KBMT89F-99     <VP2-COORD>(55) --> <VP2>(52)
rule #   9  E-KBMT89F-9      <S2>(56) --> <IMP>(54)
rule #   7  E-KBMT89F-7      <S/PRE-SENT>(57) --> <S2>(56)
rule #  22  E-KBMT89F-22     <S>(58) --> <S/PRE-SENT>(57)
rule #  16  E-KBMT89F-16     <S-COORD>(59) --> <S>(58)
```

```
FROM
rule # 386  E-KBMT89F-386    <$WORD$>(61) --> FROM
rule # 329  E-KBMT89F-329    <P>(65) --> <$WORD$>(61)
rule # 184  E-KBMT89F-184    <PP>(67) --> <P>(65)
rule #  71  E-KBMT89F-71     <VP>(68) --> <VP>(49) <PP>(67)
rule #  53  E-KBMT89F-53     <VP2>(69) --> <VP>(68)
rule #  34  E-KBMT89F-34     <VP-ADV-S>(70) --> <VP2>(69)
rule #  63  E-KBMT89F-63     <IMP>(71) --> <VP2>(69)
rule #  99  E-KBMT89F-99     <VP2-COORD>(72) --> <VP2>(69)
```

Here, 'from' is identified as a preposition.

```
THE
rule # 386  E-KBMT89F-386    <$WORD$>(74) --> THE
rule # 362  E-KBMT89F-362    <DET>(76) --> <$WORD$>(74)
```

```
DISKETTE
rule # 386  E-KBMT89F-386    <$WORD$>(79) --> DISKETTE
rule # 348  E-KBMT89F-348    <*N1>(80) --> <$WORD$>(79)
rule # 349  E-KBMT89F-349    <N>(81) --> <$WORD$>(79)
rule # 131  E-KBMT89F-131    <CN>(82) --> <N>(81)
rule # 219  E-KBMT89F-219    <N-COORD>(83) --> <N>(81)
rule # 112  E-KBMT89F-112    <N1>(84) --> <CN>(82)
rule # 109  E-KBMT89F-109    <N2>(86) --> <DET>(76) <N1>(84)
rule # 215  E-KBMT89F-215    <N1-COORD>(88) --> <N1>(84)
rule # 104  E-KBMT89F-104    <N3>(91) --> <N2>(86)
rule # 211  E-KBMT89F-211    <N2-COORD>(92) --> <N2>(86)
rule # 100  E-KBMT89F-100    <NP>(96) --> <N3>(91)
rule # 168  E-KBMT89F-168    <PP>(100) --> <P>(65) <NP>(96)
rule # 207  E-KBMT89F-207    <NP-COORD>(101) --> <NP>(96)
rule #  71  E-KBMT89F-71     <VP>(104) --> <VP>(49) <PP>(100)
rule # 172  E-KBMT89F-172    <PP-COORD>(105) --> <PP>(100)
rule #  53  E-KBMT89F-53     <VP2>(106) --> <VP>(104)
rule #  34  E-KBMT89F-34     <VP-ADV-S>(107) --> <VP2>(106)
rule #  63  E-KBMT89F-63     <IMP>(108) --> <VP2>(106)
rule #  99  E-KBMT89F-99     <VP2-COORD>(109) --> <VP2>(106)
rule #   9  E-KBMT89F-9      <S2>(110) --> <IMP>(108)
rule #   7  E-KBMT89F-7      <S/PRE-SENT>(111) --> <S2>(110)
rule #  22  E-KBMT89F-22     <S>(112) --> <S/PRE-SENT>(111)
rule #  16  E-KBMT89F-16     <S-COORD>(113) --> <S>(112)
```

*<*N1> operates at the lexical level. It allows the input word to be the first item in a compound noun.*

DRIVE
```
    rule #  386  E-KBMT89F-386    <$WORD$>(115) --> DRIVE
    rule #  347  E-KBMT89F-347    <*N2>(116) --> <$WORD$>(115)
    rule #  349  E-KBMT89F-349    <N>(119) --> <$WORD$>(115)
    rule #  346  E-KBMT89F-346    <N>(121) --> <*N1>(80) <*N2>(116)
    rule #  131  E-KBMT89F-131    <CN>(125) --> <N>(119)
    rule #  219  E-KBMT89F-219    <N-COORD>(126) --> <N>(119)
    rule #  112  E-KBMT89F-112    <N1>(129) --> <CN>(125)
    rule #  111  E-KBMT89F-111    <N2>(131) --> <N1>(129)
    rule #  215  E-KBMT89F-215    <N1-COORD>(132) --> <N1>(129)
    rule #  104  E-KBMT89F-104    <N3>(135) --> <N2>(131)
    rule #  211  E-KBMT89F-211    <N2-COORD>(136) --> <N2>(131)
    rule #  100  E-KBMT89F-100    <NP>(139) --> <N3>(135)
    rule #  207  E-KBMT89F-207    <NP-COORD>(141) --> <NP>(139)
    rule #  131  E-KBMT89F-131    <CN>(143) --> <N>(121)
    rule #  219  E-KBMT89F-219    <N-COORD>(144) --> <N>(121)
    rule #  112  E-KBMT89F-112    <N1>(145) --> <CN>(143)
    rule #  109  E-KBMT89F-109    <N2>(147) --> <DET>(76) <N1>(145)
    rule #  215  E-KBMT89F-215    <N1-COORD>(149) --> <N1>(145)
    rule #  104  E-KBMT89F-104    <N3>(152) --> <N2>(147)
    rule #  211  E-KBMT89F-211    <N2-COORD>(153) --> <N2>(147)
    rule #  100  E-KBMT89F-100    <NP>(157) --> <N3>(152)
    rule #  168  E-KBMT89F-168    <PP>(161) --> <P>(65) <NP>(157)
    rule #  207  E-KBMT89F-207    <NP-COORD>(162) --> <NP>(157)
    rule #  172  E-KBMT89F-172    <PP-COORD>(164) --> <PP>(159)
    rule #   71  E-KBMT89F-71     <VP>(165) --> <VP>(49) <PP>(161)
    rule #  172  E-KBMT89F-172    <PP-COORD>(166) --> <PP>(161)
    rule #   53  E-KBMT89F-53     <VP2>(167) --> <VP>(165)
    rule #   34  E-KBMT89F-34     <VP-ADV-S>(168) --> <VP2>(167)
    rule #   63  E-KBMT89F-63     <IMP>(169) --> <VP2>(167)
    rule #   99  E-KBMT89F-99     <VP2-COORD>(170) --> <VP2>(167)
    rule #    9  E-KBMT89F-9      <S2>(171) --> <IMP>(169)
    rule #    7  E-KBMT89F-7      <S/PRE-SENT>(172) --> <S2>(171)
    rule #   22  E-KBMT89F-22     <S>(173) --> <S/PRE-SENT>(172)
    rule #   16  E-KBMT89F-16     <S-COORD>(174) --> <S>(173)
```

PERIOD
```
    rule #  386  E-KBMT89F-386    <$WORD$>(176) --> PERIOD
    rule #  380  E-KBMT89F-380    <@PERIOD>(177) --> <$WORD$>(176)
    rule #   27  E-KBMT89F-27     <END-PUNC>(178) --> <@PERIOD>(177)
    rule #    5  E-KBMT89F-5      <START>(179) --> <CARD-NUM>(2)
                                  <@PERIOD>(15) <S>(173)
                                  <END-PUNC>(178)
```

<*N2> operates at lexical level to allow input word to be the second item in a compound noun. Then, <N>(121) is the f-structure containing lexically identified compound noun information for 'diskette drive'.

Number of 'semantic candidates' identifies number of ambiguities for the complete sentence. There are no ambiguities here. The node number is the topmost node; it corresponds to <START>(179).

```
1 (1) semantic candidate found  node # 179
```

```
((sem
   (*sem*
    ((number-bullet
       (($is-token-of any-number) ($id (*id* 15))
        ($map-data (*map* { map-str (any-number-map) } ))
        (cardinality 1)))
     (clausal-mark +) (mood imperative) (tense present)
     (source
       ((reference definite) (number singular)
        ($map-data (*map* { map-str diskette drive } ))
        ($is-token-of diskette-drive) ($id (*id* 41))))
     (theme
       ((reference definite) (number singular)
        ($map-data (*map* { map-str tape } ))
        ($is-token-of sticky-tape) ($id (*id* 20))))
     (agent *reader) ($map-data (*map* { map-str remove } ))
     ($is-token-of remove) ($id (*id* 19)))))
  (number-bullet
   ((root 1) (value 1)
    (sem
     (*sem*
      (($is-token-of any-number) ($id (*id* 15))
       ($map-data (*map* { map-str (any-number-map) } ))
       (cardinality 1))))))
 (obj
  ((case acc)
   (sem
    (*sem*
     ((reference definite) (number singular)
      ($map-data (*map* { map-str tape } ))
      ($is-token-of sticky-tape) ($id (*id* 20)))))
   (ref definite) (det ((root the) (ref definite))) (root tape)
   (count no) (person 3) (number singular) (meas-unit no)
   (proper no)))
 (valency trans) (mood imperative) (tense present) (form inf)
 (ppadjunct
  ((prep from)
   (sem
    (*sem*
     ((reference definite) (number singular)
      ($map-data (*map* { map-str diskette drive } ))
      ($is-token-of diskette-drive) ($id (*id* 41))))))
   (ref definite) (det ((root the) (ref definite)))
   (root diskette_drive) (person 3) (number singular) (count yes)
   (proper no) (meas-unit no)))
 (root remove) (comp-type no) (passive -))
```

A complete f-structure is produced. The sem *feature contains* *sem*, *the semantic f-structure. Most semantic information is captured here.*

source
— *This slot holds information about semantic values associated with the filler of the* source *thematic role.*

obj
— *This slot contains information about syntactic entity* object; sem *here contains information associated with* object *slot's filler.*

This is a human-readable representation of the parse, used to facilitate debugging. It contains essential semantic information derived from the parse.

```
semantic candidate 1 of 1
[*remove
  (agent *reader)
  (theme [*sticky-tape
          (number singular)
          (reference definite)])
  (source [*diskette-drive
          (number singular)
          (reference definite)])
  (tense present)
  (mood imperative)
  (clausal-mark +)
  (number-bullet [*any-number (cardinality 1)])]]
```

```
;;;;;;;;;;;;;;;;;;;;;;;;;;;;;;;;;;;;;;;;;;;;;;;;;;;;;;;;
;   TREE


*  (disp-tree))
<START>(179) --> <CARD-NUM>(2) <@PERIOD>(15) <S>(173) <END-PUNC>(178)
 <CARD-NUM>(2) --> <$WORD$>(1)
      <$WORD$>(1) --> 1
 <@PERIOD>(15) --> <$WORD$>(14)
      <$WORD$>(14) --> PERIOD
 <S>(173) --> <S/PRE-SENT>(172)
   <S/PRE-SENT>(172) --> <S2>(171)
       <S2>(171) --> <IMP>(169)
           <IMP>(169) --> <VP2>(167)
              <VP2>(167) --> <VP>(165)
                  <VP>(165) --> <VP>(49) <PP>(161)
                      <VP>(49) --> <V2>(22) <NP>(46)
                          <V2>(22) --> <V-A>(21)
                              <V-A>(21) --> <V>(20)
                                  <V>(20) --> <$WORD$>(19)
                                      <$WORD$>(19) --> REMOVE
                          <NP>(46) --> <N3>(42)
                              <N3>(42) --> <N2>(39)
                                  <N2>(39) --> <DET>(31) <N1>(38)
                                      <DET>(31) --> <$WORD$>(30)
                                          <$WORD$>(30) --> THE
                                      <N1>(38) --> <CN>(36)
                                          <CN>(36) --> <N>(35)
                                              <N>(35) --> <$WORD$>(34)
                                                  <$WORD$>(34) --> TAPE
                      <PP>(161) --> <P>(65) <NP>(157)
                          <P>(65) --> <$WORD$>(61)
                              <$WORD$>(61) --> FROM
                          <NP>(157) --> <N3>(152)
                              <N3>(152) --> <N2>(147)
                                  <N2>(147) --> <DET>(76) <N1>(145)
                                      <DET>(76) --> <$WORD$>(74)
                                          <$WORD$>(74) --> THE
                                      <N1>(145) --> <CN>(143)
                                          <CN>(143) --> <N>(121)
                                              <N>(121) --> <*N1>(80) <*N2>(116)
                                                  <*N1>(80) --> <$WORD$>(79)
                                                      <$WORD$>(79) --> DISKETTE
                                                  <*N2>(116) --> <$WORD$>(115)
                                                      <$WORD$>(115) --> DRIVE
<END-PUNC>(178) --> <@PERIOD>(177)
     <@PERIOD>(177) --> <$WORD$>(176)
          <$WORD$>(176) --> PERIOD
```

This tree displays the analysis rules used in the correct parse of the sentence. The tree is also represented as figure A.2.

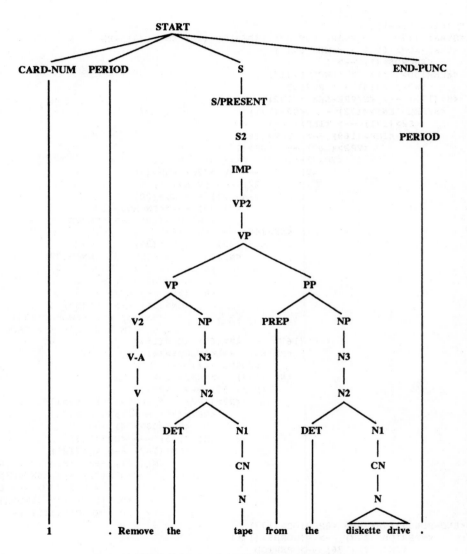

Figure A.2: **Tree structure of parsed sentence.**

A.3   Augmentation

By way of an introduction to this part of the trace, note at the outset that $id *is a parser-defined slot for f-structure indices; it is used for semantic unification at the end of the parse. The value of this slot is represented by* *id.

  $map-data *is a pointer to the dictionary to specify mapping rules, in this case for the concepts* *remove, *sticky-tape *and so on. It acquires the set of mapping rules for the English words* *"remove," "tape" and so forth.* any-number-map *is the name of the set of mapping rules for "1."*

```
Processing ...
```

```
Parse:
(*remove ($id (*id* 5)) ($map-data remove) (agent *reader)
  (theme
      (*sticky-tape
          ($id (*id* 6)) ($map-data tape) (number singular)
          (reference definite)))
  (source
      (*diskette-drive
          ($id (*id* 27)) ($map-data diskette drive)
          (number singular) (reference definite)))
  (tense present) (mood imperative) (clausal-mark +)
  (number-bullet
      (*any-number
          (cardinality 1) ($map-data any-number-map) ($id (*id* 1)))))
```

The augmentor begins processing parser output (see the discussion of format conversion in chapter 8). Only semantics and selected syntactic features used by the augmentor are shown here.

```
Bare ILT:
[clause1377
    (speechactid
        [speech-act1375
            (time time1376)
            (space)
            (direct?)
            (speech-act)])
    (propositionid
        [*remove
            (number-bullet
                [*any-number
                    (cardinality 1)])
            (mood imperative)
            (tense present)
            (source
                [*diskette-drive
                    (reference definite)
                    (number singular)])
            (theme
                [*sticky-tape
                    (reference definite)
                    (number singular)])
            (agent *reader)])]
```

Next, the reading is converted into linked FRAMEKIT frames. The display highlights the tree structure of the ILT, i.e., contains information only from parser output. This is a "bare ILT."

After applying the pattern matcher, the reading's ILT *consists of the frames shown here (the* value *facets and* common *views have been elided for brevity and clarity).*

Each frame identifies its type in an ilt-type *slot; all except* speech-act *also identify the clause to which they belong; note the* clauseid *slots.*

The $map-data *field allows the augmentor to refer to the actual source string, giving rise to the concept for the frame.*

```
applying conversions to ILT
ILT to augment:
(clause1377
    (main-clause yes)
    (number-bullet role1374)
    (ilt-type clause)
    (speechactid speech-act1375)
    (propositionid proposition1371)
    (clauseid clause1377)
    (frame-maker augmentor))
(role1374
    (reference definite)
    (roleid role1374)
    (ilt-type role)
    (propositionid proposition1371)
    (clauseid clause1377)
    (parent-frame proposition1371)
    ($id 1)
    ($map-data (any-number-map))
    (cardinality 1)
    (is-a *any-number)
    (is-token-of *any-number)
    (frame-maker augmentor))
(speech-act1375
    (time time1376)
    (space)
    (direct? yes)
    (speech-act request-action)
    (ilt-type speech-act)
    (speechactid speech-act1375)
    (frame-maker augmentor))
(proposition1371
    (time (at time1376))
    (agent agent1379)
    (propositionid proposition1371)
    (ilt-type proposition)
    (clauseid clause1377)
    (clausal-mark +)
    (mood imperative)
    (source role1373)
    (theme role1372)
    ($map-data remove)
    ($id 5)
    (is-a *remove)
    (is-token-of *remove)
    (frame-maker augmentor))
(agent1379
    (reference definite)
    (ilt-type role)
    (is-token-of *reader)
    (clauseid clause1377)
    (roleid role1378)
    (propositionid proposition1371)
    (frame-maker augmentor))
```

```
(role1373
    (roleid role1373)
    (ilt-type role)
    (propositionid proposition1371)
    (clauseid clause1377)
    (parent-frame proposition1371)
    (reference definite)
    (number singular)
    ($map-data diskette drive)
    ($id 27)
    (is-a *diskette-drive)
    (is-token-of *diskette-drive)
    (frame-maker augmentor))
(role1372
    (roleid role1372)
    (ilt-type role)
    (propositionid proposition1371)
    (clauseid clause1377)
    (parent-frame proposition1371)
    (reference definite)
    (number singular)
    ($map-data tape)
    ($id 6)
    (is-a *sticky-tape)
    (is-token-of *sticky-tape)
    (frame-maker augmentor))

Final ILT:
[clause1377
    ($sentence$ Sentence 11: 1 period Remove the tape from the
                               diskette drive period )
    (main-clause yes)
    (number-bullet
        [*any-number
            (reference definite)
            (cardinality 1)])
    (speechactid
        [speech-act1375
            (time time1376)
            (space)
            (direct? yes)
            (speech-act request-action)])
    (propositionid
        [*remove
            (time (at time1376))
            (agent
                [*reader
                    (reference definite)])
            (source
                [*diskette-drive
                    (reference definite)])
            (theme
                [*sticky-tape
                    (reference definite)])])]]
```

Since there is only one reading, the above ILT is immediately passed to the generator (stripping out some house-keeping slots used only by the augmentor). Sentence 11 gives the sentence's number from the corpus.

A.4   Generation

```
* (gen-aug-file "11.ilt")
```

The generator prints out the names of the ILT frames to be generated.

```
FrameList: (clause1377 role1374 speech-act1375 proposition1371
            agent1379 role1373 role1372)

Clauses: (clause1377)

Trying to realize clause1377 as non-lexical.
```

There is no explicit lexeme associated with a clause frame; the frame relates all information (proposition, speech-act, etc.) associated with the single ILT clause.

```
Recursively realizing number-bullet of clause1377: role1374
Trying to realize role1374 as (N).

Candidate set for role1374: NIL

Mapping role1374.

F-Structure for role1374:
((value 1) (root 1))

Trying to realize proposition1371 as (V)
```

The generator uses a realization heuristic that attempts to generate proposition heads as verbal heads in Japanese.

```
Candidate set for proposition1371: (torinozoku)
   candidates from (V): (torinozoku)
   proper subcategorization: (torinozoku)
   ordered entries: (torinozoku 1.01)
   best penalties: (torinozoku 1.01)
   final choice: "torinozo"

Recursively realizing theme of proposition1371: role1372
Trying to realize role1372 as (N).
```

Then, another heuristic is used to generate roles within propositions as Japanese noun phrases.

```
Candidate set for role1372: (teepu)
   candidates from (N): (teepu)
   proper subcategorization: (teepu)
   ordered entries: (teepu 0)
   best penalties: (teepu 0)
   final choice: "teepu"

Mapping role1372.

F-Structure for role1372:
((root teepu) (cat N) (wh -))

Recursively realizing source of proposition1371: role1373
Trying to realize role1373 as (N).

Candidate set for role1373: (deisukettodoraibu)
   candidates from (N): (deisukettodoraibu)
   proper subcategorization: (deisukettodoraibu)
   ordered entries: (deisukettodoraibu 0)
   best penalties: (deisukettodoraibu 0)
   final choice: "de-isuketto doraibu"
```

```
Mapping role1373.

F-Structure for role1373:
((root deisukettodoraibu) (cat N) (wh -))

Recursively realizing agent of proposition1371: agent1379
Trying to realize agent1379 as (N).

Candidate set for agent1379: (yuuzaa)
  candidates from (N): (yuuzaa)
  proper subcategorization: (yuuzaa)
  ordered entries: (yuuzaa 0)
  best penalties: (yuuzaa 0)
  final choice: "yuuzaa"

Mapping agent1379.

F-Structure for agent1379:
((root yuuzaa) (cat N) (wh -))
Mapping proposition1371.
-------------------------------------------------
Frame: proposition1371 Lex: torinozoku
FS: ((vtype V-5dan-ki) (subcat trans) (cat V) (root torinozoku))
(defrule j *proposition
   :any
   (null (frame-accessor frame (quote clauseid) (quote focus)))
   (feature passive -)
   (feature subj-case ga)
   ((expr
     (cond
       ((lex-feature-p (quote subcat) !lex (quote trans2)) (quote ni))
       (t (quote o))))
    => (feature obj-case))
   (feature obj2-case ni)
```

This rule fires on propositions that don't have a filled focus *slot, and it adds to the sentential f-structure appropriate values for the features* passive, subj-case, obj-case *and* obj-case2.

```
Predicate returns T.
Feature (passive -) added.
Feature (subj-case ga) added.
Feature (obj-case o) added.
Feature (obj2-case ni) added.

((obj2-case ni) (obj-case o) (subj-case ga) (passive -)
 (vtype V-5dan-ki) (subcat trans) (cat V) (root torinozoku))
-------------------------------------------------
Frame: proposition1371 Lex: torinozoku
FS: ((obj2-case ni) (obj-case o) (subj-case ga) (passive -)
     (vtype V-5dan-ki) (subcat trans) (cat V) (root torinozoku))
(defrule j *proposition
   :any
   (and
    (member
     (frame-accessor frame (quote clauseid) (quote speechactid)
      (quote speech-act))
     (quote (command request-action)))
```

This rule (i) fires on propositions whose associated speech act is a direct command or request for action, and (ii) maps the theme *slot into the syntactic* obj, *selecting the case marker.*

```
                  (equal
                   (frame-accessor frame (quote clauseid) (quote speechactid)
                    (quote direct?))
                   (quote yes)))
                 ((slot theme) => (slot obj)
                  (list !fsslot
                   (append
                    (cond
                     ((eq (frame-accessor frame (quote theme) (quote ilt-type))
                        (quote clause))
                       (quote ((wh -) (case o) (comp-form koto) (type rentai))))
                     (t (quote ((wh -) (case o)))))
                    !slotfs)))
```

Predicate returns T.
Slot obj added.

```
((obj ((wh -) (case o) (root teepu) (cat N) (wh -))) (obj2-case ni)
 (obj-case o) (subj-case ga) (passive -) (vtype V-5dan-ki)
 (subcat trans) (cat V) (root torinozoku))
-------------------------------------------------
Frame: proposition1371 Lex: torinozoku
FS: ((obj ((wh -) (case o) (root teepu) (cat N) (wh -)))
       (obj2-case ni) (obj-case o) (subj-case ga) (passive -)
       (vtype V-5dan-ki) (subcat trans) (cat V) (root torinozoku))
```

This rule maps source, goal or theme-property for any proposition except instances of *proceed-through-text.

```
(defrule j *proposition
  :any
  (not
   (equal (frame-accessor frame (quote is-token-of))
     (quote *proceed-through-text)))
  ((slot source) => (slot ppadjunct)
   (list !fsslot (cons (quote (part kara)) !slotfs)))
  ((slot goal) => (slot ppadjunct)
   (list !fsslot (cons (quote (part ni)) !slotfs)))
  ((slot theme-property) => (slot obj)
   (list !fsslot (append (quote ((wh -) (case o))) !slotfs)))
```

Predicate returns T.
Slot ppadjunct added.

```
((ppadjunct ((part kara) (root deisukettodoraibu) (cat N) (wh -)))
 (obj ((wh -) (case o) (root teepu) (cat N) (wh -))) (obj2-case ni)
 (obj-case o) (subj-case ga) (passive -) (vtype V-5dan-ki)
 (subcat trans) (cat V) (root torinozoku))
-------------------------------------------------
Frame: proposition1371 Lex: torinozoku
FS: ((ppadjunct
        ((part kara) (root deisukettodoraibu) (cat N) (wh -)))
       (obj ((wh -) (case o) (root teepu) (cat N) (wh -)))
       (obj2-case ni) (obj-case o) (subj-case ga) (passive -)
       (vtype V-5dan-ki) (subcat trans) (cat V) (root torinozoku))
```

```
(defrule j *proposition
  :any
  t
  (feature causative -)
```

Predicate returns T.
Feature (causative -) added.

```
((causative -)
 (ppadjunct ((part kara) (root deisukettodoraibu) (cat N) (wh -)))
 (obj ((wh -) (case o) (root teepu) (cat N) (wh -))) (obj2-case ni)
 (obj-case o) (subj-case ga) (passive -) (vtype V-5dan-ki)
 (subcat trans) (cat V) (root torinozoku))
--------------------------------------------------
Frame: proposition1371 Lex: torinozoku
FS: ((causative -)
     (ppadjunct
      ((part kara) (root deisukettodoraibu) (cat N) (wh -)))
     (obj ((wh -) (case o) (root teepu) (cat N) (wh -)))
     (obj2-case ni) (obj-case o) (subj-case ga) (passive -)
     (vtype V-5dan-ki) (subcat trans) (cat V) (root torinozoku))
(defrule j *proposition
  :any
  (or
   (and
    (member
     (frame-accessor frame (quote clauseid) (quote speechactid)
      (quote speech-act))
     (quote (command request-action)))
    (equal
     (frame-accessor frame (quote clauseid) (quote speechactid)
      (quote direct?))
     (quote yes)))
   (eq (frame-accessor frame (quote time)) (quote time1))
   (and (listp (frame-accessor frame (quote time)))
    (member (car (frame-accessor frame (quote time)))
     (quote (at at-or-after)))))
  (slot time present)
```

Predicate returns T.
Slot time added.

```
((time ((root present))) (causative -)
 (ppadjunct ((part kara) (root deisukettodoraibu) (cat N) (wh -)))
 (obj ((wh -) (case o) (root teepu) (cat N) (wh -))) (obj2-case ni)
 (obj-case o) (subj-case ga) (passive -) (vtype V-5dan-ki)
 (subcat trans) (cat V) (root torinozoku))
--------------------------------------------------
Frame: proposition1371 Lex: torinozoku
FS: ((time ((root present))) (causative -)
     (ppadjunct
      ((part kara) (root deisukettodoraibu) (cat N) (wh -)))
     (obj ((wh -) (case o) (root teepu) (cat N) (wh -)))
     (obj2-case ni) (obj-case o) (subj-case ga) (passive -)
     (vtype V-5dan-ki) (subcat trans) (cat V) (root torinozoku))
```

A default feature, (causative-), is added to the sentential f-structure.

This rule determines the tense *(present) for the sentential f-structure.*

This rule assigns the mood feature (imperative) in the sentential f-structure.

```
(defrule j *proposition
  :any
  t
  ((expr
    (cond
     ((and
       (member
        (frame-accessor frame (quote clauseid) (quote speechactid)
         (quote speech-act))
        (quote (command request-action)))
       (equal
        (frame-accessor frame (quote clauseid) (quote speechactid)
         (quote direct?))
        (quote yes)))
      (quote imp))
     ((equal
        (frame-accessor frame (quote clauseid) (quote speechactid)
         (quote speech-act))
        (quote request-information))
      (quote ques))
     (T (quote dec))))
   => (slot mood))
```

```
Predicate returns T.
Slot (mood ((root imp))) added.

((mood ((root imp))) (time ((root present))) (causative -)
 (ppadjunct ((part kara) (root deisukettodoraibu) (cat N) (wh -)))
 (obj ((wh -) (case o) (root teepu) (cat N) (wh -))) (obj2-case ni)
 (obj-case o) (subj-case ga) (passive -) (vtype V-5dan-ki)
 (subcat trans) (cat V) (root torinozoku))
------------------------------------------------
F-Structure for proposition1371:
((mood ((root imp))) (time ((root present))) (causative -)
 (ppadjunct ((part kara) (root deisukettodoraibu) (cat N) (wh -)))
 (obj ((wh -) (case o) (root teepu) (cat N) (wh -))) (obj2-case ni)
 (obj-case o) (subj-case ga) (passive -) (vtype V-5dan-ki)
 (subcat trans) (cat V) (root torinozoku))

Mapping clause1377.

F-Structure for clause1377:
```

This is the final f-structure.

```
((sent-num ((value 1) (root 1))) (formal +) (mood ((root imp)))
 (time ((root present))) (causative -)
 (ppadjunct ((part kara) (root deisukettodoraibu) (cat N) (wh -)))
 (obj ((wh -) (case o) (root teepu) (cat N) (wh -))) (obj2-case ni)
 (obj-case o) (subj-case ga) (passive -) (vtype V-5dan-ki)
 (subcat trans) (cat V) (root torinozoku))
```

```
J-GG-START called
  J-GG-INTEGER called
    J-GG-DIGIT called
    J-GG-DIGIT returns @1
  J-GG-INTEGER returns @1
  J-GG-PERIOD called
  J-GG-PERIOD returns
  J-GG-SXS called
    J-GG-S called
      J-GG-PP called
        J-GG-NP called
          J-GG-N called
            GG-N-ROOT called
            GG-N-ROOT returns de-isuketto doraibu
          J-GG-N returns de-isuketto doraibu
        J-GG-NP returns de-isuketto doraibu
        J-GG-P called
        J-GG-P returns @KA@RA
      J-GG-PP returns de-isuketto doraibu@KA@RA
      J-GG-S called
        J-GG-XP called
          J-GG-NP called
            J-GG-N called
              GG-N-ROOT called
              GG-N-ROOT returns teepu
            J-GG-N returns teepu
          J-GG-NP returns teepu
          J-GG-P called
          J-GG-P returns @WO
        J-GG-XP returns teepu@WO
        J-GG-S called
          J-GG-VP called
            J-GG-V called
              J-GG-V-TE called
                J-GG-V-RENYO2-T called
                  J-GG-V-5DAN-KI called
                    GG-V-ROOT called
                    GG-V-ROOT returns torinozo
                  J-GG-V-5DAN-KI returns torinozo
                J-GG-V-RENYO2-T returns torinozo@I
              J-GG-V-TE returns torinozo@I@TE
            J-GG-V returns torinozo@I@TE@KU@DA@SA@I
          J-GG-VP returns torinozo@I@TE@KU@DA@SA@I
        J-GG-S returns torinozo@I@TE@KU@DA@SA@I
      J-GG-S returns teepu@WO torinozo@I@TE@KU@DA@SA@I
    J-GG-S returns de-isuketto doraibu@KA@RA teepu@WO torinozo@I@TE@KU@DA@SA@I
  J-GG-SXS returns de-isuketto doraibu@KA@RA teepu@WO torinozo@I@TE@KU@DA@SA@I
J-GG-START returns @1 . de-isuketto doraibu@KA@RA teepu@WO torinozo@I@TE@KU@DA@SA@I
```

"1. de-isuketto doraibu@KA@RA teepu@WO torinozo@I@TE@KU@DA@SA@I"

The f-structure produced for the clause is subsequently processed by the Japanese generation grammar (J-GG) to produce the actual output string. Each rule called by the grammar is traced, indicating the portion of the output string that each rule produces.

The final string below could be processed to produce kana-kanji characters. Also, the '@' would be used before hiragana characters.

Appendix B

Annotated Japanese-English Trace

B.1 Preamble

This appendix contains a second trace of the KBMT-89 system's analysis, augmentation and generation components. The reader is urged to consult the preamble that preceded the first trace.

Here, the source language is Japanese and the target language is English. The input is *Sisutemu yunitto no de-isuketto doraibu no rebaa o okosi te kudasai*:

(B.1) sisutemu yunitto no   de-isuketto doraibu   no   rebaa o   okosi te kudasai
        system   unit   *gen* diskette   drive   *gen* lever *acc* flip up *formal imp*
        "Flip up the system unit diskette drive load lever"

Annotations that are redundant with the first trace are generally omitted.

Recall that the parser is in character-based mode for Japanese. Each roman character from the transliteration is displayed as it is parsed (cf. Chapter 4). So, for instance, the system begins postulating structures as soon as it parses the string 'si' because *si* is legal Japanese entity (e.g., depending on context, it could mean "do"). Several rules are fired (rules 412, 411, 453, etc.). They would, if eventually needed, point to *si*'s possible paradigms, given as MIZEN and RENYO. These

285

structures are later discarded when the more complete parse reveals the string 'si' to be a part of the word *sisutemu* ("system").

The KBMT-89 system was designed in part for eventual handling of Japanese ideographs. Special symbols are therefore prepended to certain strings: @si would be used for the hiragana form; $si for the kanji form;[1] and @^ would be the marker for various single-character hiragana consonant clusters.

Note that the following trace includes some analysis rules that differ from those in the previous trace. These JLEX rules make reference to the Japanese lexicon file that is compiled with the grammar. Entries are indexed by part of speech. So, the following rule

```
rule #1708 JLEX-NF-200    <N-ROOT>(47) --> SISUTEMU
```

is used to access information about the noun *sisutemu*.

As in the previous appendix, most abbreviations are transparent. Some marginal cases and exceptions are: COP designates a copula; NP+ is used to introduce NP coordination, and S+ sentential coordination; <XP> designates an NP plus case marker; and V-...DAN (where the ellipsis is replaced by an integer) identifies a Japanese verb class.

Note that the parser output at the end of section B.2 consists of three ambiguities or "semantic candidates." These were produced by an early implementation of the KBMT-89 system but are retained in the trace to illustrate connections between the analyzer and the concept lexicon and to display the augmentor's disambiguating processes. The ambiguities were produced because the concept lexicon entry for *load-lever* and *diskette drive* contained frames with two slots that modifiers can map to, namely, part-of and spatial-3d-part-of. By eliminating the latter, which is independently desirable, the ambiguities are eliminated.

---

[1]The kanji would not necessarily mean "do." Because there are several possible readings for the kanji character, each is indexed with an integer, as in $KU1.

B.2   Analysis

```
parsing sentence:
sisutemu yunitto no de-isuketto doraibu no rebaa o okosi te kudasai

S
I
 rule #1162  JKBMT89F-2324    @SI(12) --> SI
 rule # 412  JKBMT89F-824     <V-MIZEN1>(13) --> @SI(12)
 rule # 453  JKBMT89F-906     <V-RENYO1>(15) --> @SI(12)
 rule # 452  JKBMT89F-904     <V-RENYO1>(15, was 16) --> @SI(12)
 rule # 471  JKBMT89F-942     <V-RENYO2-T>(17) --> @SI(12)
 rule # 470  JKBMT89F-940     <V-RENYO2-T>(18) --> @SI(12)
 rule # 245  JKBMT89F-490     <V>(19) --> <V-RENYO1>(15)
 rule #  47  JKBMT89F-94      <VP>(20) --> <V>(19)
 rule #  43  JKBMT89F-86      <VP>(20, was 21) --> <V>(19)
 rule #  34  JKBMT89F-68      <S>(22) --> <VP>(20)
 rule #   9  JKBMT89F-18      <S+>(23) --> <S>(22)

S
U
 rule #1164  JKBMT89F-2328    @SU(40) --> SU


T
E
M
U
 rule #1708  JLEX-NF-200      <N-ROOT>(47) --> SISUTEMU
 rule # 877  JKBMT89F-1754    <CN>(48) --> <N-ROOT>(47)
 rule # 889  JKBMT89F-1778    <N>(49) --> <N-ROOT>(47)
 rule #  73  JKBMT89F-146     <NP>(50) --> <N>(49)
 rule #   2  JKBMT89F-4       <START>(51) --> <NP>(50)
 rule #  14  JKBMT89F-28      <NP+>(52) --> <NP>(50)


Y
U
N
I
T
T
O
 rule #1627  JLEX-NF-38       <N-ROOT>(71) --> YUNITTO
 rule #1998  JLEX-NF-780      <N-ROOT>(72) --> SISUTEMUYUNITTO
 rule # 877  JKBMT89F-1754    <CN>(73) --> <N-ROOT>(72)
 rule # 889  JKBMT89F-1778    <N>(74) --> <N-ROOT>(72)
 rule #  73  JKBMT89F-146     <NP>(75) --> <N>(74)
 rule #   2  JKBMT89F-4       <START>(76) --> <NP>(75)
 rule #  14  JKBMT89F-28      <NP+>(77) --> <NP>(75)
```

'sisutemuyunitto' *is parsed and reduced to* `<N-ROOT>(72)`.

N
O

Here, 'no' is parsed
and 'sisutemuyunitto'
and 'no' are reduced to
<SS> (91) modifiers.

```
rule #1178 JKBMT89F-2356      @NO(86) --> NO
rule # 134 JKBMT89F-268       <COP>(88) --> @NO(86)
rule # 156 JKBMT89F-312       <P>(89) --> @NO(86)
rule #  83 JKBMT89F-166       <SS>(91) --> <NP>(75) <COP>(88)
```

D
E

```
rule #2408 JLEX-VF-566        <V-ROOT>(99) --> DE
rule #1218 JKBMT89F-2436      @DE(100) --> DE
rule # 894 JKBMT89F-1788      <V-1DAN>(101) --> <V-ROOT>(99)
rule # 137 JKBMT89F-274       <COP>(102) --> @DE(100)
rule # 164 JKBMT89F-328       <P>(103) --> @DE(100)
rule # 407 JKBMT89F-814       <V-MIZEN1>(104) --> <V-1DAN>(101)
rule # 448 JKBMT89F-896       <V-RENYO1>(105) --> <V-1DAN>(101)
rule # 466 JKBMT89F-932       <V-RENYO2-T>(106) --> <V-1DAN>(101)
rule #  77 JKBMT89F-154       <XP>(107) --> <SS>(91) <P>(103)
rule #  91 JKBMT89F-182       <PP>(108) --> <SS>(91) <P>(103)
rule # 245 JKBMT89F-490       <V>(109) --> <V-RENYO1>(105)
rule #  45 JKBMT89F-90        <VP>(110) --> <V>(109)
rule #  34 JKBMT89F-68        <S>(111) --> <VP>(110)
rule #  98 JKBMT89F-196       <SADJUNCT>(112) --> <S>(111)
```

-
I
S
U
K
E
T
T
O

```
rule #1928 JLEX-NF-640        <N-ROOT>(122) --> DE-ISUKETTO
rule # 877 JKBMT89F-1754      <CN>(123) --> <N-ROOT>(122)
rule # 889 JKBMT89F-1778      <N>(124) --> <N-ROOT>(122)
rule #  73 JKBMT89F-146       <NP>(125) --> <N>(124)
rule #  14 JKBMT89F-28        <NP+>(127) --> <NP>(125)
rule #  67 JKBMT89F-134       <NP>(128) --> <SS>(91) <NP>(125)
rule #   2 JKBMT89F-4         <START>(129) --> <NP>(128)
rule #  14 JKBMT89F-28        <NP+>(130) --> <NP>(128)
```

D
O
R
A
I
B
U

'de-isukettodoraibu'
is parsed and reduced
to <N-ROOT> (150).

```
rule #1919 JLEX-NF-622        <N-ROOT>(149) --> DORAIBU
rule #2086 JLEX-NF-956        <N-ROOT>(150) --> DE-ISUKETTODORAIBU
rule # 877 JKBMT89F-1754      <CN>(151) --> <N-ROOT>(150)
rule # 889 JKBMT89F-1778      <N>(152) --> <N-ROOT>(150)
rule #  73 JKBMT89F-146       <NP>(153) --> <N>(152)
rule #  14 JKBMT89F-28        <NP+>(154) --> <NP>(153)
```

```
rule #   67  JKBMT89F-134     <NP>(156) --> <SS>(91) <NP>(153)
rule #    2  JKBMT89F-4       <START>(157) --> <NP>(156)
rule #   14  JKBMT89F-28      <NP+>(158) --> <NP>(156)

N
O
rule #1178  JKBMT89F-2356     @NO(167) --> NO
rule #  134  JKBMT89F-268     <COP>(169) --> @NO(167)
rule #  156  JKBMT89F-312     <P>(170) --> @NO(167)
rule #   83  JKBMT89F-166     <SS>(174) --> <NP>(156) <COP>(169)

R
E
B
A
A
rule #1741  JLEX-NF-266       <N-ROOT>(186) --> REBAA
rule #  877  JKBMT89F-1754    <CN>(187) --> <N-ROOT>(186)
rule #  889  JKBMT89F-1778    <N>(188) --> <N-ROOT>(186)
rule #   73  JKBMT89F-146     <NP>(189) --> <N>(188)
rule #   14  JKBMT89F-28      <NP+>(190) --> <NP>(189)
rule #   67  JKBMT89F-134     <NP>(194) --> <SS>(174) <NP>(189)
rule #    2  JKBMT89F-4       <START>(198) --> <NP>(194)
rule #   14  JKBMT89F-28      <NP+>(199) --> <NP>(194)

O
rule #1155  JKBMT89F-2310     @O(204) --> O
rule #1202  JKBMT89F-2404     @WO(205) --> O
rule #2265  JLEX-VF-280       <V-ROOT>(206) --> O
rule #  152  JKBMT89F-304     <P>(209) --> @WO(205)
rule #   74  JKBMT89F-148     <XP>(214) --> <NP>(194) <P>(209)

O
rule #1155  JKBMT89F-2310     @O(224) --> O
rule #2265  JLEX-VF-280       <V-ROOT>(225) --> O
rule #  895  JKBMT89F-1790    <V-5DAN-KI>(228) --> <V-ROOT>(225)
rule #  897  JKBMT89F-1794    <V-5DAN-S>(229) --> <V-ROOT>(225)
rule #  903  JKBMT89F-1806    <V-5DAN-W>(230) --> <V-ROOT>(225)

K
rule #1275  JKBMT89F-2550     @^(237) --> K
rule #  456  JKBMT89F-912     <V-RENYO2-T>(238) --> <V-5DAN-W>(230) @^(237)

O
rule #2267  JLEX-VF-284       <V-ROOT>(241) --> OKO
rule #1160  JKBMT89F-2320     @KO(243) --> KO
rule #  398  JKBMT89F-796     <V-5DAN-O>(244) --> <V-5DAN-KI>(228) @KO(243)
rule #  897  JKBMT89F-1794    <V-5DAN-S>(245) --> <V-ROOT>(241)
rule #  902  JKBMT89F-1804    <V-5DAN-R>(246) --> <V-ROOT>(241)
rule #  415  JKBMT89F-830     <V-MIZEN2>(247) --> <V-5DAN-O>(244)

S
rule #1276  JKBMT89F-2552     @^(251) --> S
rule #  463  JKBMT89F-926     <V-RENYO2-T>(252) --> <V-5DAN-R>(246) @^(251)
```

At this point, 'sisutemuyunitto no' and 'de-isukettodoraibu' are reduced to <NP>(156).

'no' is parsed here. 'sisutemuyunitto no de-isukettodoraibu' and 'no' are reduced to <SS>(174) to form a single modifier.

The word 'rebaa' is parsed and reduced to <N-ROOT>(186); and 'sisutemuyunitto no de-isukettodoraibu no rebaa' is reduced to <NP>(194).

'o' is parsed and reduced to <P>(209); next 'sisutemuyunitto no de-isukettodoraibu no rebaa' and 'o' become <XP>(214).

```
I
  rule #1162 JKBMT89F-2324    @SI(254) --> SI
  rule # 366 JKBMT89F-732     <V-5DAN-I>(256) --> <V-5DAN-S>(245) @SI(254)
  rule # 459 JKBMT89F-918     <V-RENYO2-T>(257) --> <V-5DAN-S>(245) @SI(254)
  rule # 447 JKBMT89F-894     <V-RENYO1>(258) --> <V-5DAN-I>(256)
  rule # 245 JKBMT89F-490     <V>(259) --> <V-RENYO1>(258)
  rule #  43 JKBMT89F-86      <VP>(260) --> <V>(259)
  rule #  34 JKBMT89F-68      <S>(261) --> <VP>(260)
  rule #  26 JKBMT89F-52      <S>(267) --> <XP>(214) <S>(261)
  rule #   9 JKBMT89F-18      <S+>(273) --> <S>(267)
  rule #  98 JKBMT89F-196     <SADJUNCT>(274) --> <S>(267)

T
E
  rule #1172 JKBMT89F-2344    @TE(291) --> TE
  rule # 311 JKBMT89F-622     <V-TE>(292) --> <V-RENYO2-T>(257) @TE(291)
  rule # 243 JKBMT89F-486     <V>(293) --> <V-TE>(292)
  rule # 328 JKBMT89F-656     <V-KAHEN>(294) --> <V-TE>(292)
  rule #  43 JKBMT89F-86      <VP>(295) --> <V>(293)
  rule #  34 JKBMT89F-68      <S>(296) --> <VP>(295)
  rule #  26 JKBMT89F-52      <S>(302) --> <XP>(214) <S>(296)
  rule #   9 JKBMT89F-18      <S+>(308) --> <S>(302)
  rule #  97 JKBMT89F-194     <SADJUNCT>(309) --> <S>(302)

K
U
  rule #1158 JKBMT89F-2316    @KU(330) --> KU
  rule #1016 JKBMT89F-2032    $KU1(332) --> @KU(328)
  rule # 751 JKBMT89F-1502    <NUMBER-WORD-9GATU>(334) --> $KU1(332)

D
A
  rule #1215 JKBMT89F-2430    @DA(337) --> DA

S
A
  rule #1161 JKBMT89F-2322    @SA(340) --> SA

I
  rule #1152 JKBMT89F-2304    @I(342) --> I
  rule # 205 JKBMT89F-410     <V>(343) --> <V-TE>(292) @KU(330)
                                @DA(337) @SA(340) @I(342)
  rule #  43 JKBMT89F-86      <VP>(344) --> <V>(343)
  rule #  34 JKBMT89F-68      <S>(345) --> <VP>(344)
  rule #  26 JKBMT89F-52      <S>(350) --> <XP>(214) <S>(345)
  rule #   6 JKBMT89F-12      <SXS>(351) --> <S>(350)
  rule #   9 JKBMT89F-18      <S+>(352) --> <S>(350)
  rule #   1 JKBMT89F-2       <START>(353) --> <SXS>(351)

3 semantic candidates found    node 353
```

'okosite kudasai' is parsed and reduced to <V>(343). The entire sentence is then reduced to <S>(350).

```
((sem
  (*sem*
   ((tense present)
    (theme
     ((spatial-3d-part-of
       (($is-token-of system-unit) ($id (*id* 20))
        ($map-data (*map* { map-str sisutemuyunitto } ))
        ($named-slot spatial-3d-part-of)))
      (part-of
       (($is-token-of diskette-drive) ($id (*id* 32))
        ($map-data (*map* { map-str deisukettodoraibu } ))
        ($named-slot part-of)))
      ($is-token-of load-lever) ($id (*id* 38))
      ($map-data (*map* { map-str rebaa } ))))
     (clausal-mark +) (mood imp) ($is-token-of flip-load-lever)
     ($id (*id* 68))
     (position
      (($is-token-of up-position) ($id (*id* 69))
       ($is-not-a-frame t)))
     ($map-data (*map* { map-str okosu } )))))
  (time ((root present))) (mood ((root imp))) (root okosu) (cat V)
  (vtype V-5dan-s) (formal +) (subcat trans) (passive -)
  (subj-case ga) (obj-case o) (causative -)
  (obj
   ((wh -)
    (sem
     (*sem*
      ((spatial-3d-part-of
        (($is-token-of system-unit) ($id (*id* 20))
         ($map-data (*map* { map-str sisutemuyunitto } ))
         ($named-slot spatial-3d-part-of)))
       (part-of
        (($is-token-of diskette-drive) ($id (*id* 32))
         ($map-data (*map* { map-str deisukettodoraibu } ))
         ($named-slot part-of)))
       ($is-token-of load-lever) ($id (*id* 38))
       ($map-data (*map* { map-str rebaa } )))))
    (case o)
    (xadjunct
     (*multiple*
      (*or*
       ((cop ((form no))) (cat N)
        (sem
         (*sem*
          (($is-token-of system-unit) ($id (*id* 21))
           ($map-data (*map* { map-str sisutemuyunitto } ))
           ($named-slot part-of))))
        (root sisutemuyunitto))
       ((cop ((form no))) (cat N)
        (sem
         (*sem*
          (($is-token-of system-unit) ($id (*id* 20))
           ($map-data (*map* { map-str sisutemuyunitto } ))
           ($named-slot spatial-3d-part-of)))
```

The final f-structure is output. The top level *sem* shows the semantic structure of flip-load-lever, to which 'okosu' is mapped, and the load-lever frame, which is theme of flip-load-lever. The load-lever frame contains two slots, part-of and spatial-3d-part-of.

The obj slot contains the object head, 'rebaa'. The sem slot shows the semantic structure of the noun phrase.

The xadjunct slot indicates the noun modifiers 'sisutemuyunitto' and 'deisuket-todoraibu'.

'sisutemuyunitto' can map into either of two slots, part-of or spatial-3d-part-of.

```
                               (root sisutemuyunitto)))
                          (((cop ((form no))) (cat N)
                           (sem
                            (*sem*
                             (($is-token-of diskette-drive) ($id (*id* 32))
                             ($map-data (*map* { map-str deisukettodoraibu } ))
                             ($named-slot part-of))))
                          (root deisukettodoraibu)))))
                      (cat N) (root rebaa))))
```

'deisukettodoraibu'
has one possible slot to
map to: part-of.

Semantic candidate 1 of 3

```
[*flip-load-lever
   (position up-position)
   (mood imp)
   (clausal-mark +)
   (theme [*load-lever
           (part-of [*diskette-drive])
           (spatial-3d-part-of [*system-unit])])
   (tense present)]
```

Three semantic can-
didates result. As
noted in the pream-
ble, this is because the
load-lever and
diskette-drive
frames have two slots
that modifiers can map
onto: part-of *and*
spatial-3d-part
-of. *Since selectional*
restrictions do not rule
out either frame, ambi-
guity results. Avoiding
this type of ambiguity
is trivially simple: The
concept lexicon would
be modified to limit the
fillers of these slots to
certain classes of ob-
jects.

Semantic candidate 2 of 3
```
[*flip-load-lever
   (position up-position)
   (mood imp)
   (clausal-mark +)
   (theme [*load-lever
           (part-of [*diskette-drive
                       (spatial-3d-part-of [*system-unit])])])
   (tense present)]
```

Semantic candidate 3 of 3
```
[*flip-load-lever
   (position up-position)
   (mood imp)
   (clausal-mark +)
   (theme [*load-lever
           (part-of [*diskette-drive
                       (part-of [*system-unit])])])
   (tense present)]
```

The three candidates
are passed to the
augmentor for disam-
biguation.

B.3 Augmentation

Processing ...

Parse:
```
(*flip-load-lever ($map-data okosu) (position up-position)
    ($id (*id* 81)) (mood imp) (clausal-mark +)
    (theme
        (*load-lever ($map-data rebaa) ($id (*id* 51))
        (part-of
            (*diskette-drive ($map-data deisukettodoraibu)
                             ($id (*id* 45))))
        (spatial-3d-part-of
            (*system-unit ($map-data sisutemuyunitto)
                          ($id (*id* 33))))))
    (tense present))
```

The augmentor begins format conversion on ambiguous parser output.

Bare ILT:
```
[clause2597
    (speechactid
        [speech-act2595
            (time time2596)
            (space)
            (direct?)
            (speech-act)])
    (propositionid
        [*flip-load-lever
            (tense present)
            (theme
                [*load-lever
                    (spatial-3d-part-of
                        [*system-unit])
                    (part-of
                        [*diskette-drive])])
            (mood imp)
            (position up-position)])]
```

The first of three readings is converted into linked FRAMEKIT frames for the bare ILT.

Parse:
```
(*flip-load-lever ($map-data okosu) (position up-position)
    ($id (*id* 81)) (mood imp) (clausal-mark +)
    (theme
        (*load-lever ($map-data rebaa) ($id (*id* 51))
        (part-of
            (*diskette-drive
                ($map-data deisukettodoraibu) ($id (*id* 45))
                (spatial-3d-part-of
                    (*system-unit ($map-data sisutemuyunitto)
                                  ($id (*id* 33))))))))
    (tense present))
```

Second reading is converted to FRAMEKIT *frames.*

```
Bare ILT:
[clause2604
    (speechactid
        [speech-act2602
            (time time2603)
            (space)
            (direct?)
            (speech-act)])
    (propositionid
        [*flip-load-lever
            (tense present)
            (theme
                [*load-lever
                    (part-of
                        [*diskette-drive
                            (spatial-3d-part-of
                                [*system-unit])])])])
            (mood imp)
            (position up-position)])]
```

Conversion phase concludes after extracting and converting the third reading.

```
Parse:
(*flip-load-lever ($map-data okosu) (position up-position)
    ($id (*id* 81)) (mood imp) (clausal-mark +)
    (theme
        (*load-lever ($map-data rebaa) ($id (*id* 51))
    (part-of
        (*diskette-drive
            ($map-data deisukettodoraibu) ($id (*id* 45))
            (part-of
                (*system-unit ($map-data sisutemuyunitto)
                                ($id (*id* 34))))))))
    (tense present))
```

```
Bare ILT:
[clause2611
    (speechactid
        [speech-act2609
            (time time2610)
            (space)
            (direct?)
            (speech-act)])
    (propositionid
        [*flip-load-lever
            (tense present)
            (theme
                [*load-lever
                    (part-of
                        [*diskette-drive
                            (part-of
                                [*system-unit])])])])
            (mood imp)
            (position up-position)])]
```

```
applying conversions to ILT
applying conversions to ILT
applying conversions to ILT

ILT to augment:
(clause2597
    (main-clause yes)
    (ilt-type clause)
    (speechactid speech-act2595)
    (propositionid proposition2591)
    (clauseid clause2597)
    (frame-maker augmentor))

(speech-act2595
    (time time2596)
    (space)
    (direct? yes)
    (speech-act request-action)
    (ilt-type speech-act)
    (speechactid speech-act2595)
    (frame-maker augmentor))

(proposition2591
    (time (at time2596))
    (agent agent2613)
    (mood imperative)
    (propositionid proposition2591)
    (ilt-type proposition)
    (clauseid clause2597)
    (theme role2592)
    (clausal-mark +)
    ($id 81)
    (position up-position)
    ($map-data okosu)
    (is-a *flip-load-lever)
    (is-token-of *flip-load-lever)
    (frame-maker augmentor))

(agent2613
    (reference definite)
    (ilt-type role)
    (is-token-of *reader)
    (clauseid clause2597)
    (roleid role2612)
    (propositionid proposition2591)
    (frame-maker augmentor))

(role2592
    (reference definite)
    (roleid role2592)
    (ilt-type role)
    (propositionid proposition2591)
    (clauseid clause2597)
    (parent-frame proposition2591)
```

The pattern matcher is applied to each bare ILT.

The ILT for the first reading contains the frames shown here (the value *facets and* common *views have been deleted for brevity and clarity).*

The ilt-type *slot identifies each frame's type. Additionally, each frame, except* speech-act, *uses the* clauseid *slot to identify the clause it belongs to.*

```
                    (spatial-3d-part-of role2594)
                    (part-of role2593)
                    ($id 51)
                    ($map-data rebaa)
                    (is-a *load-lever)
                    (is-token-of *load-lever)
                    (frame-maker augmentor))

                (role2594
                    (reference definite)
                    (roleid role2594)
                    (ilt-type role)
                    (propositionid proposition2591)
                    (clauseid clause2597)
                    (parent-frame role2592)
                    ($id 33)
                    ($map-data sisutemuyunitto)
                    (is-a *system-unit)
                    (is-token-of *system-unit)
                    (frame-maker augmentor))

                (role2593
                    (reference definite)
                    (roleid role2593)
                    (ilt-type role)
                    (propositionid proposition2591)
                    (clauseid clause2597)
                    (parent-frame role2592)
                    ($id 45)
                    ($map-data deisukettodoraibu)
                    (is-a *diskette-drive)
                    (is-token-of *diskette-drive)
                    (frame-maker augmentor))

                (clause2604
                    (main-clause yes)
                    (ilt-type clause)
                    (speechactid speech-act2602)
                    (propositionid proposition2598)
                    (clauseid clause2604)
                    (frame-maker augmentor))

                (speech-act2602
                    (time time2603)
                    (space)
                    (direct? yes)
                    (speech-act request-action)
                    (ilt-type speech-act)
                    (speechactid speech-act2602)
                    (frame-maker augmentor))

                (proposition2598
                    (time (at time2603))
```

When the parser includes a $map-data field, the field appears in the frame to allow the augmentor to refer to the actual source string giving rise to the frame's concept.

Second reading results in the frames shown here.

```
    (agent agent2615)
    (mood imperative)
    (propositionid proposition2598)
    (ilt-type proposition)
    (clauseid clause2604)
    (theme role2599)
    (clausal-mark +)
    ($id 81)
    (position up-position)
    ($map-data okosu)
    (is-a *flip-load-lever)
    (is-token-of *flip-load-lever)
    (frame-maker augmentor))

(agent2615
    (reference definite)
    (ilt-type role)
    (is-token-of *reader)
    (clauseid clause2604)
    (roleid role2614)
    (propositionid proposition2598)
    (frame-maker augmentor))

(role2599
    (reference definite)
    (roleid role2599)
    (ilt-type role)
    (propositionid proposition2598)
    (clauseid clause2604)
    (parent-frame proposition2598)
    (part-of role2600)
    ($id 51)
    ($map-data rebaa)
    (is-a *load-lever)
    (is-token-of *load-lever)
    (frame-maker augmentor))

(role2600
    (reference definite)
    (roleid role2600)
    (ilt-type role)
    (propositionid proposition2598)
    (clauseid clause2604)
    (parent-frame role2599)
    (spatial-3d-part-of role2601)
    ($id 45)
    ($map-data deisukettodoraibu)
    (is-a *diskette-drive)
    (is-token-of *diskette-drive)
    (frame-maker augmentor))

(role2601
    (reference definite)
    (roleid role2601)
```

```
        (ilt-type role)
        (propositionid proposition2598)
        (clauseid clause2604)
        (parent-frame role2600)
        ($id 33)
        ($map-data sisutemuyunitto)
        (is-a *system-unit)
        (is-token-of *system-unit)
        (frame-maker augmentor))
```

Third reading pro-
duces these frames.

```
(clause2611
        (main-clause yes)
        (ilt-type clause)
        (speechactid speech-act2609)
        (propositionid proposition2605)
        (clauseid clause2611)
        (frame-maker augmentor))

(speech-act2609
        (time time2610)
        (space)
        (direct? yes)
        (speech-act request-action)
        (ilt-type speech-act)
        (speechactid speech-act2609)
        (frame-maker augmentor))

(proposition2605
        (time (at time2610))
        (agent agent2617)
        (mood imperative)
        (propositionid proposition2605)
        (ilt-type proposition)
        (clauseid clause2611)
        (theme role2606)
        (clausal-mark +)
        ($id 81)
        (position up-position)
        ($map-data okosu)
        (is-a *flip-load-lever)
        (is-token-of *flip-load-lever)
        (frame-maker augmentor))

(agent2617
        (reference definite)
        (ilt-type role)
        (is-token-of *reader)
        (clauseid clause2611)
        (roleid role2616)
        (propositionid proposition2605)
        (frame-maker augmentor))
```

```
(role2606
    (reference definite)
    (roleid role2606)
    (ilt-type role)
    (propositionid proposition2605)
    (clauseid clause2611)
    (parent-frame proposition2605)
    (part-of role2607)
    ($id 51)
    ($map-data rebaa)
    (is-a *load-lever)
    (is-token-of *load-lever)
    (frame-maker augmentor))

(role2607
    (reference definite)
    (roleid role2607)
    (ilt-type role)
    (propositionid proposition2605)
    (clauseid clause2611)
    (parent-frame role2606)
    (part-of role2608)
    ($id 45)
    ($map-data deisukettodoraibu)
    (is-a *diskette-drive)
    (is-token-of *diskette-drive)
    (frame-maker augmentor))

(role2608
    (reference definite)
    (roleid role2608)
    (ilt-type role)
    (propositionid proposition2605)
    (clauseid clause2611)
    (parent-frame role2607)
    ($id 34)
    ($map-data sisutemuyunitto)
    (is-a *system-unit)
    (is-token-of *system-unit)
    (frame-maker augmentor))

Augmenting ILTs
Generating composite ILT
```

After combining the three readings into a composite, the resulting structure will be used to perform some disambiguations and then be searched for the points on which the readings differ.

```
The composite ILT for this sentence is
(make-frame composite2618
        (propositionid (value composite2619)
                (subframe (composite2619 clause2611 clause2604 clause2597)))
        (ilt-type (values ((clause) clause2611 clause2604 clause2597)))
        ($sentence$
                (values (("sentence 40:  sisutemu yunitto no de-isuketto
                                doraibu no rebaa o okosi te kudasai")
                        clause2611 clause2604 clause2597)))
        ($equivalences (values (clause2597 clause2597 clause2604 clause2611)))
        (clauseid
                (values (nil clause2597 clause2604 clause2611))
                (value composite2618))
        (frame-maker
                (values (nil clause2597 clause2604 clause2611))
                (value augmentor)))
```

Proposition frames of all three readings are equivalent, as can easily be seen from the composite. Each slot has the same filler in all three readings, or points at a subframe in each. Thus there is no need to create a menu for this composite frame (see chapter 8).

```
(make-frame composite2619
        ($equivalences
                (values (proposition2591 proposition2605 proposition2598
                                proposition2591)))
        (is-token-of
                (values ((*flip-load-lever) proposition2605 proposition2598
                                proposition2591)))
        (position
                (values ((up-position) proposition2605 proposition2598
                                proposition2591)))
        (theme
                (value composite2621)
                (subframe (composite2621 proposition2605 proposition2598
                                proposition2591)))
        (ilt-type
                (values ((proposition) proposition2605 proposition2598
                                proposition2591)))
        (agent
                (value composite2620)
                (subframe (composite2620 proposition2605 proposition2598
                                proposition2591)))
        (clauseid
                (values (nil proposition2591 proposition2598 proposition2605))
                (value composite2618))
        (frame-maker
                (values (nil proposition2591 proposition2598 proposition2605))
                (value augmentor)))
```

```
(make-frame composite2621
      ($equivalences
            (values (role2606 role2606) (role2599 role2599)
                  (role2592 role2592)))
      (is-token-of
            (values ((*load-lever) role2606 role2599 role2592)))
      (part-of
            (value composite2623)
            (subframe (composite2623 role2606 role2599 role2592)))
      (spatial-3d-part-of
            (values (nil role2599 role2606))
            (value composite2622)
            (subframe (composite2622 role2592)))
      (ilt-type
            (values ((role) role2606 role2599 role2592)))
      (reference
            (values ((definite) role2606 role2599 role2592)))
      (clauseid
            (values (nil role2592 role2599 role2606))
            (value composite2618))
      (frame-maker
            (values (nil role2592 role2599 role2606))
            (value augmentor)))
(make-frame composite2623
      (part-of
            (values (nil role2593 role2600))
            (value composite2699)
            (subframe (composite2699 role2607)))
      (spatial-3d-part-of
            (values (nil role2593 role2607))
            (value composite2646)
            (subframe (composite2646 role2600)))
      ($equivalences
            (values (role2607 role2607) (role2600 role2600)
                  (role2593 role2593)))
      (is-token-of
            (values ((*diskette-drive) role2607 role2600 role2593)))
      (ilt-type
            (values ((role) role2607 role2600 role2593)))
      (reference
            (values ((definite) role2607 role2600 role2593)))
      (clauseid
            (values (nil role2593 role2600 role2607))
            (value composite2618))
      (frame-maker
            (values (nil role2593 role2600 role2607))
            (value augmentor)))

(make-frame composite2699
      ($equivalences (values (role2608 role2608)))
      (is-token-of (values ((*system-unit) role2608)))
      (ilt-type (values ((role) role2608)))
      (reference (values ((definite) role2608)))
      (clauseid (values (nil role2608)) (value composite2618))
      (frame-maker (values (nil role2608)) (value augmentor)))
```

Now we can examine the composite frame corresponding to the ILTs' theme *frames. Note that one reading contained a subframe for the* spatial-3d -part-of *slot, while the other two did not contain that slot.*

```
(make-frame composite2646
      ($equivalences (values (role2601 role2601)))
      (is-token-of (values ((*system-unit) role2601)))
      (ilt-type (values ((role) role2601)))
      (reference (values ((definite) role2601)))
      (clauseid (values (nil role2601)) (value composite2618))
      (frame-maker (values (nil role2601)) (value augmentor)))

(make-frame composite2622
      ($equivalences (values (role2594 role2594)))
      (is-token-of (values ((*system-unit) role2594)))
      (ilt-type (values ((role) role2594)))
      (reference (values ((definite) role2594)))
      (clauseid (values (nil role2594)) (value composite2618))
      (frame-maker (values (nil role2594)) (value augmentor)))

(make-frame composite2620
      ($equivalences
          (values (agent2617 agent2617) (agent2615 agent2615)
                  (agent2613 agent2613)))
      (is-token-of
          (values ((*reader) agent2617 agent2615 agent2613)))
      (ilt-type
          (values ((role) agent2617 agent2615 agent2613)))
      (reference
          (values ((definite) agent2617 agent2615 agent2613)))
      (clauseid
          (values (nil agent2613 agent2615 agent2617))
          (value composite2618))
      (frame-maker
          (values (nil agent2613 agent2615 agent2617))
          (value augmentor)))
```

Each frame in the composite is checked for ambiguities that may be removed; there is no possibility of removing the correct reading at this stage.

```
applying safe eliminations to COMPOSITE2699
applying safe eliminations to COMPOSITE2646
applying safe eliminations to COMPOSITE2623
applying safe eliminations to COMPOSITE2622
applying safe eliminations to COMPOSITE2621
applying safe eliminations to COMPOSITE2620
applying safe eliminations to COMPOSITE2619
applying safe eliminations to COMPOSITE2618
```

Next, the augmentor scans the composite ILT again; here it is possible to remove the correct reading (see chapter 8).

```
applying potentially unsafe eliminations to COMPOSITE2699
applying potentially unsafe eliminations to COMPOSITE2646
applying potentially unsafe eliminations to COMPOSITE2623
applying potentially unsafe eliminations to COMPOSITE2622
applying potentially unsafe eliminations to COMPOSITE2621
applying potentially unsafe eliminations to COMPOSITE2620
applying potentially unsafe eliminations to COMPOSITE2619
applying potentially unsafe eliminations to COMPOSITE2618
```

```
determining ambiguous case roles for COMPOSITE2618
determining ambiguous case roles for COMPOSITE2619
determining ambiguous case roles for COMPOSITE2621
determining ambiguous case roles for COMPOSITE2623
determining ambiguous case roles for COMPOSITE2699
determining ambiguous case roles for COMPOSITE2646
determining ambiguous case roles for COMPOSITE2622
determining ambiguous case roles for COMPOSITE2620
```

Augmentor now builds the disambiguation menus by scanning the composite ILT.

```
User selected (part-of for (*system-unit)) from menu 1
determining ambiguous case roles for COMPOSITE2623
0 menus remaining
```

Here the menus are displayed. The user makes a selection, and the composite frame from which the menu was built is disambiguated.

```
Final ILT:
[clause2611
    ($sentence$ Sentence 40:   sisutemu yunitto no de-isuketto
                               doraibu no rebaa o okosi te kudasai)
    (main-clause yes)
    (speechactid
        [speech-act2609
            (time time2610)
            (space)
            (direct? yes)
            (speech-act request-action)])
    (propositionid
        [*flip-load-lever
            (time (at time2610))
            (agent
                [*reader
                    (reference definite)])
            (theme
                [*load-lever
                    (reference definite)
                    (part-of
                        [*diskette-drive
                            (reference definite)
                            (part-of
                                [*system-unit
                                    (reference definite)])])])
            (position up-position)])]
```

After disambiguation, a single reading remains. This reading is passed to the generator after housekeeping slots (not shown here) are deleted.

B.4   Generation

```
* (gen-aug-file  "40.j.ilt")

FrameList: (clause2611 speech-act2609 proposition2605 agent2617
              role2606 role2607 role2608)

Clauses: (clause2611)
```

No explicit lexeme is associated with a clause frame.

```
Trying to realize clause2611 as non-lexical

Trying to realize proposition2605 as (V)
```

The generator uses a realization heuristic in an attempt to produce proposition heads as verbal heads in Japanese.

```
Candidate set for proposition2605: (flip-down flip-up)
   candidates from (V): (flip-down flip-up)
   proper subcategorization: (FLIP-DOWN FLIP-UP)
   ordered entries: (FLIP-UP 0.67) (FLIP-DOWN 1.15)
   best penalties: (FLIP-UP 0.67)
   final choice: "flip"
```

Generator uses realization heuristic in attempt to generate roles within propositions as Japanese noun phrases.

```
Candidate set for role2606: (load-lever)
   candidates from (N): (load-lever)
   proper subcategorization: (load-lever)
   ordered entries: (load-lever 0)
   best penalties: (load-lever 0)
   final choice: "load lever"

Recursively realizing part-of of role2606: role2607
Trying to realize role2607 as (N ADJ).

Candidate set for role2607: (diskette-drive)
   candidates from (n adj): (diskette-drive)
   proper subcategorization: (diskette-drive)
   ordered entries: (diskette-drive 0)
   best penalties: (diskette-drive 0)
   final choice: "diskette drive"

Recursively realizing part-of of role2607: role2608
Trying to realize role2608 as (N ADJ).

Candidate set for role2608: (system-unit)
   candidates from (N ADJ): (system-unit)
   proper subcategorization: (system-unit)
   ordered entries: (system-unit 0)
   best penalties: (system-unit 0)
   final choice: "system unit"

Mapping role2608.

F-Structure for role2608:
((number singular) (ref definite) (count yes) (root system_unit))

Mapping role2607.
```

```
F-Structure for role2607:
((number singular) (ref definite)
 (pre-nom-noun
  ((number singular) (ref definite) (count yes) (root system_unit)))
 (count yes) (root diskette_drive))

Mapping role2606.

F-Structure for role2606:
((number singular) (ref definite)
 (pre-nom-noun
  ((number singular) (ref definite)
   (pre-nom-noun
    ((number singular) (ref definite) (count yes)
     (root system_unit)))
   (count yes) (root diskette_drive)))
 (count yes) (root load_lever))

Recursively realizing agent of proposition2605: agent2617
Trying to realize agent2617 as (N).

Candidate set for agent2617: (reader you your)
  candidates from (N): (reader)
  proper subcategorization: (reader)
  ordered entries: (reader 0)
  best penalties: (reader 0)
  final choice: "reader"

Mapping agent2617.

F-Structure for agent2617:
((ref definite) (human +) (number singular) (person 2) (count yes)
 (root (*or* pro reader)))

Mapping proposition2605.
-------------------------------------------------
Frame: proposition2605 Lex: flip-UP
FS: ((particle up) (valency trans) (cons-double p) (root
flip_up))

(defrule e *proposition
  :exclusive
  (and (frame-accessor frame (quote agent))
   (frame-accessor frame (quote theme))
   (or
    (eq (frame-accessor frame (quote clauseid) (quote focus))
     (quote agent))
    (null (frame-accessor frame (quote clauseid) (quote focus))))
   (lex-feature-p (quote valency) !lex (quote trans))
   (not (eq (frame-accessor frame (quote agent)) (quote unknown))))
  ((slot agent) => (slot subj))
  ((slot theme) => (slot obj)))
```

This rule maps agent *to syntactic subject and* theme *to syntactic object when* agent *is in focus or when a focus value is absent.*

```
Predicate returns T.
Slot subj added.
Slot obj added.

((obj
  ((number singular) (ref definite)
   (pre-nom-noun
    ((number singular) (ref definite)
     (pre-nom-noun
      ((number singular) (ref definite) (count yes)
       (root system_unit)))
     (count yes) (root diskette_drive)))
   (count yes) (root load_lever)))
 (subj
  ((ref definite) (human +) (number singular) (person 2) (count yes)
   (root (*or* pro reader))))
 (particle up) (valency trans) (cons-double p) (root flip_up))
-----------------------------------------------
Frame: proposition2605 Lex: flip-up
FS: ((obj
      ((number singular) (ref definite)
       (pre-nom-noun
        ((number singular) (ref definite)
         (pre-nom-noun
          ((number singular) (ref definite) (count yes)
           (root system_unit)))
         (count yes) (root diskette_drive)))
       (count yes) (root load_lever)))
     (subj
      ((ref definite) (human +) (number singular) (person 2)
       (count yes) (root (*or* pro reader))))
     (particle up) (valency trans) (cons-double p) (root flip_up))
```

This rule adds the appropriate tense *feature to the syntactic f-structure.*

```
(defrule e *proposition
   :any
   (or
    (if (listp (frame-accessor frame (quote time)))
     (eq (first (frame-accessor frame (quote time))) (quote at))
     (eq (frame-accessor frame (quote time)) (quote time1)))
    (equal (fs-feature (quote passive) !fs) (quote +)))
   (feature tense present)
```

```
Predicate returns T.
Feature (tense present) added.

((tense present)
 (obj
  ((number singular) (ref definite)
   (pre-nom-noun
    ((number singular) (ref definite)
     (pre-nom-noun
      ((number singular) (ref definite) (count yes)
       (root system_unit)))
     (count yes) (root diskette_drive)))
   (count yes) (root load_lever)))
```

```
 (subj
  ((ref definite) (human +) (number singular) (person 2) (count yes)
   (root (*or* pro reader)))))
 (particle up) (valency trans) (cons-double p) (root flip_up))
--------------------------------------------------
Frame: proposition2605 Lex: flip-up
FS: ((tense present)
     (obj
      ((number singular) (ref definite)
       (pre-nom-noun
        ((number singular) (ref definite)
         (pre-nom-noun
          ((number singular) (ref definite) (count yes)
           (root system_unit)))
         (count yes) (root diskette_drive)))
       (count yes) (root load_lever)))
     (subj
      ((ref definite) (human +) (number singular) (person 2)
       (count yes) (root (*or* pro reader)))))
     (particle up) (valency trans) (cons-double p) (root flip_up))

(defrule e *proposition
    :any
    t
    ((expr
      (cond
       ((and
         (or
          (equal
           (frame-accessor frame (quote clauseid) (quote speechactid)
            (quote speech-act))
           (quote command))
          (equal
           (frame-accessor frame (quote clauseid) (quote speechactid)
            (quote speech-act))
           (quote request-action)))
         (equal
          (frame-accessor frame (quote clauseid) (quote speechactid)
           (quote direct?))
          (quote yes)))
        (quote imperative))
       ((equal
         (frame-accessor frame (quote clauseid) (quote speechactid)
          (quote speech-act))
         (quote request-info))
        (quote interrogative))
       (t (quote declarative)))))
     => (feature mood))
```

This rule adds the appropriate mood to the f-structure.

```
Predicate returns T.
Feature (mood imperative) added.

((mood imperative) (tense present)
 (obj
  ((number singular) (ref definite)
```

```
      (pre-nom-noun
        ((number singular) (ref definite)
         (pre-nom-noun
           ((number singular) (ref definite) (count yes)
            (root system_unit)))
         (count yes) (root diskette_drive)))
       (count yes) (root load_lever)))
    (subj
      ((ref definite) (human +) (number singular) (person 2) (count yes)
       (root (*or* pro reader))))
    (particle up) (valency trans) (cons-double p) (root flip_up))
------------------------------------------------
Frame: proposition2605 Lex: flip-up
FS: ((mood imperative) (tense present)
      (obj
        ((number singular) (ref definite)
         (pre-nom-noun
           ((number singular) (ref definite)
            (pre-nom-noun
              ((number singular) (ref definite) (count yes)
               (root system_unit)))
            (count yes) (root diskette_drive)))
         (count yes) (root load_lever)))
      (subj
        ((ref definite) (human +) (number singular) (person 2)
         (count yes) (root (*or* pro reader))))
      (particle up) (valency trans) (cons-double p) (root flip_up))
```

Here, the appropri-
ate necessity *fea-*
ture is added to the f-
structure; it is based
on whether the speech
act is direct.

```
(defrule e *proposition
  :any
  t
  ((expr
    (cond
      ((and
        (equal
         (frame-accessor frame (quote clauseid) (quote speechactid)
          (quote speech-act))
         (quote command))
        (equal
         (frame-accessor frame (quote clauseid) (quote speechactid)
          (quote direct?))
         (quote no)))
       (quote +))
      (t (quote -))))
   => (feature necessity))
```

```
Predicate returns T.
Feature (necessity -) added.

((necessity -) (mood imperative) (tense present)
  (obj
    ((number singular) (ref definite)
     (pre-nom-noun
       ((number singular) (ref definite)
        (pre-nom-noun
```

```
      ((number singular) (ref definite) (count yes)
        (root system_unit)))
      (count yes) (root diskette_drive)))
    (count yes) (root load_lever)))
  (subj
    ((ref definite) (human +) (number singular) (person 2) (count yes)
      (root (*or* pro reader))))
  (particle up) (valency trans) (cons-double p) (root flip_up))
------------------------------------------------
F-Structure for proposition2605:

((necessity -) (mood imperative) (tense present)
  (obj
    ((number singular) (ref definite)
      (pre-nom-noun
        ((number singular) (ref definite)
          (pre-nom-noun
            ((number singular) (ref definite) (count yes)
              (root system_unit)))
          (count yes) (root diskette_drive)))
      (count yes) (root load_lever)))
  (subj
    ((ref definite) (human +) (number singular) (person 2) (count yes)
      (root (*or* pro reader))))
  (particle up) (valency trans) (cons-double p) (root flip_up))

Mapping clause2611.

F-Structure for clause2611:
((necessity -) (mood imperative) (tense present)
  (obj
    ((number singular) (ref definite)
      (pre-nom-noun
        ((number singular) (ref definite)
          (pre-nom-noun
            ((number singular) (ref definite) (count yes)
              (root system_unit)))
          (count yes) (root diskette_drive)))
      (count yes) (root load_lever)))
  (subj
    ((ref definite) (human +) (number singular) (person 2) (count yes)
      (root (*or* pro reader))))
  (particle up) (valency trans) (cons-double p) (root flip_up))
```

The final f-structure.

```
                    GG-START called
                   GG-@CAP called
                   GG-@CAP returns @CAP
                   GG-S called
                    GG-S1 called
                     GG-S2 called
                      GG-IMP called
                       GG-VP1 called
                        GG-VP called
                         GG-V2 called
                          GG-V-A called
                           GG-V called
                           GG-V returns FLIP
                           GG-PARTICLE called
                           GG-PARTICLE returns UP
                          GG-V-A returns FLIP UP
                         GG-V2 returns FLIP UP
                         GG-NP called
                          GG-N3 called
                           GG-N2 called
                            GG-DET called
                            GG-DET returns THE
                            GG-N1 called
                             GG-AP called
                              GG-PNN called
                               GG-AP called
                                GG-PNN called
                                 GG-N called
                                 GG-N returns SYSTEM_UNIT
                                GG-PNN returns SYSTEM_UNIT
                               GG-AP returns SYSTEM_UNIT
                               GG-N called
                               GG-N returns DISKETTE_DRIVE
                              GG-PNN returns SYSTEM_UNIT DISKETTE_DRIVE
                             GG-AP returns SYSTEM_UNIT DISKETTE_DRIVE
                             GG-N called
                             GG-N returns LOAD_LEVER
                            GG-N1 returns SYSTEM_UNIT DISKETTE_DRIVE LOAD_LEVER
                           GG-N2 returns THE SYSTEM_UNIT DISKETTE_DRIVE LOAD_LEVER
                          GG-N3 returns THE SYSTEM_UNIT DISKETTE_DRIVE LOAD_LEVER
                         GG-NP returns THE SYSTEM_UNIT DISKETTE_DRIVE LOAD_LEVER
                        GG-VP returns FLIP UP THE SYSTEM_UNIT DISKETTE_DRIVE LOAD_LEVER
                       GG-VP1 returns FLIP UP THE SYSTEM_UNIT DISKETTE_DRIVE LOAD_LEVER
                      GG-IMP returns FLIP UP THE SYSTEM_UNIT DISKETTE_DRIVE LOAD_LEVER
                     GG-S2 returns FLIP UP THE SYSTEM_UNIT DISKETTE_DRIVE LOAD_LEVER
                    GG-S1 returns FLIP UP THE SYSTEM_UNIT DISKETTE_DRIVE LOAD_LEVER
                   GG-END-PUNC called
                    GG-@PERIOD called
                    GG-@PERIOD returns PERIOD
                   GG-END-PUNC returns PERIOD
                  GG-S returns FLIP UP THE SYSTEM_UNIT DISKETTE_DRIVE LOAD_LEVER PERIOD
                 GG-START returns @CAP FLIP UP THE SYSTEM_UNIT DISKETTE_DRIVE LOAD_LEVER PERIOD


         "Flip up the system unit diskette drive load lever."
```

The f-structure produced for the clause is processed by the generation grammar (GG) to produce the final output string. Each rule called by the grammar is traced, indicating the part of the output string that each rule produces.

Appendix C

Running the Translation System

This appendix gives a brief operational overview of the tasks involved in starting and running the KBMT-89 translation. The system consists of several parts, each of which needs to be loaded individually. Running each part on a separate workstation has improved performance. Various parts may be omitted if they will not be used. The parsers and generators should be loaded first, the augmentor last. The following protocol is offered to give a feel for the procedure. Additional details about the KBMT-89 implementation and configuration are given in chapters 8 and 9.

1. Load the parsers for the source and target languages.

   - English parser: enter `parser-e`
   - Japanese parser: enter `parser-j`

2. Load the generators for the desired source and target languages.

   - English generator: `generator-e`
   - Japanese generator: `generator-j`

3. Load the augmentor: `augmentor`

Once everything is loaded, configure the augmentor for the current session by responding to the prompts that appear in the window at the bottom of the screen. The user has to respond to several inquiries:

1. *Ontology directory:* Enter the location of the concept lexicon.

2. *Ontology file:* Enter the name within the above directory of the file containing the concept lexicon.

3. *Source language:* Enter the language in which sentences will be entered, which is also the language used for most interaction with the program.

4. *Get parse from a file:* Press the Y key to use previously prepared parses, N to have the parser produce new parses.

   (a) *Directory containing parses:* If Y was pressed, the user needs to specify where to find the prepared parses. The name of the directory containing the parses is entered.

   (b) *File extension:* The parses are stored in files with names of the form `num.ext`.

5. *Directory containing corpus:* If the user has a pre-existing set of sentences to work with, he or she specifies the directory in which this set of sentences is stored. If the user does not have such a set, `/dev` should be entered.

6. *Corpus file:* Enter the name of the file containing the set of sentences. If `/dev` was entered for the previous question, `null` should be entered now.

7. *Target language:* Specify the target language; it may be the same as the source language.

8. *Send output to a file:* Type Y to store the augmentor's results in files or N to have the translation generated immediately.

9. *Directory for storing* ILTs: Specify where to store the augmentor's results or the data needed for immediate generation.

10. *Generate paraphrases for verification:* Enter Y to see a paraphrase of the original sentence before generating the translation.

11. *Temp directory for "Graphical* ILT": Specify where to store the data that must be transmitted in order to display an interlingua text graphically.

12. *Activate pronoun resolver:* To translate a connected set of sentences from some text rather than a sequence of unrelated sentences, enter Y to enable pronoun resolution.

(a) *Configure pronoun resolver:* If the previous question was answered with a Y, the user will be asked whether the pronoun resolver should be configured. In most cases, the pronoun resolver will function best with the default settings.

13. *Verbosity of trace:* Specify level of detail. The augmentor maintains a trace of its activities in a separate window which is usually hidden behind the input panel. The larger the integer entered, the more detailed the trace will be, at some expense in execution speed. For values of 1 or more, the trace window will be moved and expanded to occupy most of the query area.

14. *File for logging translations:* Specify a file. A list of all sentences translated and their translations is stored in this file.

Bibliography

Allen, J.F. 1984. Towards a General Theory of Action and Time. *Artificial Intelligence* 23:123-154.

Andrews, A. 1982. The Representation of Case in Modern Icelandic. In J. Bresnan (ed.), *The Mental Representation of Grammatical Relations*. Cambridge, Mass.: MIT Press, 427-503.

Arnold, D. and L. des Tombe. 1987. Basic Theory and Methodology in EUROTRA. In S. Nirenburg (ed.), *Machine Translation: Theoretical and Methodological Issues*. Cambridge: Cambridge University Press, 114-135.

Ashley, K. Forthcoming. Reasoning with Cases and Hypotheticals in HYPO. *International Journal of Man-Machine Studies*.

Ashley, K. and E. Rissland. 1988. A Case-Based Approach to Modeling Legal Expertise. *IEEE Expert* (Fall): 70-77.

Bennett, W.S. 1982. The Linguistic Component of METAL. Working Paper, Linguistic Research Center, University of Texas, Austin.

Brachman, R. and H. Levesque (eds.). 1985. *Readings in Knowledge Representation*. Los Altos, Calif.: Morgan Kaufmann.

Brachman, R. and J. Schmolze. 1985. An Overview of the KL-ONE Knowledge Representation System. *Cognitive Science* 9:171-216.

Bresnan, J. 1982a. Control and Complementation. In J. Bresnan (ed.), *The Mental Representation of Grammatical Relations*. Cambridge, Mass.: MIT Press, 282-390.

Bresnan, J. 1982b. The Passive in Lexical Theory. In J. Bresnan (ed.), *The Mental Representation of Grammatical Relations*. Cambridge, Mass.: MIT Press, 3-86.

Bresnan, J. 1989. The Syntactic Projection Problem and the Comparative Syntax of Locative Inversion. In K. Chen and C. Huang (eds.), *Journal of Information Science and Engineering*. Special issue, R.O.C. Computational Linguistics Workshops II, 287-304.

315

Bresnan, J., P.-K. Halvorsen and J. Maling. 1987. Logophoricity and Bound Anaphors. Manuscript, Stanford University, Stanford, Calif.

Bresnan, J. and J. Kanerva. 1989. Locative Inversion in Chichewa: A Case Study of Factorization in Grammar. *Linguistic Inquiry* 20:1-50.

Carbonell, J.G. 1983a. Learning by Analogy: Formulating and Generalizing Plans from Past Experience. In J.G. Carbonell, T. Mitchell and R. Mychalski (eds.), *Machine Learning: An Artificial Intelligence Approach*, Volume I. Palo Alto, Calif.: Tioga Press, 137-161.

Carbonell, J.G. 1983b. Discourse Pragmatics in Task-Oriented Natural Language Interfaces. In Proceedings of the 21st Annual Meeting of the Association for Computational Linguistics (ACL-83), 164-168.

Carbonell, J.G. 1986. Derivational Analogy: A Theory of Reconstructive Problem-Solving and Expertise Acquisition. In J.G. Carbonell, T. Mitchell and R. Mychalski (eds.), *Machine Learning, An Artificial Intelligence Approach*, Volume II. Los Altos, Calif.: Morgan Kaufman, 371-392.

Carbonell, J.G., W.M. Boggs, M.L. Mauldin and P.G. Anick. 1985. The Xcalibur Project, A Natural Language Interface to Expert Systems and Data Bases. In S. Andriole (ed.), *Applications in Artificial Intelligence*. Princeton: Petrocelli Books.

Carbonell, J.G. and R. Brown. 1988. Anaphora Resolution: A Multi-Strategy Approach. In Proceedings of 12th International Conference on Computational Linguistics (COLING-88), Budapest, 96-101.

Carbonell, J.G., R.E. Cullingford and A.V. Gershman. 1981. Steps toward Knowledge-Based Machine Translation. *IEEE Transactions on Pattern Analysis and Machine Intelligence*, July, 376-392.

Carbonell, J.G. and P.J. Hayes. 1987. Natural Language Understanding. In S.C. Shapiro (ed.), *Encyclopedia of Artificial Intelligence*. New York: John Wiley & Sons, 660-677.

Carbonell, J.G. and R. Joseph. 1985. The FRAMEKIT Reference Manual. Internal Paper, Computer Science Department, Carnegie Mellon University, Pittsburgh, Pa.

Carbonell, J.G., S.E. Morrisson, M.R. Kee, W.M. Boggs and M.L. Mauldin. 1983. Xcalibur Working Document 5: The Semantic Representation II. Internal Paper, Computer Science Department, Carnegie Mellon University, Pittsburgh, Pa.

Carbonell, J.G. and M. Tomita. 1985. New Approaches to Machine Translation. Technical Report, Computer Science Department, Carnegie Mellon University, Pittsburgh, Pa.

Carbonell, J.G. and M. Tomita. 1987. Knowledge-Based Machine Translation, The CMU Approach. In S. Nirenburg (ed.), *Machine Translation: Theoretical and Methodological Issues*. Cambridge: Cambridge University Press, 68-89.

Chomsky, N. 1957. *Syntactic Structures*. The Hague: Mouton.

Chomsky, N. 1981. *Lectures on Government and Binding*. Dordrecht: Foris.

Cumming, S. 1986. The Lexicon in Text Generation. Paper presented at the Linguistic Society of America's Linguistics Institute Workshop on the Lexicon, New York.

Dalrymple, M. 1989. Anaphoric Binding: Syntactic Constraints and Semantic Interpretation. Thesis proposal, Stanford University, Stanford, Calif.

Defrise, C. 1989. Lexical Description for NLP: The Case of the French Adverb *Presque*. *Machine Translation* 4:195-232.

Defrise, C. and S. Nirenburg. 1989. Aspects of Text Meaning. Technical Report, Center for Machine Translation, Carnegie Mellon University, Pittsburgh, Pa.

Ducrot, O. 1980. *Les échelles argumentatives*. Paris: Minuit.

Farwell, D. and Y. Wilks. 1991. Ultra: A Multi-lingual Machine Translator. In Proceedings of MT Summit III, Washington, D.C.

Fass, D. 1986a. Collative Semantics. In Proceedings of 11th International Conference on Computational Linguistics (COLING-86), Bonn, 341-343.

Fass, D. 1986b. Collative Semantics: A Description of the Meta5 Program. Technical Report. Computer Research Laboratory, New Mexico State University, Las Cruces.

Fass, D. 1988. Collative Semantics: A Study in the Discrimination of Meaning. CSS/LCCR Technical Report.

Fillmore, C.J. 1968. The Case for Case. In E. Bach and R.T. Harms (eds.), *Universals in Linguistic Theory*. New York: Holt, Rinehart and Winston, 1-88.

Forbus, K. 1983. Qualitative Reasoning About Space and Motion. In D. Gentner and A. Stevens (eds.), *Mental Models*. Hillsdale, N.J.: Lawrence Erlbaum Associates, 53-73.

Gazdar, G., E. Klein, G. Pullum and I. Sag. 1985. *Generalized Phrase Structure Grammar*. Cambridge, Mass.: Harvard University Press.

Grosz, B. and C. Sidner. 1985. The Structures of Discourse Structure. Technical Report, BBN Laboratories, Inc., Cambridge, Mass.

Hausser, R. 1988. Left-Associative Grammar: An Informal Outline. *Computers and Translation* 3:23-67.

Hayes, P., A. Hauptmann, J.G. Carbonell and M. Tomita. 1987. Parsing Spoken Language: A Semantic Caseframe Approach. Technical Report, Center for Machine Translation, Carnegie Mellon University, Pittsburgh, Pa.

Hobbs, J. 1985. Introduction. In J. Hobbs and R. Moore (eds.), *Formal Theories of the Commonsense World*. Norwood, N.J.: Ablex, xi-xxii.

Hobbs, J. 1986. Overview of the Tacitus Project. *Computational Linguistics* 12:220-222.

Hobbs, J. and R. Moore (eds.). 1985. *Formal Theories of the Commonsense World.* Norwood, N.J.: Ablex.

Hutchins, W. 1986. *Machine Translation: Past, Present, Future.* Chichester, UK: Ellis Horwood Ltd.

International Business Machines Corp. 1983. *Guide to Operations Manual* for IBM Personal Computer XT. Boca Raton, Fla.: IBM Corporation.

International Business Machines Corp. 1986. *IBM maruti-suteishion 5560 shisutemu sousa gaido* ("IBM multi-station 5560 system operation guide"). Tokyo: IBM Corporation.

Jackendoff, R. 1977. $\overline{X}$ *Syntax: A Study of Phrase Structure.* Cambridge, Mass.: The MIT Press.

Jackendoff, R. 1983. *Semantics and Cognition.* Cambridge, Mass.: The MIT Press.

Jacobs, P. 1985. PHRED: A Generator for Natural Language Interfaces. *Computational Linguistics* 11:218-242.

Kaplan, R. and J. Bresnan. 1982. Lexical Functional Grammar: A Formal System for Grammatical Representation. In J. Bresnan (ed.), *The Mental Representation of Grammatical Relations.* Cambridge, Mass.: MIT Press, 173-281.

Kaplan, R. and A. Zaenen. 1989. Long-Distance Dependencies, Constituent Structure, and Functional Uncertainty. In M.R. Baltin and A.S. Kroch (eds.), *Alternative Conceptions of Phrase Structure.* Chicago: University of Chicago Press, 17-42.

Kay, M. 1985. Parsing in Functional Unification Grammar. In D. Dowty, L. Karttunen and A. Zwicky (eds.), *Natural Language Parsing: Psychological, Computational, and Theoretical Perspectives.* Cambridge: Cambridge University Press, 251-278.

Kittredge, R. and R. Grishman (eds.). 1986. *Analyzing Language in Restricted Domains.* Hillsdale, N.J.: Lawrence Erlbaum Associates.

Kolodner, J. 1984. *Retrieval and Organizational Strategies in Conceptual Memory: A Computer Model.* Hillsdale, N.J.: Lawrence Erlbaum Associates.

Leavitt, J. 1991. The DIBBS User's Guide. Technical Memo, Center for Machine Translation, Carnegie Mellon University, Pittsburgh, Pa.

Leavitt, J. and E. Nyberg. 1990. The DIBBS BlackBoard Control Architecture and Its Application to Distributed Natural Language Processing. In Proceedings of IEEE Tools for Artificial Intelligence 1991, Washington, D.C., 202-208.

Lenat, D., M. Prakash and M. Shepherd. 1985. Cyc: Using Common Sense Knowledge to Overcome Brittleness and Knowledge Acquisition Bottlenecks. *AI Magazine* 6:65–85.

Levin, B. 1989. English Verbal Diathesis. Lexicon Working Papers 32. Lexicon Project, Center for Cognitive Science, MIT, Cambridge, Mass.

Levin, L. 1982. Sluicing: A Lexical Interpretation Procedure. In J. Bresnan (ed.), *The Mental Representation of Grammatical Relations*. Cambridge, Mass.: MIT Press, 590-654.

Levin, L. 1985. Identifying Non-Nominative Subjects in LFG. In Proceedings of the Eastern States Conference on Linguistics, 313-324.

Levin, L. 1987. Toward a Linking Theory of Relation Changing Rules in LFG. CSLI Report No. CSLI-87-115, Center for the Study of Language and Information, Stanford, Calif.

McKeown, K. 1985. *Text Generation*. Cambridge: Cambridge University Press.

Marcus, M. 1987. Words in Generation. In Proceedings of TINLAP-3, Las Cruces, N. Mex.

Mitamura, T. 1989. The Hierarchical Organization of Predicate Frames for Interpretive Mapping in Natural Language Processing. Ph.D. dissertation, Department of Linguistics, University of Pittsburgh, Pittsburgh, Pa.

Mohanan, K.P. 1982. Grammatical Relations and Clause Structure in Malayalam. In J. Bresnan (ed.), *The Mental Representation of Grammatical Relations*. Cambridge, Mass.: MIT Press, 504-589.

Mohanan, K.P. 1983. Functional and Anaphoric Control. *Linguistic Inquiry* 14:641-674.

Monarch, I.A. and J.G. Carbonell. 1987. CoalSORT: A Knowledge-Based Interface. *IEEExpert*, Spring, 39-53.

Musha, H. 1987. Syntactic Predictions in the Recognition of English. Technical Report, Center for Machine Translation, Carnegie Mellon University.

Nirenburg, S. (ed.). 1985. Proceedings of the Conference on Theoretical and Methodological Issues in Machine Translation of Natural Languages. Colgate University, Hamilton, N.Y.

Nirenburg, S. (ed.). 1987a. *Machine Translation: Theoretical and Methodological Issues*. Cambridge: Cambridge University Press.

Nirenburg, S. 1987b. A Distributed Generation System for Machine Translation. Technical Report, Center for Machine Translation, Carnegie Mellon University, Pittsburgh, Pa.

Nirenburg, S., J.G. Carbonell, M. Tomita and K. Goodman. 1991. *Knowledge-Based Machine Translation*. San Mateo, Calif.: Morgan Kaufmann.

Nirenburg, S. and C. Defrise. Forthcoming. Application-Oriented Computational Semantics. In R. Johnson and M. Rosner (eds.), *Computational Linguistics and Formal Semantics*. Cambridge: Cambridge University Press.

Nirenburg, S. and K. Goodman (eds.). 1989. KBMT-89 Project Report. Technical Report, Center for Machine Translation, Carnegie Mellon University, Pittsburgh, Pa.

Nirenburg, S. and K. Goodman. 1990. Treatment of Meaning in MT Systems. In Proceedings of the Third International Conference on Theoretical and Methodological Issues in Machine Translation of Natural Languages, University of Texas, Austin, 171-188.

Nirenburg, S., R. McCardell, E. Nyberg, P. Werner, S. Huffman, E. Kenschaft and I. Nirenburg. 1988a. DIOGENES-88. Technical Report No. 88-107, Center for Machine Translation, Carnegie Mellon University, Pittsburgh, Pa.

Nirenburg, S., I. Monarch, T. Kaufmann, I. Nirenburg and J.G. Carbonell. 1988b. Acquisition of Very Large Knowledge Bases. Technical Report No. 88-108, Center for Machine Translation, Carnegie Mellon University, Pittsburgh, Pa.

Nirenburg, S., E. Nyberg and E. Kenschaft. 1987b. Inexact Frame Matching for Lexical Selection in Natural Language Generation. Technical Memo, Center for Machine Translation, Carnegie Mellon University, Pittsburgh, Pa.

Nirenburg, S. and J. Pustejovsky. 1988. Processing Aspectual Semantics. In Proceedings of Annual Meeting of the Cognitive Science Society, Montreal.

Nirenburg, S. and V. Raskin. 1987a. The Analysis Lexicon and the Lexicon Management System. *Computers and Translation* 2:177–188.

Nirenburg, S. and V. Raskin. 1987b. The Subworld Concept Lexicon and the Knowledge Base Management System. *Computational Linguistics* 13:276–289.

Nirenburg, S., V. Raskin and A. Tucker. 1986. On Knowledge-Based Machine Translation. In Proceedings of 11th International Conference on Computational Linguistics (COLING-86), Bonn, 627-632.

Nirenburg, S., V. Raskin and A. Tucker. 1987a. The Structure of Interlingua in TRANSLATOR. In S. Nirenburg (ed.), *Machine Translation: Theoretical and Methodological Issues*. Cambridge: Cambridge University Press, 90-113.

Nyberg, E. 1988. FRAMEKIT User's Guide. Technical Memo, Center for Machine Translation, Carnegie Mellon University, Pittsburgh, Pa.

Perlmutter, D. 1979. Working 1's and Inversion in Italian, Japanese, and Quechua. In Proceedings of the Berkeley Linguistic Society, 277-324.

Perlmutter, D. (ed.). 1983. *Studies in Relational Grammar 1*. Chicago: The University of Chicago Press.

Polanyi, L. and R. Scha, 1986. A Model of Natural Language Discourse. In L. Polanyi (ed.), *The Structure of Discourse*. Norwood, N.J.: Ablex.

Pollard, C. and I. Sag. 1987. *An Information-Based Syntax and Semantics*. Volume I, *Fundamentals*. CSLI Lecture Notes 13. Chicago: The University of Chicago Press.

Pustejovsky, J. 1987. An Integrated Theory of Discourse Analysis. In S. Nirenburg (ed.), *Machine Translation: Theoretical and Methodological Issues*. Cambridge: Cambridge University Press, 168-191.

Pustejovsky, J. 1988a. The Geometry of Events. In C. Tenny (ed.), *Studies in Generative Approaches to Aspect*. Cambridge, Mass.: MIT Center for Cognitive Studies.

Pustejovsky, J. 1988b. Event Semantic Structure. Technical Report, Computer Science Department, Brandeis University, Waltham, Mass.

Pustejovsky, J. and S. Nirenburg. 1987. Lexical Selection in the Process of Language Generation. In Proceedings of 25th Annual Meeting of the Association for Computational Linguistics (ACL-87), Stanford, Calif., 201-206.

Quirk, R., S. Greenbaum, G. Leech and J. Svartvik. 1985. *A Comprehensive Grammar of the English Language*. London: Longman.

Radford, A. 1988. *Transformational Grammar: A First Course*. Cambridge: Cambridge University Press.

Schank, R. 1982. *Dynamic Memory*. Cambridge: Cambridge University Press.

Shieber, S. 1986. *An Introduction to Unification-Based Approaches to Grammar*. CSLI Lecture Notes 4. Chicago: University of Chicago Press.

Simpson, J. and J. Bresnan. 1982. Control and Obviation in Warlpiri. In Proceedings of the 1st West Coast Conference on Formal Linguistics.

Slocum, J. 1985. Survey of Machine Translation: Its History, Current Status, and Future Prospects. *Computational Linguistics* 11:1-17.

Slocum, J. (ed.). 1988. *Machine Translation Systems*. Cambridge: Cambridge University Press.

Spector, A., R. Pausch and G. Bruell. 1988. Camelot: A Flexible, Distributed Transaction Processing System. In Proceedings of Compcon 88, 432-437.

Spector, A. and K. Swedlow. 1987. The Guide to the Camelot Distributed Transaction Facility: Release 1. Computer Science Department, Carnegie Mellon University, Pittsburgh, Pa.

Takeda, K. 1990. Bi-Directional Grammars for Machine Translation. In Proceedings of Seoul International Conference on Natural Language Processing, Seoul, 162-167.

Tojo, S. 1988. A Computational Model of Verb Complex Translation. Technical Report, Center for Machine Translation, Carnegie Mellon University, Pittsburgh, Pa.

Tomabechi, H. 1987. Direct Memory Access Translation: A Theory of Translation. Technical Report, Center for Machine Translation, Carnegie Mellon University, Pittsburgh, Pa.

Tomita, M. 1984. Disambiguating Grammatically Ambiguous Sentences by Asking. In Proceedings of 10th International Conference on Computational Linguistics (COLING-84), Stanford, Calif., 476-480.

Tomita, M. 1985. *Efficient Parsing for Natural Language*. Boston: Kluwer.

Tomita, M. 1986. Sentence Disambiguation by Asking. *Computers and Translation* 1:39-51.

Tomita, M. and J.G. Carbonell. 1986. Another Stride Towards Knowledge Based Machine Translation. In Proceedings of 11th International Conference on Computational Linguistics (COLING-86), Bonn, 633-639.

Tomita, M. and J.G. Carbonell. 1987. The Universal Parser Architecture for Knowledge-Based Machine Translation. Technical Report, Center for Machine Translation, Carnegie Mellon University, Pittsburgh, Pa.

Tomita, M., M. Kee, T. Mitamura and J.G. Carbonell. 1987. Linguistic and Domain Knowledge Sources for the Universal Parser Architecture. In Proceedings of the International Conference on Terminology and Knowledge Representation, Trier, 191-203.

Tomita, M. and K. Knight. 1988. Pseudo Unification and Full Unification. Technical Memo, Center for Machine Translation, Carnegie Mellon University, Pittsburgh, Pa.

Tomita, M., T. Mitamura, H. Musha and M. Kee. 1988. The Generalized LR Parser/Compiler Version 8.1: User's Guide. Technical Memo, Center for Machine Translation, Carnegie Mellon University, Pittsburgh, Pa.

Tomita, M. and E. Nyberg. 1988. Generation Kit and Transformation Kit Version 3.2 User's Manual. Technical Memo, Center for Machine Translation, Carnegie Mellon University, Pittsburgh, Pa.

Tsuji, H. 1988. Problem Solver with Strategies for Clearing Goal Stack and Forestalling State Space. Technical Report, Center for Machine Translation, Carnegie Mellon University, Pittsburgh, Pa.

Tucker, A., S. Nirenburg and V. Raskin. 1986. Discourse, Cohesion and Semantics of Expository Text. In Proceedings of 11th International Conference on Computational Liguistics (COLING-86), Bonn, 181-183.

Tulving, E. 1985. How Many Memory Systems are There? *American Psychologist* 40:385-398.

Vasconcellos, M. and M. Leon. 1985. SPANAM and ENGSPAN: Machine Translation at the Pan American Health Organization (PAHO). *Computational Linguistics* 11:122-136.

Vauquois, B. 1975. *La Traduction automatique à Grenoble*. Paris: Dunod.

Wedekind, J. 1988. Generation as Structure Driven Derivation. In Proceedings of 12th International Conference on Computational Linguistics (COLING-88), Budapest, 732-737.

Westcoat, M. 1987. Practical Instructions for Working with the Formalism of Lexical Functional Grammar. In J. Bresnan (ed.), *Lexical Functional Grammar*, Course Material for the 1987 Linguistic Institute. Stanford, Calif., 3-39.

Wheeler, P. 1984. Changes and Improvements to the European Commission's SYSTRAN System, 1976-1983. In Proceedings of the International Conference on the Methodology and Techniques of Machine Translation. Cranfield Institute of Technology, UK.

Wilensky, R. 1984. KODIAK—A Knowledge Representation Language. In Proceedings of the 6th Annual Conference of the Cognitive Science Society, 344-352.

Wilks, Y.A. 1973. An Artificial Intelligence Approach to Machine Translation. In R.C. Schank and K.M. Colby (eds.), *Computer Models of Thought and Language*. San Francisco: W.H. Freeman and Company, 114-151.

Wilks, Y.A. 1975. A Preferential, Pattern-Seeking Semantics for Natural Language Inference. *Artificial Intelligence* 6:53-74.

Winograd, T. 1983. *Language as a Cognitive Process*. Volume I: *Syntax*. Reading, Mass.: Addison-Wesley.

Zaenen, A. 1987. The Place of *bevallen* (please) in the Syntax of Dutch. Center for the Study of Language and Information, Stanford University, Stanford, Calif.

Zarechnak, M. 1979. The History of Machine Translation. In B. Henisz-Dostert, R. Ross McDonald and M. Zarechnak (eds.), *Machine Translation*. Trends in Linguistics: Studies and Monographs, Volume XI, The Hague: Mouton, 3-87.

Index